Hiking the
Carolina Mountains

- Appalachian Trail
- Blue Ridge Parkway
- Dupont State Forest
- Great Smoky Mountains National Park
- Pisgah & Nantahala National Forests
- Upstate South Carolina

And much more

by
Danny Bernstein

milestone
press

almond, nc

Text copyright 2007 by Danny Bernstein
Maps copyright 2007 by Milestone Press, Inc.
All rights reserved
Second printing June 2007

Milestone Press, PO Box 158, Almond, NC 28702

Book design by Denise Gibson/Design Den
www.designden.com

Cover photos by Mary Ellen Hammond
Back cover author photo by Bruce Bente

Interior photos by the author except as follows:
Lenny Bernstein: pp. 17, 25, 206; Jean Gard: p. 222;
Mary Ellen Hammond: pp. 6, 7, 10, 12, 16, 31, 67, 83-87,
92, 95, 96, 104, 107, 113, 133, 134, 138, 151, 165 (trail sign),
181, 183, 186, 201, 320; Ashok Kudva: p. 301 (Gray's lily);
Jim Reel: p. 19

Library of Congress Cataloging-in-Publication Data

Bernstein, Danny, 1946-
  Hiking the Carolina mountains : Appalachian Trail, Blue
Ridge Parkway, DuPont State Forest, Great Smoky Mountains
National Park, Pisgah & Nantahala National Forests, upstate
South Carolina and much more / by Danny Bernstein.
    p. cm.
  Includes bibliographical references and index.
  ISBN 978-1-889596-19-8 (alk. paper)
  1. Hiking–North Carolina–Guidebooks.
  2. Mountains–North Carolina–Guidebooks.
  I. Title.
GV199.42.N66B47 2007
796.5209756–dc22

                              2007000087

P-P-1

This book is dedicated
to all the trail maintainers, volunteer and professional,
who keep our hiking trails clear, clean, and signed.
Without them, there would be few trails and little hiking.

Acknowledgements

Many people helped me at every stage of this project.

I am grateful to the members of the Carolina Mountain Club who accompanied me on many hikes specifically for this book: Bruce Bente, Lenny Bernstein, Tom Bindrim, Tommie Boston, Stuart English, Jean Gard, Ashok Kudva, Gail Lamb, Marianne Newman, Jim Reel, Becky Smucker, Dave Wetmore, and Mark Zimmerman.

Mary Ellen Hammond and Jim Parham at Milestone Press helped me turn my hiking enthusiasm into a book, and I thank them for their expertise and patience.

Tommy Hays, Director of the Great Smokies Writing Program, encouraged me to think like a writer. Dr. Dan Pierce of the UNC-Asheville History Department first got me excited about the history of Southern Appalachia several years ago. The rangers at every one of the parks and forests I visited answered my questions enthusiastically and steered me in the right direction.

To my husband, Lenny, thank you for your love, advice, patience, devotion, and companionship during this project—and always.

Contents

Where To Find the Hikes

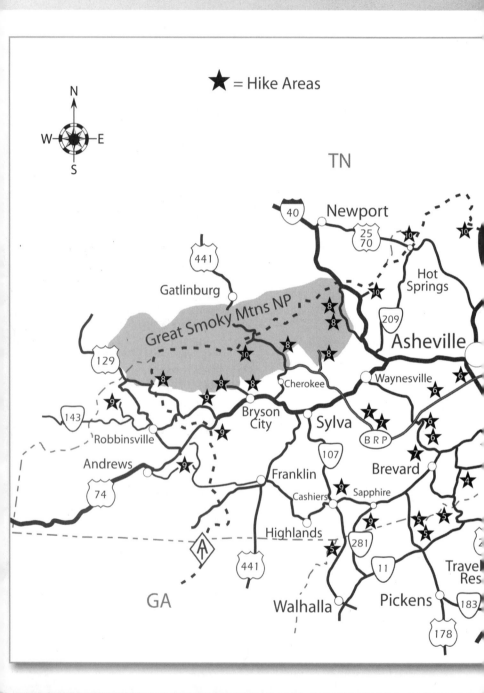

★ = Hike Areas

Area Covered

Tennessee
Asheville   North Carolina
Greenville
South
Carolina
Georgia

Introduction

Hiking the Carolina Mountains

If you are browsing through this book, you already know the pleasures of hiking. Perhaps you moved to the western Carolinas and want to learn about your new surroundings in the mountains. You may have lived here for a long time, maybe all your life, and want to expand your hiking area. Or you've gone to the same popular spots many times—Mt. Pisgah, Joyce Kilmer Memorial Loop, Graveyard Fields, Raven Cliff Falls—and are ready to explore new territory. Whether you are a visitor with a limited amount of time, or a newcomer or a native, this book will help you find and choose great hikes without having to do a lot of research. It has all the information you need to get you to the trailhead and begin walking.

A Hiker's Paradise

The western Carolina mountains are a hiker's paradise, boasting three National Park units—(Great Smoky Mountains National Park, Blue Ridge Parkway, and the Carl Sandburg Home National Historic Site)—, three national forests— (Pisgah, Nantahala, and Sumter)—, and several state parks and forests. Thanks to the range of altitude in these mountains, from 1,000 ft. elev. in the Green River

Hiking in the Carolina mountains is as good as hiking gets.

Game Lands to 6,684 ft. elev. on top of Mt. Mitchell, you can hike comfortably year-round.

A Long Human History

This region has not been a true wilderness for a very long time. First, the Cherokee Indians farmed and burned the forests to encourage the increase of game. In the late 18th century, pioneers moved down from the North and East. In the 1880s, loggers arrived here after they had finished clear-cutting the Upper Midwest and the Northeast. As a result, there is little old-growth forest in existence here today.

In the 20th century, people moved out of the areas that are now national park and national forest. Signs of human habitation—cemeteries, stonewalls, chimneys, and railroad ties—are found along the trails. Some buildings are still intact and maintained. On one trail you can even see old cars that have been rusting away since the 1940s. These artifacts do not spoil the experience; instead they make exploration more stimulating and mysterious.

I treasure every spike, every railroad grade, and every cabin on the trail as much as I treasure the trees and wildflowers. Let's not pretend that we are walking in untouched wilderness. You can see nature rebounding after many years. Some stretches of land, devastated by fires, are filling in with shrubs.

Finding Solitude

Yet wildness hangs on in the rhododendrons and mountain laurels, the signature flowers of the area, which, depending on the altitude, can be found in bloom from late March until August. Wildness is still felt in the native flowers from the first bloodroot in early March to the last asters and goldenrods in the fall. The Carolina mountains have a diversity of plant species greater than any found in all of Europe.

The roads and parking lots are sometimes congested in the Smokies, and the visitor center at Caesars Head can be very busy on a Sunday afternoon. But if you hike a couple of miles out from the trailhead, you will not feel cramped. According to a formula from *Backwoods Ethics* by Guy and Laura Waterman, "crowds diminish according to the square of the distance from the nearest road and the cube of the elevation above it." In other words, the farther off the road you go and the higher you climb, the fewer people you will see. Several popular hikes are included in this book because there is a good reason why they are so popular: a short climb to a 360-degree view or an outstanding waterfall surrounded by lush mosses.

Discovering the Southern Appalachians

I came to western North Carolina after hiking extensively in the Northeast for over 30 years and completing, among other hiking challenges, the Appalachian Trail. I didn't plan to hike the A.T. But in the 1970s my husband Lenny and I walked our first small section in the White Mountains of New Hampshire and started a card file with that one entry.

We added miles slowly while peak bagging other peaks in the Northeast. A weekend backpack here, a couple of days there, and the miles added up. When the drive to the trailhead became an overnight trip, we spent our annual vacations chipping away at A.T. miles. Many A.T. hikers give themselves a trail name, but we had a motto which we signed in logbooks in A.T. shelters: *Georgia to Maine in 25 years*. And that's almost how long it took us to complete the Appalachian Trail. In the process, we discovered hiking in the Southern Appalachians, with its open views on balds, smooth instead of rocky trails, switchbacks which contour a mountain rather than going straight up, and rushing creeks and waterfalls. We were soon hooked on the area.

After moving to Asheville, I completed the **South Beyond 6000 (SB6K)**, the 40 mountains over 6,000 ft. elev. in the Southern Appalachians, and now I am working on the **Smokies 900**, hiking all the trails in the Great Smoky Mountains National Park. I moved to these mountains to hike and that's what I do, several times a week. With over 2,000 miles of trails, there is a lifetime's worth of hiking exploration to do in the western Carolinas.

Besides actually being on the trail, I take a multidisciplinary approach to learning the area, using books, maps, the web, GPS, history and natural history

Many hikes will take you to mountain summits where the views are outstanding.

courses, and hiking clubs with experienced hikers to consult.

From hundreds of possible hikes, I have chosen for this book what I think are the best and most varied hikes of the area—and it wasn't easy. I didn't rely solely on my own opinion. I am a hike leader for the Carolina Mountain Club, the oldest and most active hiking club in the Carolina Mountains. The CMC leads three to four hikes a week, year-round. Through the combined knowledge of club members, club schedulers plan the best hikes for each season, and I have profited from their collective knowledge.

Highlights of this guidebook

- Many guidebooks describe individual trails only, expecting readers to put trail pieces together into day hikes. This book provides the hikes already organized. Hikes usually involve more than one trail.

- Each hike description includes total distance and altitude gain, which in my opinion is a better measure of difficulty than labeling the hike easy, moderate, or strenuous. Total distance, ascents, and descents were recorded with a GPS. I leave it to you to decide whether gaining 1,000 ft. elevation over ten miles is easy, or if climbing 1,000 ft. over one mile is strenuous.

- This book covers areas which have historically not received much publicity, including:
  - The **Nantahala National Forest**, south and west of the Smokies,
  - **Upstate South Carolina** in the Blue Ridge Escarpment, a delightful but underdocumented area with well-maintained state parks,
  - **Dupont State Forest**, a new North Carolina state forest with outstanding waterfalls,
  - The **Montreat Wilderness**, owned by the Mountain Retreat Association, which has created a conservation easement and allows the public on its trails.

- This book includes hikes of all lengths, from less than 5 miles to more than 13 miles.

- Only a few hikes involve shuttles, which often depend on having two cars. Having two cars for a hike is a great luxury and not realistic for many people.

- The hikes are placed in a historical context. Understanding the historical background of the area you're hiking in will enrich your day on the trail. In some areas such as the North Shore of Fontana Lake in the Smokies, the effects of history are still being felt and debated today.

- Movies filmed or set in the location of a particular hike are listed along with novels set in the area. North Carolina is the third most popular state for filming movies, and much of this is due to the remote and wild beauty of its mountains.

- You'll find a glossary of hiking terms in the back of the book, listing definitions of words and phrases commonly used in trail guides and by hikers.

Take care when crossing streams. In the western Carolina mountains, rocks are often slippery with moss. It's no fun hiking in wet boots, and even less fun doing it with a twisted ankle.

Hiking safety and skills

There are many books on developing hiking skills, but this is not one of them. However, several frequently asked questions and other issues related to hiking in the Carolina mountains are worth addressing here.

What if I see a bear?

• Consider yourself very lucky. Most black bears are shy and will run away at the first sign or sound of people. Usually, the most you might see is a black rump crossing the trail and disappearing into the woods. But if you do encounter a bear coming toward you on the trail, the following is the recommended response.
• Give the bear plenty of room and leave it alone.
• Do not get close to the bear and do not try to feed it.
• Try to stand your ground.

Do not run or turn your back to the bear.
• Do not crouch. Make yourself as big as possible by raising your arms and yelling.
• The bear will usually run away. In the unlikely event that it does not, fight back and throw rocks at the bear.

What if I meet a snake?

Again, count yourself lucky, since snakes are shy and will slither off the trail and into the grass very quickly. The timber rattlesnake and copperhead are the only poisonous snakes in this area. Avoid confrontation with a snake by staying on the trail. If you see a snake, give it plenty of room to get away. Hiking boots which go over the ankle are also good protection against snakes.

What about bees, wasps, and other stinging insects?

If you think you are allergic to stinging insects, ask your doctor to prescribe an epinephrine pen and carry it in your first aid kit along with an over-the-counter antihistamine. Yellow jackets can be a problem in late summer and early fall.

Do I have to worry about poison ivy?

"Leaves of three, let it be." Poison ivy is prolific in the Southern Appalachians and is typically seen on the edges of trails, not deep in the woods. In the winter, the thick fuzzy vines around a tree trunk can also give you a rash. Poison ivy usually does not grow above 3,000 ft. elev., but in a few places you may see it as high as 4,500 ft. Learn to identify it and stay away from it. If you think you've been in contact with poison ivy, wash yourself well with a strong soap, such as brown laundry soap, as soon as you get home.

Is it safe to drink the water?

There is no place in the United States where it is entirely safe to drink water directly from streams, no matter how fast the water is running. On a day hike, bring all your water from home. You need two quarts—more on a long and strenuous hike. If you need extra water while on the trail, you must treat it. Some hikers carry water filters for that purpose. I carry iodine tablets which come in small bottles. Pop a tablet in a quart of water, wait 20 minutes, and you have potable water. If you don't like the taste, after the 20 minutes add some lemonade powder to disguise the iodine taste.

Altitude and weather

There are no flat trails in the western Carolinas. If you are a flatlander, start out with a shorter hike than you would back home.

Altitude determines weather, temperature, climate, the flora and fauna you will see, and the clothes you will need. As you go up and down these mountains, weather changes. Climbing 3,000 ft. in elevation is the climatic equivalent of traveling 750 miles north, and the temperature drops one degree with every 250 ft. above sea level. The top of Mt. Mitchell—at 6,684 ft. the highest mountain east of the Mississippi—is 26 degrees colder than it would be at sea level (if the western Carolina mountains had any areas at sea level). If you plan to go up in altitude, take a fleece sweater or jacket, because it will be colder on top than at the trailhead.

Different altitudes affect flora and fauna. At the lowest

altitudes, spring flowers appear in early March. At 6,000 ft. elev., you can see these same species of flowers in late May. The reverse occurs in the fall. Go to the top of Cold Mountain in the Shining Rock Wilderness in early September for autumn color; in November you can still enjoy fall foliage at Paris Mountain State Park in upstate South Carolina.

Make sure you dress in layers, especially for those high-altitude hikes.

The leave-no-trace ethic

For dayhikers, "leave no trace" is as simple as it sounds: leave nothing in the woods. In addition to packing out your candy wrappers, do not

Waterfalls are beautiful, but view them from a distance. Every year people get hurt trying to climb them.

throw organic waste such as apple cores or banana or orange peels into the woods. According to the Leave No Trace Center for Outdoor Ethics, banana peels take up to a year to disintegrate; orange peels take up to two years.

Take a "trail break"—a euphemism for going to the toilet in the woods—off the trail and well away from any water source. Bring along a sealable plastic bag to carry out your used toilet paper.

When you're hiking, stay on the trail. You'll protect the plants and cut down on erosion. With so many maintained trails to explore, there is no need to go crashing through the woods.

Historical artifacts

Because you are hiking through areas that have been inhabited, you may see historical artifacts such as rusty buckets and railroad paraphernalia on the trail. Please leave them in place. Of course, you are most welcome to pick up and carry out any soda cans and bottles you find.

Can I take my dog on the trail?

In most places mentioned in this book, dogs are permitted on the trails but should be under control at all times. You should carry a leash with you. If dogs are not allowed in an area, this restriction is mentioned in the Rules section. Dogs are not allowed on trails in the Great Smoky Mountains National Park.

Hunting

If you look at the hunting season calendar, you'll see that you can hunt some kind of animal almost any time of the year. However, when people talk about hunting season, they are usually referring to the bear and boar season or the deer season, both of which occur between October and the beginning of January. Hunters and hikers can coexist in the woods. Hikers should wear orange vests and hats and stay on the trails; hunting is not allowed in state or national parks.

It may look a bit scary, but a suspension bridge offers a safe way across a gorge or stream.

Be Prepared

What to bring on a day hike

Bringing the proper equipment will add greatly to your personal enjoyment and safety, and the enjoyment and safety of your group. This stuff is essential if you're going out in the woods for more than a couple of hours. Make sure that you are comfortable with your equipment and that you know how to use and carry it properly. Do not carry anything in your hands; do not tie a jacket around your waist. Everything should fit in your daypack. Carry your wallet and keys in your daypack at all times. Do not depend on anyone else to lend you gear or carry your gear for you.

Contents of your daypack should include:

- Two quarts of water in plastic water bottles, such as nalgene (not soda bottles)
- Lunch and snacks
- Rain jacket (no matter what the forecast)
- Long-sleeved shirt (ditto)
- Sunglasses
- Sun hat
- Insect repellent
- Sunscreen
- Tissues
- Personal first aid kit
- Small flashlight
- Plastic bag for trash
- Map (know how to use it)
- Compass (ditto)

Being prepared means just that. You never know what you might encounter on a hike in the high country. Snow can occur in the upper elevations in fall, winter, and spring.

If it is not the height of a warm summer, add:

- Hiking sweater or jacket (wool or fleece)
- Hat and gloves (wool or fleece)
- Rain pants

Wear:

- Shorts or light pants and a short-sleeved t-shirt as the bottom layer
- Hiking boots, well broken-in, that go over the ankles
- Good hiking socks (not sports socks)
- Sun hat with a wide brim
- Bandanna (keep it handy)

Dress in layers

Your first layer should be a short-sleeved t-shirt (synthetic, not cotton) even if it seems cool in the morning; you will warm up. Your second layer should be a long-sleeved shirt, also synthetic. If you need additional layers, you'll have your warm hiking sweater and rain jacket in your daypack. Shorts give you more mobility and keep you cooler; long pants provide more protection from insects and brush. Jeans are a bad idea for hiking; the heavy cotton fabric will keep you wet longer.

Eating on the trail

A simple lunch starts with a sandwich and a piece of fruit. Small cans of tuna fish or sardines are easy to carry if you remember to bring along a fork and a couple of plastic

This hiker is ready. Notice the proper attire for a summer hike; a day pack holds extra layers.

bags to wrap the empty cans in afterwards. Add cookies, an energy bar, and trail mix (nuts, chocolate, raisins, and other dried fruit) and you have your body fuel for the day. Chocolate tastes great on the trail, but buy the harder, dark variety or you'll end up with chocolate sauce on a hot day.

How To Use This Guide

The book is organized by hiking area, generally from east to west. All the hikes within an entity, Great Smoky Mountains National Park, for example, are listed together, even though the Park encompasses many mountains.

Each region description contains its own history and introduction, including:

Rules/fees: Wilderness area rules, entrance fees, and whether dogs are permitted.

Facilities: Visitor centers, toilets, and picnic tables, if any.

Closest town: Helpful if you're looking for a meal or lodging after the hike. Sometimes, the closest lodging is a campground.

Website: Official website, if one exists.

Related books and movies: Novels and movies set in the area, and movies filmed in the area.

Area map:
For each hiking area a general map is included to give you an idea of where the hikes are and the roads you'll use to get to them. You'll want to refer to a general road map as well.

For each hike, all the details at a glance

Type of hike: There are numerous types and they are named accordingly.
Loop – Walking a closed circular route without retracing your steps.
Out and back – Walking to a certain point, turning around, and returning to the start the way you came.
Shuttle – A one-way hike that requires placing a car at the end of the hike before you begin walking. An efficient way of organizing a shuttle hike is for all cars to drive to the endpoint and leave half the cars there. All hikers then get in the remaining cars and drive to the starting trailhead to begin the hike.
Lollipop – A loop hike with a "tail" which is hiked both ways.
Figure-eight – Two loops that intersect, so you come to the same point twice in the course of the hike.

Distance: The total mileage of the hike as described, including any side trips. The distance of each hike was calculated with a GPS. In assessing difficulty of a hike, many hikers look at distance first.

Total ascent/descent: Total vertical rise and fall in elevation over the whole hike, whether it is in a single uphill stretch or over many ups and downs. Except for shuttle hikes, the total descent is equal to the ascent.

Highlights: A list of what you can expect to experience on a hike, for example: views, waterfall, cabin, artifacts, rock formations, wildflowers.

Topographic map: There is a topographic map available from the U.S. Geological Survey for every section of the United States. Some hikers like topo maps because they seem more official. For most of us, a trail map is more helpful.

Trail map: The name of the official trail map for each hike. You can buy most maps in outdoor stores or on the web, but sometimes the official map is available only in a visitor center. Trail numbers, if any, on hikes in this guide correspond to those on the official trail map.

Land managed by: This item lists the agency in control of the land on which the trail is located, for example, the Great Smoky Mountains National Park or the Nantahala National Forest.

Directions to the trailhead: Directions to trailhead from the closest auto road are given based on the official North Carolina or South Carolina road map.

Difficulty

Hikes in this book are not rated by difficulty. Distance and total ascent must be taken together to indicate the difficulty of the hike. For people who have knee problems, total descent is also important. Within a hike description, steep sections are noted.

Maps

In each hike description you'll find two maps. The small map accompanying the directions is intended to show the roads that will get you to the trailhead. You may not always find these roads on a state road map. The larger map shows the hiking route. It will serve you well as a stand-alone map or in conjunction with the official trail map listed.

The Changing Trail

Trails sometimes close because of a blowdown, or a flood destroys a bridge, or a rock slide creates an obstruction. New trails open up and bridges get repaired. To avoid surprises, call the ranger station or other supervising authority before you go. Telephone numbers are listed in Appendix B. To read and report updates, please visit my website, www.hikertohiker.com.

And now—just go out and hike!

Mount Mitchell

Guyot's methods were time-consuming,
physically demanding, and far more meticulous
than those employed by either Mitchell or
Clingman. Remaining on the mountains for
days at a stretch, Guyot took many barometric
readings for each peak he climbed.

— Timothy Silver,
Mount Mitchell and the Black Mountains

Mount Mitchell

Essential Facts

Rules/fees:
Pets must be on a leash no longer than 6 ft.

Facilities:
Museum, gift shop, snack bar, restrooms, restaurant in Mt. Mitchell State Park

Closest town:
Burnsville, NC

Website:
www.ils.unc.edu/parkproject/visit/momi/home.html

Related book:
Mount Mitchell and the Black Mountains by Timothy Silver

The Black Mountains have been a source of fascination for explorers and tourists for over 200 years. André Michaux, an 18th-century French botanist, was sent to search American forests for new species of trees with which to rebuild the forests of France. Michaux made several trips to the Southern Appalachians in the 1780s. He climbed the Blacks and, just as importantly for us, he documented his adventures. Michaux is credited, at least in popular mythology, as being the first European to climb the Blacks. He named them

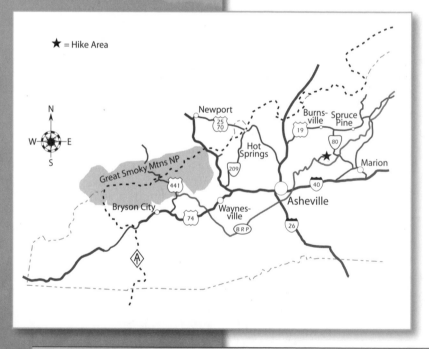

The sign says it all: Mt. Mitchell is the highest peak in the East.

"La Montagne Noire"—what we call the Black Mountains.

Elisha Mitchell, a minister and scientist who came from Connecticut to teach at the University of North Carolina in Chapel Hill in 1818, was captivated by Michaux's journals. At the time, Mt. Washington in New Hampshire was believed to be the highest mountain in the East, a belief alive and well today among much of the hiking community in the Northeast. Mitchell began exploring and measuring the Carolina mountains and in 1835 showed that the crest of the Black Mountains was higher. But exactly which mountain was the highest?

On subsequent trips, Mitchell climbed various peaks in the Blacks and named the present day Mt. Gibbes/Clingmans Peak—a mountain now easily recognized because of its transmission towers—as the highest. Thomas Clingman, a congressman and one of Elisha Mitchell's former students, claimed that he was the first to climb the mountain. The two men fought a battle of words which was recorded by the press and attracted as much attention as any modern-day celebrity scandal.

In 1857, Mitchell, by then 64 years old and determined to clear his reputation as the one who had first climbed the highest mountain in the East, undertook another climbing trip there. He and his party took a tourist track partway up the mountain, staying in cabins from which he explored the nearby mountains for days. On his last day, Mitchell went off by himself and was caught in a thunderstorm.

Though the record of his route is hazy, he slipped on a rocky ledge above a waterfall and fell to his death. His pocket watch, broken by the fall, stopped at 8:10:56 pm. It was several days before his body was recovered. Public sentiment made Elisha Mitchell a hero and affixed the name Mitchell to the highest mountain, where he is now buried. However, Clingman was not forgotten in mountain history. His name was given to the highest point in Tennessee, Clingmans Dome, in Great Smoky Mountains National Park, as well as to Clingmans Peak in the Blacks.

Loggers arrived in the Blacks in the 1880s, about the same time they came to the rest of western North Carolina. Before railroads, the timber was hauled out in wagons. By 1911, construction started on a railroad from the town of Black Mountain to the summit of Mt. Mitchell to more efficiently transport the prized fir and spruce trees. In 1915 North Carolina's Governor Craig, concerned about the devastation caused by the logging, called for a small area around Mt. Mitchell to become North Carolina's first state park. There was still plenty of timber to cut outside the new state park in what is now Pisgah National Forest.

In the same year, the Mt. Mitchell Railroad started passenger service to accommodate the growing number of tourists who wanted to reach the highest point in the East. At that time the train journey took three hours from Mt. Mitchell Station in present-day Black Mountain to Camp Alice, which had a dining hall and tents and was a half-mile hike from the summit of Mt. Mitchell. Tourists then hiked to the top. Camp Alice had a dining hall and tents and was a passenger destination. But once the logging stopped in 1922, the railroad was no longer profitable and closed down soon after, along with Camp Alice.

The new age of the automobile had begun, and that year a toll road was opened to the top of Mt. Mitchell, using the same road beds as the railroad. The road was only wide enough for one-way traffic, so cars went up in the morning and started down after 3:30 pm. The route is approximated by Old Mitchell Toll Rd., a trail which now starts in Montreat and climbs to the top of Mt. Mitchell. Most hikers use the Graybeard Trail to access Old Mitchell Toll Rd. for a hike of about 14 miles.

Tourists used the Toll Road until 1940. By then you could get to the summit of Mt. Mitchell by both the Blue Ridge

Mt. Mitchell trails conquer steep sections with innovative steps.

aphid-like insect. The adelgids, which probably came from Central Europe on ornamental trees in the early 1900s, were not found in the Southern Appalachians until the 1950s. Acid rain also contributes to the death of the trees on the mountain. The dying trees are not attractive, but don't let that discourage you from walking up to the top of Mt. Mitchell, the highest point east of the Mississippi.

For some, the battle over which is the tallest mountain is not over. Some peakbaggers, aided by mathematicians, want to redefine the way we rank mountains. Instead of measuring a mountain by its height above sea level, they want to use the concept of prominence. The most prominent peaks have a noticeable separation between them and nearby higher peaks. Under that definition, Mt. Mitchell is no longer the most prominent peak in the East because there are so many other tall mountains around it. Instead, Mt. Washington, the only 6,000-footer in the Northeast, becomes again the tallest, most prominent peak, and Mt. Marcy in New York State outranks Clingmans Dome in Tennessee.

Parkway and a state road now known as NC 128. No one was going to pay to drive up to the mountain if they could get there for free. Hiking around Mt. Mitchell these days is hiking through history, with trail names such as Camp Alice, Old Mitchell, and Commissary. The goal is always the tower on top of Mt. Mitchell.

There has been an observation tower on top of Mt. Mitchell since the early 1850s. The last one, built in 1960, was constantly being repaired, and a new, more accessible structure is planned to open in 2007. From the top of the mountain you can see the majestic fir trees being reduced to bare matchsticks by the balsam wooly adelgid, an

Camp Alice Loop

This loop takes in so much in 4.5 miles: history, ridge views, and a spruce-fir forest. You'll get to the top of Mt. Mitchell, the highest mountain east of the Mississippi, where you can stop for a snack and hot drink. On the way down you can even have a sit-down lunch, since there's a restaurant on the trail with outstanding views—and stopping for a meal during a hike is a very European way of walking in the mountains. The loop is completely within Mt. Mitchell State Park, and the trail is impeccably maintained with signboards at every junction.

Getting to the trailhead:
From the Blue Ridge Parkway, milepost 355.3, turn up NC 128 (Mt. Mitchell Rd.). Drive about 2.5 miles to the park office.

Type of hike: Loop

Distance: 4.5 miles

Total ascent: 1,170 ft.

Highlights: Highest mountain in the East, SB6K, history, spruce-fir forest

USGS map:
Mt. Mitchell, Montreat

Trail map: Mt. Mitchell State Park map available at the Mt. Mitchell visitor center

Land managed by:
Mt. Mitchell State Park, NC.

The Hike

The park office, at 6,100 ft. elev., is at Stepps Gap. The office complex, with information and restrooms, is the place to pick up a free trail map. The Commissary Trail [orange diamond blazes] starts to the right of the park office, as you face the building.

This trail was part of the Mt. Mitchell Railroad and later the Mt. Mitchell Motor Road. Railroad buffs have found railroad paraphernalia on this trail as late as the 1990s. Commissary Trail, graveled all the way to the Camp Alice junction, gently descends among rhododendron, maple, and Fraser fir. To the right, you have outstanding southwestern ridge views. If you walk this trail in mid-June, you'll also catch a spectacular display of Catawba rhododendrons in bloom.

At 0.4 miles (6,000 ft. elev.), at an opening in the trees created by several boulders, look right to the transmission towers on top of Clingmans Peak. The trail turns gently left and you can see the restaurant and the Mt. Mitchell tower, two destinations on this hike. With the wind blowing through the open pasture, the views, and the buildings in the distance, you may feel as if you're in Switzerland rather than in North Carolina.

You lose the views at 0.8 mile as the trail closes in. Fraser fir, the most abundant tree here, lines the trail along with rhododendron growing diagonally from among the rocks.

At 1.2 miles, you'll reach the Camp Alice Trail [blue square blazes] and the Mountains-to-Sea Trail [white circles]. Camp Alice was an overnight destination

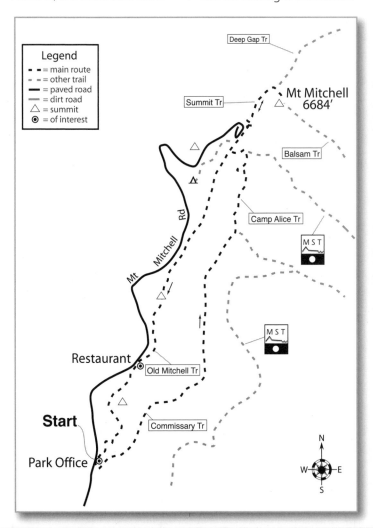

constructed about 1914 for tourists who came up on the Mt. Mitchell Railroad. It had a large dining room and platform tents for sleeping. From here, visitors walked to the top of Mt. Mitchell. Just beyond the junction, Lower Creek cascades in from the left.

Turn left on the Camp Alice Trail. (Continuing straight on the Commissary Trail would take you to Commissary Ridge, which ends in a campsite in Pisgah National Forest.) The Camp Alice Trail is short but steep, climbing into a rocky fir forest with little undergrowth. Ferns and Jack-in-the-pulpits peek out among the downed trees that have been cleared and pushed to the side. The trail makes a sharp right at 1.5 miles.

At 1.7 miles (6,240 ft. elev.), the trail ends, intersecting with Old Mitchell Trail [yellow circle blazes]. Take Old Mitchell Trail to the right as it starts to go up immediately; the trail to the left is how you will come down on your return. Ignore one confusing blue blaze which leads directly into an area of jumbled downed trees.

The Old Mitchell Trail makes a left at 1.9 miles and comes out into the open to obstructed views on the left. You can see the transmission tower on Clingmans Peak, which will be in view for most of the hike. Soon after, you'll reach the Campground Spur

Trail at 6,440 ft. elev. and make a right. You can now hear cars and motorcycles going up the Mt. Mitchell Rd.

Back in the woods for a short while, you'll climb uphill on rocky steps. You know you're getting close to the top when the trees get shorter, you can see daylight above, and tourists—some wearing flip-flops, come down and ask, "Where does this go to?"

At 2.3 miles (6,600 ft. elev.), you reach the Mt. Mitchell Trail leading to the Summit Trail. To your left are concessions (museum, gift shop, snack bar) and restrooms. Make a right turn and pass the Environmental Education Center on the left, which offers programs for the public on summer weekends. On sunny days, this area attracts visitors from all over the world. Turn right on the Summit Trail [no blazes] to the top. At 2.4 miles (6,684 ft. elev.), you're at the top of the highest mountain in the east. Standing on a rock looking southwest, you can see the restaurant buildings, Clingmans Peak, and the Mt. Mitchell Road.

Retrace your steps and turn left on the Old Mitchell Trail, the trail you'll be taking all the way back. At 2.8 miles, turn left at the junction with the Campground Spur Trail to continue on the Old Mitchell Trail. At the intersection with

Catawba rhododendron blooms in June on Mt. Mitchell.

the Camp Alice Trail (3.0 miles), make a right and continue to follow the yellow circles.

The trail, covered in pine needles, goes down rocky steps. At 3.1 miles (6,200 ft. elev.), you'll see a new Old Mitchell Trail sign nailed to a tree. Wooden planks have been placed on the trail where needed. Climb a wooden ladder (held securely on a concrete base) to work your way past boulders and big logs bordering the trail. At 3.3 miles you'll cross under power lines, where you can see the wide gravel Commissary Trail below. At 3.5 miles you parallel the road, and the trail becomes smooth and covered with small pebbles for a short while. It then ascends gently through false hellebore, blackberry cane, and bluets.

The first indication that you're approaching civilization is at 3.6 miles—a propane tank for the restaurant ahead. Follow the gravel road into the parking area, and turn left at the sidewalk leading to the restaurant entrance. The restaurant, open May through October, offers table service only.

Leaving the restaurant, follow the yellow blazes as the trail goes straight ahead across the lawn. At 3.9 miles, it climbs through fir trees and comes out into the open, then takes its final descent. Across Mt. Mitchell Rd., a gated road leads to the transmission towers atop Clingmans Peak. Come out on the road and make a left turn to get back to the park office and your car, to end the hike.

Mount Mitchell

*F*ollowing the Mountains-to-Sea Trail (MST) east from NC 128 to the top of Mt. Mitchell and down to Black Mountain Campground, you'll be hiking up on an old railroad bed and past the site of Camp Alice, which offered rustic lodging to tourists from about 1914 into the late 1920s. The climate at the top of the hike feels more like Canada than typical Southern Appalachia. On the way down, you'll see the forest change from fir and spruce to oak and hickory.

Though it is possible to drive within a few hundred feet of the summit of Mt. Mitchell, this hike is an opportunity to experience at close range the differences in climate and environment as you descend almost 4,000 ft. in elevation.

Getting to the trailhead:
The hike starts on NC 128 and ends at the Black Mountain Campground. First, place a car at Black Mountain Campground. To get there, take the Blue Ridge Parkway north past milepost 348. Exit to the left on unpaved FS 2074 as it descends past several campsites. At a triangle formed by three roads, go straight. The campground is 3.3 miles from the Blue Ridge Parkway.

Then park the remaining car at the trailhead on NC 128 (Mt. Mitchell Rd.). Drive back up from Black Mountain Campground to the Blue Ridge Parkway. Go south for 7.9 miles to NC 128 at milepost 355.3. Turn right on NC 128 and drive 0.6 mile to a gravel parking area on the right.

Type of hike: Shuttle

Distance: 11.4 miles

Total ascent/descent: 1,590 ft./3,840 ft.

Highlights: Views, SB6K, ecological changes, history, highest mountain in the East

USGS map: Mt. Mitchell, Celo, and Montreat

Trail map: South Toe River, Mt. Mitchell, and Big Ivy Trail Maps, USDA Forest Service; and Mt. Mitchell State Park map available at the Mt. Mitchell Visitor Center

Land managed by: Pisgah National Forest, Appalachian District; and Mt. Mitchell State Park

The Hike
Walk down the road (NC 128) and look for the MST signs [with white circle blazes] on low posts. Turn left, head

down the rock steps, and note three posts sticking out of the ground. You'll cross a small creek where a wand says "#191 - Buncombe Horse Trail." Continue on a gentle railroad grade trail and cross a second creek at 0.3 miles. Bluets, mountain laurel, and rhododendron line the trail as it crosses several small creeks.

As you walk, imagine riding to the top of Mt. Mitchell on a railroad car or in your private auto in the 1920s. Much of the land would have been logged so you would have views not available now that the forest has returned.

As you come out of the green tunnel, there are intermittent, semi-open views on the right. Wild hydrangea and strawberries abound, but the Fraser firs on the right are victims of the balsam wooly

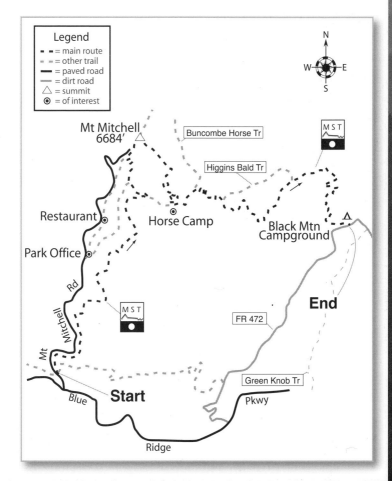

Legend
- = main route
- = other trail
— = paved road
— = dirt road
△ = summit
◉ = of interest

N
W — E
S

Mt Mitchell 6684' △

Buncombe Horse Tr

M S T

Higgins Bald Tr

Restaurant ◉

◉ Horse Camp

△

Black Mtn Campground

Park Office ◉

Mitchell Rd

M S T

FR 472

End

Green Knob Tr

Mt

Blue **Start**

Pkwy

Ridge

adelgid, a non-native, invasive insect. At 2.5 miles, the trail turns gently left to skirt a hill lined with rhododendron, balsam, and violets. There is a view of Green Knob Tower to the northwest. (See *Green Knob Tower* hike, p. 37.)

At 3.0 miles, you'll start seeing the Mt. Mitchell tower, surrounded by dead trees, and cross a low cascade on rocks at 3.3 miles. Pass an open field on the right with outstanding views—it looks like a pasture. The trail has entered Mt. Mitchell State Park.

At 3.6 miles, make a sharp left to stay on the MST. The trail to the right continues as the Buncombe Horse Trail. You are walking now on a wide jeep road with open views at the nicely

Rough steps lead you to the very top of Mt. Mitchell.

graveled Camp Alice site.

You'll arrive at a small cascade on Lower Creek on your right at 3.9 miles. Turn right here to stay on the MST—which is also the Camp Alice Trail, blazed blue. (If you stayed straight on the gravel road, it is 1.2 miles to the park office.)

Follow trail steps through Fraser firs as you ascend 900 ft. in elevation to the summit. There are no views here. At 4.3 miles, the MST joins the Old Mitchell Trail [yellow blazes]. (If you made a left here you'd reach the park office in 1.5 miles.) Follow the yellow blazes another 0.5 mile to the summit. At 4.4 miles, the trail emerges from the woods. Looking at the view, the peak on the left with the transmission tower is Clingmans Peak; you can see a small stretch of the Blue Ridge Parkway from here. Make a right turn to stay on the MST. (The left is a spur trail to the campground.)

At 4.7 miles, you've arrived at the tourist section of Mt. Mitchell State Park—a right takes you on the side trail to the observation tower; a left takes you to the museum (well worth your time), a snack bar, and bathrooms.

Continuing right, you'll pass the Environmental Education Center on the left, which holds special programs and can be booked for groups. Continue up to the tower.

Parts of the trail take you through a tangle of rhododendron and trees.

Take a right at the fork here and follow the tourists—the MST continues down.

At the base of the tower (4.8 miles), Dr. Elisha Mitchell, for whom this peak was named, lies in a grave surrounded by a black metal fence. Mitchell was originally buried in Asheville, but in 1858 his remains were reburied here at the top of Mt. Mitchell.

Retrace your steps from the tower trail and turn right to get back on the MST, which converges with the Balsam Nature Trail for a short while, and the Mt. Mitchell Trail. Pass a rock outcropping and other formations on the right as you descend into the spruce fir forest. Take a right at the sign to Black Mountain Campground (the sign says 5.5 miles; Balsam Nature Trail continues to the left.).

The wide and rough trail descends quickly on wooden steps through a stand of dead fir trees. At 6.2 miles, you'll make a sharp left as the trail leaves Mt. Mitchell State Park and enters Pisgah National Forest. It emerges from the woods occasionally, allowing obstructed views through fir and rhododendron.

On the left at 6.5 miles, look for a deep cavern with an overhang, after which you'll come out to a southwestern view of the Blue Ridge Parkway and then head back into the woods. Make a left turn at the horse camp to stay on the MST. At 6.9 miles, cross a large flat camping area and the beginning of the

Commissary Ridge Trail. There are several good campsites here. The Buncombe Horse Trail takes off on the left; the MST continues right along with the Mt. Mitchell Trail.

At 7.2 miles, as you cross under the power lines, there are outstanding southeastern views on your left, with ridge after ridge of mountains as you look toward Charlotte. Then you enter woods with limited views to the east as the trail switchbacks over rocky, root-covered terrain, heading deeper into this green, catacomb-like forest.

At 8.3 miles (4,890 ft. elev.), traverse a small area where many spruce trees have fallen with their roots upended by a microburst—a sudden, violent downdraft of air over a small area, rather like a mini-tornado—which can do significant damage to trees.

At the split with the Higgins Bald Trail, the MST [here #190A] goes right. There are confusing yellow markers on both sides of the split; follow the white circle blazes. The Higgins Bald Trail is a loop off the MST, so if you make a mistake, you'll still end up on the MST.

At 8.7 miles, the trail turns left and enters a field which is filling in with forgotten Christmas trees, mountain laurel, silverbell, and wild hydrangea. When you reach a flat campsite under hemlocks, veer to the left and follow

faint MST signs. The area through the campsite can be confusing. Stay to the left and cross Setrock Creek. The trail continues northeast and goes under the power line at a switchback. At 9.1 miles, the dry trail skirts the ridge and continues downhill. At 9.5 miles, the two legs of the split have rejoined. The trail turns right (south) and continues descending. High ridge views are visible through the trees.

You're in a maple forest as the trail switchbacks down. At 11.1 miles, the trail makes a sharp left and descends on good steps. Ignore a trail which goes up to the right.

Cross the road at the edge of the Black Mountain Campground. Continue on the MST, which now also has blue blazes and follows a creek downstream. Go through the campground and make a right turn over the bridge to the trailhead by the information board to end the hike.

Green Knob Tower

Looking for solitude? On the Green Knob Trail, you can be in your own world. As you near the top of the hike, you'll be rewarded with outstanding western views of Mt. Mitchell and Clingmans Peak. The Green Knob Tower is listed on the National Historic Lookout Register (similar in concept to the National Register of Historic Places), which recognizes both active and inactive fire towers and ground lookouts. Green Knob tower is just one example of a lookout no longer used for fire watching that remains a popular destination. Though you can also get to Green Knob Tower by walking just half a mile from Green Knob Tower Overlook on the Blue Ridge Parkway, this hike provides an excellent alternative with a challenging walk in a quiet forest.

Getting to the trailhead:
The trailhead is at the Black Mountain Campground. Take the Blue Ridge Parkway north past milepost 348. Exit to the left on unpaved FS 2074 as it goes downhill and passes campsites. At a triangle formed by three roads, go straight. The Campground is 3.3 miles from the Parkway. The trail starts in back of the information board.

Type of hike: Out and back

Distance: 5.7 miles

Total ascent: 2,310 ft.

Highlights: views of mountain ridges, tower, solitude

USGS map: Old Fort

Trail map: South Toe River, Mount Mitchell & Big Ivy Trail Maps, USDA Forest Service.

Land managed by:
Pisgah National Forest, Appalachian District; and Blue Ridge Parkway

The Hike
The trail starts at the back of the information board outside the Black Mountain Campground at about 2,990 ft. elev. The Green Knob Trail [#182 – yellow blazes] and the River Loop Trail [#200] follow the same path in a dry hemlock forest with an understory of rhododendron. At 0.3 mile, the trail makes a right turn to follow the yellow blazes and continues uphill. This is not the split between the two trails. (The left trail goes to a flat road, so if you are not climbing and the walking is too relaxed, you've probably missed the turn to the right.) At 0.4 mile, you'll arrive at the split between the two

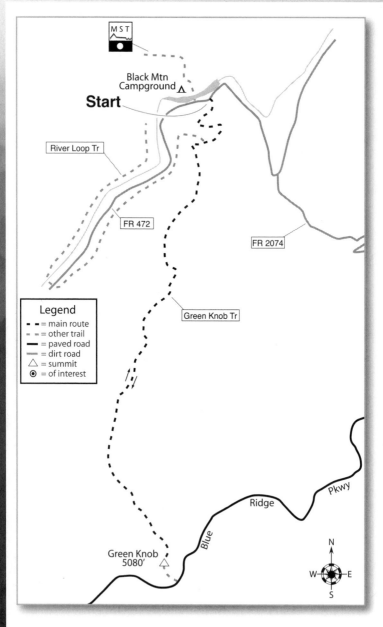

MST

Black Mtn Campground △

Start

River Loop Tr

FR 472

FR 2074

Green Knob Tr

Legend
– – = main route
– – = other trail
▬ = paved road
= dirt road
△ = summit
◉ = of interest

Blue

Ridge

Pkwy

Green Knob
5080' △

N
W ◉ E
S

trails. Take the left fork. (The right fork, marked River Loop, parallels and crosses the South Toe River and comes back to the campground in less than 3 miles.)

The trail climbs steeply through galax, mountain laurel, and rhododendron, heading southwest toward the Blue Ridge Parkway. Soon the trail flattens out. A huge log with large woodpecker holes lies across the trail. The trail alternates between steep and gentle climbs. Notice the sparkles of mica on the ground. The shiny mineral was used industrially for electrical insulation.

You'll reach a rocky area at 1.2 miles with a limited view of a knob; then lose that view as the trail steeply descends. As you start up again, you'll be walking among large hemlock, maple, and Fraser magnolia. Periodically the trail flattens as it changes direction. At 1.4 miles, the trail descends steeply again, and you can use this downhill for a well-earned rest.

Soon you'll enter a cool hemlock forest, likely to have a welcome breeze in the summer. Climbing upward at 1.9 miles, you'll welcome the first switchback. Once out of the green tunnel of hemlocks, you're under an open sky at 4,500 ft. elev. On your left, you'll pass a large boulder with a beech tree growing out of it. A little later, look right for your first ridge views of Clingmans Peak with its transmission towers, and Mt. Mitchell, the highest mountain east of the Mississippi. The trail then goes back into the forest while skirting the

hillside filled with trillium, Indian cucumber, and galax.

At 2.4 miles, you'll have extended views of the Black Mountains. The buildings you see are the various structures on top of Mt. Mitchell, including a restaurant, visitor center, and museum. You'll know you're getting close to the top because you can hear motorcycles below on the Blue Ridge Parkway. Soon on the left, a great view of the northeast valley opens up as the trail continues its climb, and a short rocky field

Blazes in Transition

The blazing for the Green Knob Trail is in transition, but don't let that stop you. The Green Knob Trail was originally blazed white, and the wand at the trailhead and your map may still show it as white. However, the Appalachian District of Pisgah National Forest is in the process of converting blazes for all the trails in its district to yellow, with the exception of the Mountains-to-Sea Trail. The yellow blazes with the occasional old white paint may be disconcerting. However, if you follow the yellow blazes, ignore the white paint, and pay attention to the one trail junction, you'll have no trouble.

The Green Knob firetower is one of the few remaining classic "dunce cap" towers.

provides more outstanding views to your right, including the Blue Ridge Parkway. When you come back to this rocky spot on your return, you may have to sit down to negotiate the trail. Up ahead, a pitch pine stands alone.

At 2.8 miles, the trail comes out in the open and the tower is straight ahead on a short side trail. (The side trail makes a left and continues down for 0.5 mile to the Blue Ridge Parkway at the Green Knob parking overlook—milepost 350.4.)

On top, at 5,080 ft.elev., piles of brambles have been cut to keep the area open. Look for hawks and turkey vultures circling overhead.

According to information provided by the National Historic Lookout Register, Green Knob Tower is one of the few remaining classic "dunce cap" pyramid-roof towers, once common in southern national forests. The 32-ft. steel tower with a cab and catwalk was built by the Civilian Conservation Corp in 1932 and restored in 1996. An old refrigerator, storage box with electrical equipment, and broken windows have been left inside the cab. From the catwalk on top of the tower, you'll get a 360-degree panorama, including a view of the Blue Ridge Parkway snaking though the forest.

Retrace your steps to return to the trailhead and end the hike.

Alternate route: For a quick way up to the Green Knob Tower, park at the Green Knob overlook on the Blue Ridge Parkway at milepost 350.4 (4,760 ft. elev.) Walk on the grassy sides of the Blue Ridge Parkway heading north for a few hundred feet. Cross the road and look for a Green Knob Trail wand. The trail ascends 0.5 mile and 320 ft. in elevation to the tower site.

Black Mountain

We celebrate your founding, Montreat: Those
visionary men and women who, with your help,
discovered the beauty and the potential alive in
your rolling mountains and flowing streams.

—From the litany for Montreat
Centennial Celebration Sunday

Black Mountain

Essential Facts

Rules/fees:
Organized groups not connected with Montreat are asked to request permission to use the trails by calling 828-669-2911 ext. 328 or emailing wilderness@montreat.org

Facilities:
Bookshop, gift store, nature center

Closest town:
Black Mountain, NC

Website:
www.montreat.org/wilderness.htm

Related book:
A Flowing Stream: An Informal History of Montreat, NC 1897-1997
by Elizabeth Maxwell

Western North Carolina is peppered with Christian retreats and conference centers of various Protestant denominations, dating back to the end of the 19th century. The area was attractive because of the climate and railroad lines; land was cheap and so was local labor. For churchgoers, the mountains were a place for quiet reflection where you could feel closer to God. Spending time in a retreat center felt more like being a pilgrim than a tourist.

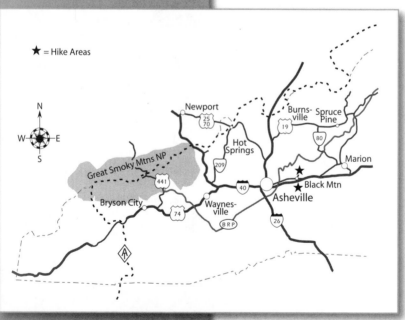

These days you don't have to be Christian or even religious to stay in one of these facilities. They operate as conference centers, catering to groups and family reunions that use them as an inexpensive base for their own programs. They serve meals and have amenities like tennis courts and lakes for recreation. Most of the conference centers in western North Carolina also have trails on their grounds and allow the public to hike with the understanding that these lands are private.

Montreat

In 1897, John C. Collins, a Congregationalist minister from Connecticut, bought 4,500 acres in the Swannanoa Valley from failed sheep ranchers. Collins and his partners chartered the Mountain Retreat Association and envisioned a "community and health resort with places for dwellings,…rest, recreation, Christian work and fellowship." The land was close to the Black Mountain railroad station and close to the mountains where, it was felt, God resided. Flat Creek, which runs through Montreat, provided fresh water. From the beginning individuals bought land and built summer cottages.

In 1907, the whole property was sold to the Presbyterian Church, which still manages the conference center and college. Montreat (short

Lookout Point is a favorite destination for those hiking at Montreat.

for mountain retreat) is now a conference center, college, history center, campgrounds, and town. Until 1967, everyone who entered Montreat paid a fee; the iconic stone arches of the toll gate are still the image of Montreat. The gate was attended by boys who collected a fee from everyone who came in, including residents—it was a "gated" community and residents liked the protection. Later Montreat incorporated, the better to be able to levy taxes and apply for government funding. Today Montreat College has almost 400 students, and 630 people live in Montreat year-round.

Montreat is a great year-round hiking area with open summits in the winter. Though the Montreat Wilderness has only a modest number of trail miles on its 2,500 acres, it connects to other watersheds and lands. Flat Creek, which is anything but flat, starts near the summit of Graybeard Mountain and gathers its water and momentum from various streams and rivulets. It then flows into the town, paralleling Assembly Drive. For a short walk, take a tour on foot through the town and college, starting at Lake Susan opposite the Assembly Inn on Assembly Drive, the center of Montreat. You can visit the L. Nelson Bell Library, named for Ruth Bell Graham's father, Billy Graham's father-in-law.

From Lake Susan, you can also drive up or walk up Greybeard Trail Rd. (although the accepted spelling is Graybeard, it is spelt with

Plastic diamond blazes mark the Montreat trails.

an "e" on the street sign) to the Walker C. Jones Wildlife Sanctuary and go around the small pond, which was the original water supply for Montreat. Sitting on a bench in the autumn, watching the red and gold leaves fall into the water, you can appreciate why people are attracted to this spot.

You do not have to be a Presbyterian to live in Montreat; anyone with the ability to pay can buy a house. Concerned with future development, the Mountain Retreat Association sold the development and timber rights to the Southern Appalachian Highland Conservancy via a conservation easement. This legal agreement between landowner and land trust permanently limits a property's use. The Montreat Wilderness ecosystem is protected from human manipulation in perpetuity while still allowing for hiking on trails, camping, birding, and fishing.

This land is contiguous with more than 125,000 acres of other protected forest lands and park lands, including the Blue Ridge Parkway and Mt. Mitchell State Park. If you take the Graybeard Trail to Old Mitchell Toll Rd. and connect to trails in Mt. Mitchell State Park, you can hike all the way to the top of Mt. Mitchell, about 14 miles one way.

Welcoming arched stone gates have become a familiar symbol of Montreat.

YMCA Blue Ridge Assembly

Just south of Black Mountain and on the other side of I-40, you'll find the YMCA Blue Ridge Assembly. It was founded in 1906 as a place in the mountains where men and women, regardless of race or nationality, could come together for training and inspiration. Known simply as the Blue Ridge Assembly, it is now available for conferences and retreats.

BRA's oldest building, Robert E. Lee Hall, with its rocking chairs and tall white columns, dominates the campus. The Assembly continues to be a training ground for college students and brings in 100 college-aged men and women from the world over to work in all areas of the conference center. Although certainly not extensive, the BRA trail system provides good views of Mt. Mitchell and the eastern ridges.

Pot Cove Loop

This loop highlights the various aspects of the Montreat community: town, wilderness area, logging, and college. The hike starts up Greybeard Trail Rd., a residential street. It then plunges into the Boggs Wilderness, crisscrossing Flat Creek several times until you find yourself at Pot Cove on Old Mitchell Toll Rd., originally the route of a logging railroad up to Mt. Mitchell. The last part of the loop takes you through Montreat College, a small Christian College which opened in 1916. The Chapel of the Prodigal with its outstanding fresco by Ben Long is definitely worth a stop.

Distance: 6.1 miles

Total ascent: 1,200 ft.

Highlights: views of mountain ridges, town, and college

USGS map: Montreat

Trail map: Montreat map available at the Montreat Bookshop in the Montreat Conference Center

Land managed by: Montreat Wilderness Area

The Hike

From Lake Susan, walk north on Greybeard Trail Rd. which follows Flat Creek. Every house on the road is unique, built in a different era from the next. At the top of the road, you'll see a parking area. If you happen to have two cars and could set a shuttle here, it would save you a mile walk at the end. Take a short diversion left into the Walker C. Jones Wildlife Sanctuary and go around the small pond, the original water supply for Montreat.

Coming back down on Graybeard Trail, continue to the signboard and the bridge on the right. Cross Flat Creek on the bridge and take the relocated Graybeard Trail. The trail was built in 2004, but it feels brand new; the dirt is fresh and soft underfoot. The Graybeard Trail, marked by blue diamonds and lined with rhododendron and galax, parallels the cascades and mossy rocks of Flat Creek.

Getting to the trailhead:

Take I-40 east to exit 64 at Black Mountain. Make a left on NC 9 and drive north through Black Mountain. Continue on NC 9 to the Montreat gates on Assembly Dr. Turn right on Lookout Dr. and park.

Type of hike: Loop

★=Start

Assembly Dr
★ Lookout Rd
Montreat
NC 9
US 70
Black Mtn
I-40
Exit 64

At the junction, take a right to stay on the Graybeard Trail and enter the Boggs Wilderness. (If you want a very short loop [1.9 miles], take a left here on Harry Bryan Trail and a left on the Julia Woodward Trail. The two trails allow for a nice gentle walk in the Bell forest. The Julia Woodward Trail ends at a small waterfall flowing between two boulders on Slaty Branch Creek.) Now you are on the original section of trail at the first of four Flat Creek crossings; here the trail is wider and less manicured. To cross, rock hop or use the logs that have been carefully placed across the creek. As you go up, keep an eye out for waterfalls, cascades, and natural rock sculptures, all worthy of a stop and a photo.

After the fourth creek crossing, the trail gets rough for a short but steep section reaching Old Trestle Rd. This trail was part of the logging railroad route that went from Black Mountain to Mt. Mitchell

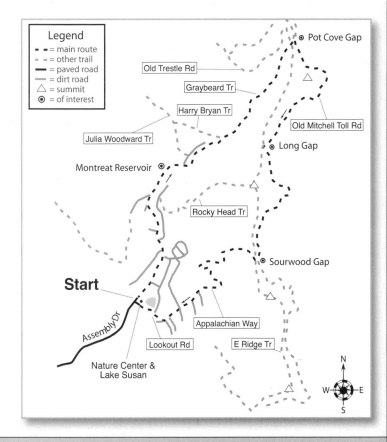

You'll have to do some rock hopping to cross Flat Creek.

in the early 1900s. Cross Old Trestle Rd. and continue on Graybeard Trail to Toll Rd. at Pot Cove Gap at 2.5 miles. Toll Rd. follows the general route of a logging railroad, built in 1913, which also transported tourists to the flanks of Mt. Mitchell and Camp Alice. When logging was no longer profitable, a one-way toll road for autos was built; passenger cars went up in the morning and came down in the afternoon.

At Pot Cove Gap, look up to see a pot hanging from a rusty nail on the large tree. Was there a family living here who left a pot? Was it just a prank? Perhaps the best explanation is that there was a train accident at that spot. It was the custom to memorialize the railroad men who died by hanging their lunch pails on a nail hammered into a tree. The gap is a good place to stop, take a snack break, and drink in the views.

Turn right and head down the Toll Rd., admiring the eastern ridge views all the way. Blue Ridge Pinnacle is behind you and to the left. It is said that on a clear day, you can see the peaks above Linville Gorge. You'll pass the bear hunting club with its trailer and several dog houses.

At the next gap, Sourwood Gap, take a right onto Appalachian Way at 4.5 miles. Follow Appalachian Way as it turns left and steeply downward to the gate. Passing through the gate, with a tank on your left, you are back on a Montreat town road.

The first few houses on the road are huge, with double and triple wrap-around decks. As you go descend and enter a different neighborhood, the houses get older and smaller. As you arrive at the college campus, look for the Chapel of the Prodigal on the left. Inside, the 16-ft. fresco *The Return of the Prodigal* by North Carolina fresco master Ben Long is worth a visit. Turn right onto Lookout Rd. to get to the main road, and to your car to finish the hike.

Lookout Rock

The highlight of the hike is the Lookout Rock, a stone outcropping which was described by an early resident as "a cone of ice cream turned out on the edge of the mountain." The views from the top of the Montreat and Swannanoa valleys and the Seven Sisters are spectacular. Seven Sisters is a local name for Middle Mountain, a four-mile ridge with more than seven peaks that descend from Graybeard Mountain to the north to Tomahawk Mountain to the southwest.

Getting to the trailhead: Take I-40 to exit 64 at Black Mountain. Make a left on NC 9 and head north through Black Mountain. Continue on NC 9 to the Montreat gates on Assembly Dr. Turn right on Lookout Rd. and park.

Type of hike: Loop

Distance: 4.7 miles

Total ascent: 1,040 ft.

Highlights: Views of Seven Sisters ridge, solitude for most of the hike, history

★ =Start

Assembly Dr
★ Lookout Rd
Montreat
NC 9
US 70   Black Mtn
I-40   Exit 64

USGS map: Montreat

Trail map: Montreat map available at the Montreat Bookshop in the Montreat Conference Center

Land managed by: Montreat Wilderness Area

The Hike

Walk up Lookout Rd. through the campus, past the Chapel of the Prodigal on the right. The Chapel is definitely worth a stop to admire the famous fresco by Ben Long, depicting the Bible story of the return of the prodigal son. Then Lookout Rd. turns to gravel as it goes through a residential area, climbing steeply.

At 0.6 mile (2,940 ft. elev.), turn right into the first (lower) parking area where a wand says "Do not block road." Take the Rainbow Road Trail [orange blazes] at the far end of the parking area, not to be confused with the Rainbow Mountain Trail. The Rainbow Road Trail turns right and goes gently downhill among rhododendron and numerous wildflowers.

The Rainbow Road Trail is one of only two trails that allow mountain biking (the other is Old Mitchell Toll Rd.). However, the trail doesn't feel as if it gets much bike use. It's a pleasant trail filled with rhododendron, hemlock, sourwood, Fraser magnolia, and poplar, with occasional seepages cutting across it.

At 1.1 miles, the trail starts climbing a little and becomes a broken rocky road with winter views to the right.

At 1.6 miles, you'll reach the intersection with the Rainbow Mountain Trail extension, which goes into the woods to the right. This short trail was built to avoid the climb to Rainbow Mountain, since there are no views from that mountain. Stay left and reach the second intersection with Rainbow Mountain Trail at 1.8 miles (3,220 ft. elev.). At 2.2 miles, ignore the driveway you'll pass on the right. The Rainbow Road Trail continues left and up.

At 2.4 miles, you'll reach a four-way intersection; Old Trestle Rd. goes left. A trail coming in from the extreme right should be ignored; it's not on the map. Go straight (a soft right) on Old Mitchell Toll Rd. [unblazed].

Old Mitchell Toll Rd. ascends gently, with winter views to your right. The Toll Road was the route of a logging railroad and later an auto toll road to Mt. Mitchell. For a challenging 14-mile hike, you could follow this trail to the Blue Ridge Parkway, pass the Camp Alice site, and continue to the summit of Mt. Mitchell.

Pass a trail on the right which goes into the Ridgecrest Tranquility Trail system. The Ridgecrest Conference

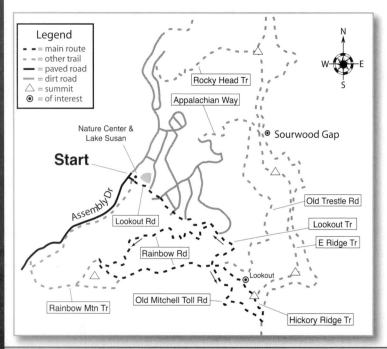

Center, another Christian retreat, has trails which join those of Montreat; you can do a loop which includes both conference centers.

At 3.1 miles, make a left on the Hickory Ridge Trail [blue blazes] and climb the steps built in 2006 by the staff of the Montreat Nature Center. The Hickory Ridge Trail, steep, short, and narrow, goes through nettles. At 3.3 miles, you'll reach Lookout Mountain (3,760 ft. elev.) at a T junction with no views. Make a left on the East Ridge Trail [gray blazes]; you may meet other hikers on their way back from the Lookout. The trail descends steeply through a few rocky spots. At 3.4 miles, the trail makes a sharp left and arrives at Lookout Rock.

From here on a clear day you can see the Seven Sisters, the Montreat valley, and Graybeard Mountain. Lookout Rock is often a hiking destination for those staying at the conference center.

Returning from Lookout Rock on Lookout Trail, follow the yellow blazes on the rocky and steep downhill. Looking straight ahead (northwest) as you descend on the rocks, you can see Assembly Hall, the largest building in Montreat, sometimes referred to as "the castle." As you continue down, more buildings become visible. Two sets of solid wooden stairs help you descend. Soon the rocks disappear,

Figuring out what wildflowers you are looking at is part of the fun of the hike.

but the trail remains steep. A wooden fence on your left is intended to prevent people from shortcutting the trail. This is the busiest trail section in Montreat.

Cross Old Trestle Rd. at 3.7 miles and continue down the Lookout Trail. The end of the trail (4.1 miles) is at a parking area with an information board. Make a soft right onto Lookout Rd. and head back to the parking lot to finish the hike.

Graybeard Mountain

A hike up Graybeard Mountain illustrates both the human and natural history of the area. Old roads, railroad tracks, a shelter, and current residences show that people have been in the area for a long time. On top of Graybeard Mountain, you'll have views of ridges upon ridges all the way to Mt. Mitchell. The Montreat Wilderness has preserved and protected the natural resources and beauty of its holdings. People living in the shadow of the mountain explain that they often can predict rain when the mountain's summit is covered in clouds, resembling a gray beard.

Getting to the trailhead:
Take I-40 east to exit 64 at Black Mountain. Take NC 9 north through the town of Black Mountain. Continue on NC 9 and enter the Montreat gates. Drive on Assembly Drive, past Lake Susan on the right. Continue on Greybeard Trail Rd. to its end and park opposite the Walker C. Jones Sanctuary.

Type of hike: Partial loop

Distance: 8 miles

Total ascent: 2,180 ft.

Highlights: Views, history, cabins, and shelter

USGS map: Montreat

Trail map: Montreat map available at the Montreat Bookshop in the Montreat Conference Center

Land managed by: Montreat Wilderness Area

Special challenge: It is not a good idea to hike the Old Mitchell Toll Rd. during bear hunting season, between mid-October and early January. For more info, check with the N.C. Wildlife Resources Commission at www.ncwildlife.org.

The Hike
The hike starts opposite the Walker C. Jones Wildlife Sanctuary. Take a short diversion left into the Sanctuary, encircled by rosebay rhododendron, and go around the small pond, the original water supply for Montreat.

Back on the Graybeard Trail, continue to the signboard and the bridge on the right. Cross Flat Creek on the bridge and take the Graybeard Trail [blue diamond blazes], which was relocated in 2004. The soil is fresh and soft underfoot. The Graybeard Trail, lined with rhododendron and galax, parallels the cascades and mossy rocks of Flat Creek.

At the junction with the Harry Bryan Trail, take a right to stay on the Graybeard Trail and enter the Lou and Wade Boggs Memorial Wilderness, dotted with dwarf crested iris, speckled wood lily, and Christmas fern. Now you're on the original section of trail at the first of four Flat

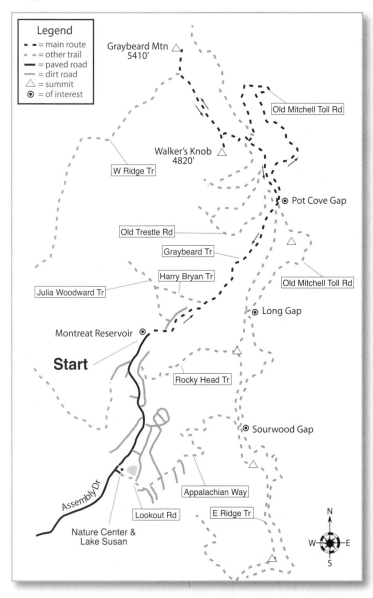

Legend
- ▪ ▪ = main route
- ▪ ▪ = other trail
- ▬ = paved road
- ▬ = dirt road
- △ = summit
- ⊙ = of interest

Graybeard Mtn △
5410'

Old Mitchell Toll Rd

Walker's Knob △
4820'

W Ridge Tr

Pot Cove Gap

Old Trestle Rd

Graybeard Tr

Harry Bryan Tr

Julia Woodward Tr

Old Mitchell Toll Rd

Long Gap

Montreat Reservoir ⊙

Start

Rocky Head Tr

Sourwood Gap

Assembly Dr

Appalachian Way

Lookout Rd

E Ridge Tr

Nature Center &
Lake Susan

N
W—E
S

Creek crossings. Rock hop or use the carefully placed logs to cross the creek. In the summer, families wade in the cold, shallow pools at the bottom of the cascades; the creek crossings may get icy in the winter.

After the fourth creek crossing, the trail, rough and steep for a bit, soon reaches Old Trestle Rd. Cross Old Trestle Rd. and continue on Graybeard Trail to Old Mitchell Toll Rd. [unblazed] at Pot Cove Gap at 1.5 miles. The Toll Rd. follows the general route of a logging railroad built in 1913, which also transported tourists to the flanks of Mt. Mitchell and later to Camp Alice. When logging was no longer profitable, a one-way auto toll road was built; passenger cars went up in the morning

and down in the afternoon. At Pot Cove Gap, look up on the large tree to see a pot hanging from a rusty nail. After a train wreck, it was customary to memorialize the men who died by hanging their lunch pails from a nail in a tree. The gap is a good place for a snack and a view break.

Make a left and continue on the Graybeard Trail, which has joined the Old Mitchell Toll Rd. About 100 yd. further, the Graybeard Trail goes left. That's the way you'll come back. Continue right on the Old Mitchell Toll Rd., which eventually goes to Mt. Mitchell, 12.5 miles away. This section of the Toll Road, known locally as Dickey's Loop, was named for C.A. Dickey, one of the first men to build a logging railroad from Black Mountain to the foot of Mt. Mitchell.

At 2.4 miles (4,240 ft. elev.), pass a rippling cascade on the left. Soon after, you'll reach a wide spot on the trail and take a right to an overlook. From the overlook, the highest close-in mountain you can see looking northeast is Graybeard. It looks a long way off.

Continue climbing, and at 2.7 miles you'll pass a house trailer complete with garden, shed, and American flag. This is the home of the caretaker for the bear hunting club farther down Old Mitchell Toll Rd. You are no longer on Montreat property, but a reciprocal agreement between

Be sure to look for the pot hanging in the tree when you reach Pot Cove.

The Walker Knob shelter is a bit crude, but it keeps out the elements and some of the critters.

the hunters and the Montreat Wilderness allows the public to hike here. Pass another old house with several dog houses and ignore a trail coming in from the right. Cross a little creek, which supplies the water for the two cabins you just passed.

At 3.1 miles (4,510 ft. elev.), the trail splits. If you're curious, take a left to check out winter views and come back to Old Mitchell Toll Rd. At 3.3 miles, take a left on Old Trestle Rd. (here unsigned) which connects to the Graybeard Trail. The flat trail goes through a rhododendron tunnel. In another 0.1 mile you'll reach the junction with the Graybeard Trail, which comes in from the left. Continue straight on the Graybeard Trail, following the blue diamond blazes.

The trail descends, crosses a creek at 3.5 miles (4,490 ft. elev.), and then turns sharply right to follow the blue blazes—a sign pointing the other way says "Switchbacks." The Switchbacks is part of the Old Trestle Rd. that the Montreat maintenance crew has cleared and reopened to make it easier to access Graybeard Mountain. A narrow trail climbs in an enclosed forest among Clinton's lily, trillium, iris, Indian cucumber, fly poison, and false hellebore.

At 3.8 miles (4,750 ft. elev.), at the intersection with the Walker's Knob Trail, take a right to stay on the Graybeard Trail. The trail skirts a rocky stretch and enters an area filled with flame azalea, mountain laurel, and nettle.

You'll reach the top of Graybeard Mountain at 4.5 miles (5,410 ft. elev.). Looking straight ahead, the close-in double hump is Rocky Knob, which could be reached by continuing on Old Mitchell Toll Rd. Behind it, the hump is Pinnacle. To the left in the distance you can see the tower on Mt. Mitchell, and, farther to the left a little closer in, the transmission towers on Clingmans Peak.

Continue left for about 50 ft. to a second lookout. Then retrace your steps down the Graybeard Trail and make a right onto the Walker's Knob Trail [orange blazes] at 5.3 miles. You'll pass an enclosed shelter painted green. Based on the entries in the shelter log book, backpackers use it all year round:

> Hello Beautiful Graybeard
> Small spits of snow around
> from a fall a few days ago
> My first hike since moving
> to town a week ago

You'll reach Walker's Knob at 5.5 miles (4,820 ft. elev.), surrounded by blueberry bushes. Looking down, you can see the town of Black Mountain. The view may even be better here than on Graybeard Mountain, but as the trees continue to grow, they will eventually obscure it.

To return, retrace your steps and make a right onto the Graybeard Trail. Stay on the Graybeard Trail, ignoring the "Switchbacks." The trail makes a right at 6.0 miles, putting you on a new section of Greaybeard Trail for this hike. In less than 0.1 mile, a creek comes in from the right, tumbling over Graybeard Falls into a pool below. A campsite in an idyllic setting is on the other side of the creek.

Here the trail is wet and muddy as you come down on rocky steps through rhododendron and hemlock. At 6.5 miles (4,010 ft. elev.), you're back on Old Mitchell Toll Rd.; make a right. At Pot Cove turn right again. Follow the blue blazes to continue on the Graybeard Trail back to your car to end the hike.

High Windy

This hike is good any time of the year, but it particularly shines in the winter when the trees are bare. The loop takes you up to High Windy, the highest point on the Blue Ridge Assembly property, down to a scenic overlook, and then follows the creek west on Wolfpit Circle. Though the hike is only 6 miles, it does most of its climbing in the first 2.5 miles, making it a good workout.

Getting to the trailhead: Traveling on I-40, take exit 64, to Black Mountain and Montreat, and turn south on NC 9. Proceed less than 0.5 mile and go straight on Blue Ridge Rd. Travel 0.9 mile, turn left at the small Blue Ridge Assembly sign, and continue to the entrance. Park in the upper parking lot behind the Blue Ridge Center (do not park further up). Walk up the stairs. Make a right around Cottage Circle. Continue on Cottage Circle to the back of the Robert E. Lee building.

Type of hike: Loop

Distance: 6 miles

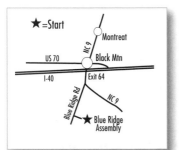

Total ascent: 1,600 ft.

Highlights: Views, chimney on top of High Windy

USGS map: Black Mountain

Trail map: A map is available from the Blue Ridge Center Guest Services Desk, in its main building.

Land managed by: YMCA Blue Ridge Assembly

Related movie: *28 Days* (2000) with Sandra Bullock

The Hike

At the trailhead, a large sign lists all the trails on the property. Take the High Windy Trail, passing the amphitheater on the right, with its large cross. Continue up the road and pass a locked gate on your left signed "Wolfpit Circle." This is where the hike will come back to close the loop.

Follow the High Windy sign and red blazes. The trail is really a wide road lined with rhododendrons, a good place for spotting early spring flowers. If there were ever enough snow here, these broad trails would be a wonderful place for cross-country skiing.

At 0.75 miles, make a right at the T to stay on the High Windy Trail. Soon you'll pass a shelter, originally built as a storm shelter for hikers caught in the rain (it is too small and too close to the trailhead for use by backpackers). At this point, most walkers take the Carolina Loop (which goes to the left), and you will probably have High Windy Trail all to yourself.

The trail alternates between very steep and almost flat as it goes up around the mountain. Before the trees leaf out, you'll have great views, particularly in flat stretches at about 1.5 miles.

At the T junction at 1.9 miles, make a left. The trail

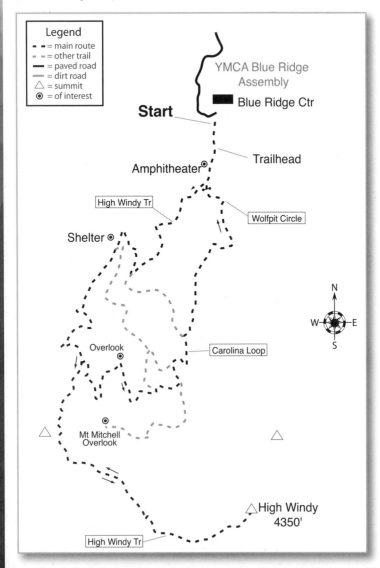

Imagine living up here atop High Windy. The folks who occupied this house had a great view but harsh weather.

the trail to the right will lead to a viewpoint of Mt. Mitchell.

Make a right on the Carolina Loop and follow the stream down. At 4.75 miles, take the blue-blazed Wolfpit Circle. Cross the stream. The trail becomes a road as you get closer to the BRA campus. When you reach the locked gate, you have completed the circle. Return to the trailhead to finish the hike.

descends for a short while but soon climbs to the top of High Windy (4,350 ft. elev.). The top is flat with a new building and transmission tower. Farther along there's an old chimney. Below, another trail connects High Windy to other (unmaintained) trails.

Returning from High Windy, look for the trail to the right with a Blue Ridge Assembly (BRA) sign, and take it. At 3.9 miles, turn right again at another BRA sign which will take you to a scenic overlook at 3,720 ft. elev. From here you are looking due north at the Blue Ridge Parkway. Ignore the first left junction and take the second left. At this point,

Mountains-to-Sea Trail

I'm a person of action. I would encourage
people of all ages to go hiking.

—Katie Nelson, at 79 years of age
the oldest person to finish the MST.

Mountains-to-Sea Trail

Essential Facts

Rules/fees:
The Mountains-to-Sea Trail (MST) does not have official entrances or visitor centers; you can get on and off the trail at hundreds of places. The MST follows the rules of the land it traverses. Note that on Blue Ridge Parkway land, camping is allowed only at designated campgrounds.

Facilities:
Varies based on the section

Closest towns:
Asheville, Brevard, Waynesville, NC

Land managed by:
The MST is part of the North Carolina State Park system, managed by the N.C. Division of Parks and Recreation. In the mountains, most of the trail is on Blue Ridge Parkway land.

Website:
www.ncmst.org

Related books:
Walking the Blue Ridge by Leonard M. Adkins; *Hiking North Carolina's Mountain-to-Sea Trail* by Allen de Hart; *Trail Profiles: The Mountains-to-Sea Trail* by Walt Weber

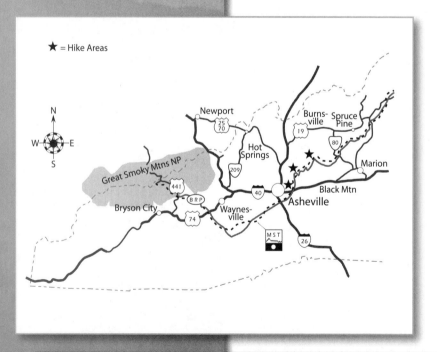

★ = Hike Areas

The Mountains-to-Sea Trail is an ambitious trail project which will eventually traverse North Carolina from Clingmans Dome at 6,643 ft. elev. in the Great Smoky Mountains National Park to Jockey's Ridge State Park on the Atlantic Ocean. The trail offers a unique trek of over 900 miles across the state of North Carolina, reaching high peaks, green valleys, cool streams, farm land, and sand dunes. However, that does not mean that the trail when completed will be a downhill walk from west to east. Currently, the MST is about half on footpaths and half on backcountry roads or N.C. Department of Transportation bike routes. The trail traverses three national parks—Great Smoky Mountains National Park, the Blue Ridge Parkway, and Cape Hatteras National Seashore—and several national forests, including Nantahala, Pisgah, and Croatan. Currently hikers have the option of biking or canoeing parts of the trail, since the footpath is not yet complete.

The Friends of the Mountains-to-Sea Trail, a nonprofit organization formed to turn the vision of the MST into a reality, organizes volunteers to build and maintain the trail across the state. They have adopted the same design and construction practices

You'll recognize the distinctive markers and white circle blazes when hiking the Mountains-to-Sea Trail.

used for the Appalachian Trail. In the mountains, the Carolina Mountain Club is currently responsible for the route from the Great Smoky Mountains National Park to the Black Mountain Campgrounds, and is building 15-mile section west of Balsam Gap. In some sections the MST can be combined with side trails to make a loop.

The logistics of traveling the whole MST are much more complicated than those of hiking the A.T. The MST has no shelters and few legal places to camp, so backpackers have to be creative in finding a place to stay for the night. Since this is a new trail still in the design and construction phase in many places, few services have sprung up to cater to MST backpackers—there are no hostels, shuttle services or all-you-can-eat buffets along the route. There are also no chat rooms, websites, blogs, published personal accounts, or mythology of walking the MST, which are essential for hikers trying to get a feeling for the trail. As of now, only eight people have walked its full length. Number 7 is Katie Nelson, a great-grandmother, and at 79 the oldest to complete the MST.

In the mountains, the MST was built using existing trails, old logging railroad grades, and carriage roads whenever possible. Altitude determines the walking conditions, making the difference between a pleasant spring walk near a bridge over the French Broad at about 2,000 ft. elev. to a cold, snowy trek on top of Silvermine Bald at 5,960 ft. Eventually, the whole MST will be a walking trail marked by white circles. The mountain section of the MST was designated as a National Recreation Trail on National Trails Day in 2005.

The Blue Ridge Parkway

In the western part of the state, the MST ascends and descends with the contour of the Blue Ridge Parkway. The trail keeps coming back to the Parkway until the road leaves North Carolina north of Stone Mountain State Park.

The Blue Ridge Parkway travels the spine of the Southern Appalachians. This 469-mile scenic route goes from the south end of Shenandoah National Park in Virginia to the entrance to the Great Smoky Mountains National Park outside of Cherokee, NC. Though most visitors drive the Parkway, you can also walk, bicycle, or ride a motorcycle, and, if you are really lucky, on rare winter days you can cross-country ski it.

In an effort to relieve the poverty brought on by the Great Depression, and because road building generates wages which immediately circulate into the local economy, the Parkway project was designed to employ as many local men as possible. Two national parks had just been created in Appalachia: Great Smoky Mountains National Park and Shenandoah National Park. In the process of creating these new public lands, timber jobs and property tax money had been lost. The states had bought the land, so the Federal Government agreed to build the road.

Historically, no single person is considered responsible for the construction of the Parkway. Senator Harry F. Byrd of Virginia suggested the idea to President Roosevelt and provided the political will

The Moutains-to-Sea Trail traverses some of North Carolina's highest ridges.

and energy to move the proposal along. Harold L. Ickes, Secretary of the Interior under President Roosevelt, implemented the project and made the difficult decisions. The National Park Service agreed to manage the road and not charge a toll.

One of the most contentious issues was the path the Parkway would take. Politicians realized the tourist potential and wanted the road to go through their territory. The road would start as an extension of the Skyline Drive, through Shenandoah National Park. There were several proposed routes through Virginia, but the Tennessee/North Carolina tug of war was the root of most of the controversy and lobbying. The proposals included going directly from Virginia to Tennessee; from Virginia to North Carolina; and from Virginia to North Carolina, veering west into Tennessee beyond Blowing Rock.

Politicians from outside the area, the mayors of Charleston, SC, and St. Petersburg, FL, in particular, weighed in with their opinions on the route, emphasizing that this was a national road, affecting more than the three states involved. Ickes held hearings, more like formal debates, where Knoxville and Asheville lobbied hard for their respective states. One Tennessee speaker went all the way back to 1780 and the Battle of Kings Mountains to prove that Tennessee was more patriotic than North Carolina. He pointed out that the three presidents who were born in North Carolina all had the good sense to move to Tennessee.

When Ickes finalized his decision on the route through North Carolina, he based it on fairness. He said that Gatlinburg was already an established entrance to the Smokies. To end the Parkway there would effectively make Gatlinburg the only entrance into the park. Moreover, North Carolina had the more scenic route and tourists would appreciate the higher elevation during the summer months.

In 1935, the first section on the Virginia/North Carolina

border was begun. The Parkway was not built in one continuous stretch but in bits and pieces where employment was most needed. Work slowed during World War II; the Parkway was finally completed in 1987 with the construction of the Linn Cove Viaduct on the side of Grandfather Mountain.

The road was meant to preserve not just the scenery, but also the history of the area. In Shenandoah National Park, the Park Service had erased all traces of mountain culture, and they would not repeat that mistake. On the Parkway they kept log cabins and gristmills that reinforce the stereotype of the solitary mountain family. They also preserved upscale homes such as those in Moses H. Cone Memorial Park and the remains of Rattlesnake Lodge (see *Lane Pinnacle* hike, p. 74).

The hiker walking the MST in the mountains will come to understand the Parkway almost as intimately as the trail—the overlooks, mileposts, and tunnels. Sometimes your hike will take you onto the road to close a circle and get back to your car. It's worth noting here that walking through a tunnel is never safe, since they are dark and narrow, and drivers won't be able to see you.

Remember also that the Blue Ridge Parkway is not an interstate. The maximum speed limit is 45 mph, and when the National Park Service decides that a section of the Parkway is too icy for safe driving, they close that section, and it usually stays closed until April. Then it's time to find another place to hike!

Craggy Gardens

The Craggy Mountains, once a candidate for wilderness designation, offer several short hikes. The Mountains-to-Sea Trail (MST) also traverses the area. If you have two cars, do the six-mile shuttle and then hike up to Craggy Pinnacle to round out the day. The trail starts at 5,260 ft. and stays above 5,000 ft. the whole way. If you only have one car, walk from the Graybeard Mountain Overlook (milepost 363.4) to Glassmine Falls Overlook (milepost 361.2) and back.

On this hike you'll pass through two overlooks on the Blue Ridge Parkway.

Getting to the trailhead:

The hike starts at Craggy Gardens picnic area and ends at Glassmine Falls Overlook on the Blue Ridge Parkway. Place a car at Glassmine Falls Overlook first. To get there drive to Blue Ridge Parkway milepost 361.2. Drive the remaining car to the Craggy Gardens picnic area at milepost 367.6. Turn right and take the road to the turn-around point and park. The MST access starts at the far end of the parking area, opposite the restrooms.

Type of hike: Shuttle

Distance: 6 miles to Glassmine Falls, less than 1 mile out and back to Craggy Pinnacle

Total ascent/descent: 1,480 ft./1,430 ft., plus 240 ft. for Craggy Pinnacle

Highlights: Mountain ridges, heath balds, wildflowers, outstanding views

USGS map: Craggy Pinnacle, Montreat

Trail map: South Toe River, Mount Mitchell & Big Ivy Trail Maps, USDA Forest Service.

Land managed by: Pisgah National Forest, Appalachian District, and the Blue Ridge Parkway

The Hike

The hike starts at the far end of the picnic area. Climb up the steps with the restrooms on your left, passing the picnic tables. You are on an access trail which intersects the MST in less than 500 ft. Continue straight and uphill on the MST, heading east.

You're on a good trail walking through blueberry, blackberry, strawberry, wild hydrangea, and rhododendron. You'll see these plants through most of the hike. On the left in the woods, you may see an old, incongruously placed gazebo.

At 0.4 mile, pass a stump on the left from which two

★=Start

Craggy Gardens
★

Milepost 361.2

Blue Ridge Parkway

I-40

Asheville

Legend
- ▪ ▪ = main route
- ▪ ▪ = other trail
- ▬ = paved road
- ═ = dirt road
- △ = summit
- ◉ = of interest

Glassmine Falls Overlook ◉

Locust Knob △

M S T

Bullhead Mtn △

Douglas Falls Tr

◉ Graybeard Mtn Overlook

Start

△ Craggy Dome

△

◉ Craggy Pinnacle
Parking

△ Picnic Area

◉ CCC Shelter

△ Craggy Gardens

N
W ✦ E
S

trees are growing—like a work of modern art. You'll reach a shelter at 0.6 mile (5,640 ft. elev.), from which you can see Craggy Dome and Craggy Pinnacle. The shelter was built in 1935 by the Civilian Conservation Corps from chestnuts logs. Most other wood would have deteriorated by now with the constant exposure to water and wind, but this timber looks solid and permanent. However, the shelter has large gaps between the boards and will not protect you much from the rain.

There are several side trails to the right that lead to the balds on Craggy Gardens. Turn right on one of these trails and wander through the maze of paths. In mid-June, when the rhododendron, azalea, and mountain laurel bloom, many families make this their destination. Turk's cap lilies transform the area into an outstanding flower garden. You can see how the bald is in the process of filling in with blueberry, laurel, and other heath plants. There's a viewpoint enclosed by a stone fence at the extreme left. Retrace your steps to the shelter.

The MST continues through the shelter and down into a rhododendron tunnel. Here the trail is part of a nature trail, with signs explaining the flora and fauna, which terminates at the Craggy Gardens Visitor Center. The MST does not go down to the visitor center.

Ignore all the herd paths to the left. At 0.9 mile, make a well-signposted left turn to continue on the MST. This turn also has a sign for Douglas Falls. The trail is now rocky, wet, and slippery, which makes it slow going—the better to admire your surroundings. It's a hard life here above 5,000 ft. elevation, especially in the winter. Gnarled trees are slanted sideways with trunks split open and sometimes filled with rocks. The trail meanders up and down through a dark tunnel of false hellebore, bluets, rhododendron, and wild hydrangea. Sometimes you'll find small pieces of quartz and mica among the moss-covered rocks.

On the right at 1.5 miles, you'll pass a condominium-sized rock with many ledges. With several caves at the bottom as ground floor apartments, this might be home for a bear in winter. Just as the trail switchbacks down, there's a comfortable sitting rock at 1.6 miles on the right.

This side of the ridge is dry and grassy with fields of trillium.

At 1.9 miles, a yellow-blazed trail on the left heads down to Douglas Falls. Stay to the right on the MST, which climbs up. You'll pass several seepages coming through from rocks on the right at 2.3 miles; the trail is constantly wet. Now you may start to hear noises from the Blue Ridge Parkway through the trees. At 3.1 miles, pass a creek going under a rock bridge, with

The Craggies

Breathtaking, incredible, spectacular: all those clichés have been used for the Craggies, and they all ring true. On days when Asheville, below to the west, is balmy, the rhododendrons are sometimes still curled up and covered with rime ice at Craggy Gardens and Craggy Pinnacle.

In June, the mountain laurel, rhododendron, and azalea at Craggy Gardens, a high-mountain bald, are an explosion of color. However, the balds are fascinating any time of the year. There is no definitive theory on how balds were originally formed, but we know that grazing by settlers' cattle kept them open. All grazing was stopped by 1950. In the fall, Craggy Pinnacle is a popular spot for viewing hawk migration.

You can get to the Glassmine Falls overlook by car on the Blue Ridge Parkway, but it is more fun to hike there.

false bugbane occasionally dotting the woods.

You may wonder about a constant droning sound. At 3.3 miles, you'll reach a maintenance building and portable power generator just off a paved service road. Though the sound detracts from the wilderness experience, you've reached a working end of the Parkway rarely seen by motorists. Walk straight (south) on the blacktop road. At 3.4 miles turn left at the MST sign, and soon you'll reach the Blue Ridge Parkway. Cross the road and follow the trail back into the woods. Though you can see the overlook to your left, stay on the trail; you'll find it's worth it to resist the temptation.

Reach a split-log fence on the right and continue to the Graybeard Mountain Overlook at 3.6 miles. According to the sign, you're at 5,592 ft. elev. and looking down on Graybeard Mountain across the valley. Graybeard is the highest mountain in the Montreat Wilderness, located outside Black Mountain. (See *Graybeard Mountain* hike, p. 54.)

Continue across the parking lot and back into the woods. The trail climbs gently through yellow birches. Though you may note herd paths going off to the right, stay left on the main path. Walk through several small groves of spruces—flat areas with little undergrowth—which are interspersed with gently ascending, rhododendron-lined sections.

At 4.0 miles, you'll pass through a large stand of spruces where you need to follow the white circles closely because the trail is covered in pine needles. At

4.5 miles (5,720 ft. elev.), enter a heath bald in the process of filling in. In September, ripe blueberries here attract many pickers—if bears have not gotten to them first. Soon after on the right, pass a huge boulder with a fringe of blueberry plants on top.

You'll reach a second heath bald with outstanding views to the left at 4.8 miles. In late June, purple-fringed orchid—an occasional, almost rare flower that blooms at high elevation—may be in evidence.

Visiting Craggy Pinnacle

From Glassmine Falls driving south on the Parkway, turn right at milepost 364.1 into the parking area for Craggy Pinnacle. This walk, less than 0.5 mile to the top with 240 ft. of ascent, attracts tourists and residents alike for its panoramic views.

Use the 360-degree view to orient yourself: Craggy Dome to the north, the Parkway to the south, the Asheville watershed to the east. To the west: the Pisgah range, with Mt. Pisgah and its distinctive tower; farther on is Tennessee. On the return, turn left and take in the lower view. The Blue Ridge Parkway built a rock enclosure at each viewpoint to keep tourists from trampling the fragile endangered plants. Stay inside the enclosures—the views are just as good from both.

Gentians also bloom here in the early fall. Three magnificent rocky southeastern viewpoints follow in close succession, each better than the one before. You'll be looking down into the Asheville watershed against a background of mountains. Lunch Rock at 5.1 miles has the best expanse of rock ledges and is a great place for the obvious—lunch. All three views are filling in mostly with mountain laurels, so don't wait too long to try this hike.

The trail goes down into a dark, spooky stand of spruces where most of the bottom branches are dead. You're paralleling the Blue Ridge Parkway, and at 5.7 miles, you can see the road. Descend to a wooden fence which stays between you and the road. At 5.9 miles turn right, head back into the woods, and pass under a buckeye tree. As the trail climbs, you'll stay to the left.

Come down on a grassy trail at 6.0 miles to the Glassmine Falls Overlook to end the hike. Glassmine Falls is referred to as a dry falls because it has water only after a good rainfall.

Extra: You may want to finish the hike with a view from the paved observation area, a less-than-100-yd. walk north from the overlook parking lot.

Lane Pinnacle

On this hike you'll follow the Mountains-to-Sea Trail east from Bull Gap at 3,100 ft. to Lane Pinnacle at 5,230 ft. The trail is generally in good condition, with great winter views. It's easy to follow the white circles all the way up. Bull Gap may have been named for the last bull elk or the last bull buffalo, depending on which legend you choose.

Part of the hike is on an old carriage road with several gentle switchbacks. Rock tripe, the large, leathery lichens growing on rocks here, looks like lettuce and can be eaten when boiled—for emergency use only.

Getting to the trailhead:
Take the Blue Ridge Parkway to milepost 375.6 at Bull Gap. Turn at the brown Weaverville/ Vance Birthplace sign. The trailhead is 1.0 miles from this turn. At the T, turn right on Ox Creek Rd. The trailhead is the second one on this road. Look for the white circle blazes of the Mountains-to-Sea Trail.

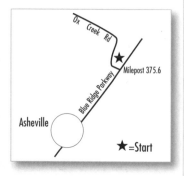

Take the short access trail and turn left onto the MST.

Type of hike: Out and back

Distance: 10 miles

Total ascent: 2,900 ft.

Highlights: Views of mountain ridges, lake, historical house remains

USGS map: Craggy Pinnacle

Trail map: *Trail Profiles: The Mountains-to-Sea Trail* by Walt Weber

Land managed by:
Pisgah National Forest, Appalachian District, and Blue Ridge Parkway

The Hike
After 1.4 miles of hiking, you'll reach the site of Rattlesnake Lodge site at 3,700 ft. elev. Rattlesnake Lodge was the summer home of Asheville physician and outdoor activist Chase P. Ambler. Built in 1903 and occupied until 1920, the building burned to the ground in the late 1920s. The retaining walls and foundations for its tennis courts, swimming pool, and caretaker's cabins will give you a good feel for the lifestyle of another era's rich and famous—famous in Asheville, at least. In those days, Ambler's wife and children went up to the Lodge as soon as school let out in the spring and returned to Asheville in the fall. Dr. Ambler came up on weekends. From the porch of the main house,

guests could look down the mountainside into the Swannanoa River basin.

Chase Ambler owned land from Bull Gap to Lane Pinnacle and supervised the building of a horse trail from his property to Mt. Mitchell in 1908. It was hoped that this trail would be part of the proposed "Crest of the Blue Ridge Highway," the precursor of the Blue Ridge Parkway.

Although the road was started in 1912, it didn't get far. However, much of Ambler's trail became part of the MST. At the center of the site, a display board erected by the Carolina Mountain Club shows a map, pictures, and descriptions of the old Lodge and outbuildings.

Continue past the main lodge site to reach an intersection. The trail leading right descends 0.4 miles to the Parkway at the Tanbark Ridge tunnel (milepost 374.4). It's the shortest route between the Lodge and the Parkway.

Leaving Rattlesnake Lodge, continue climbing the flanks of Bull Mountain and cross a branch of Bull Creek. You'll reach Rich Knob at 3.4 miles. Beware of the barbed wire just off the trail on the left. Enjoy the downhill, because soon you'll climb Wolf Den, the next knob at 4.2 miles. You'll go through the Lemon Squeezer, where the trail passes between two rocks.

There's another downhill and one last climb to Lane

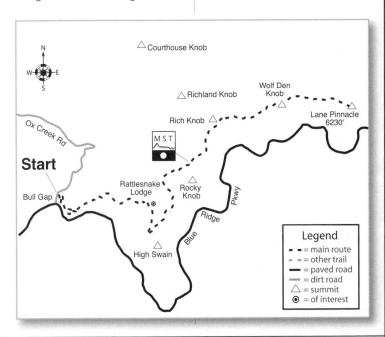

Pinnacle, your destination at 5,230 ft. elev. The mountain was named for Charles Lane, who worked in an iron mine on its north slope. From the rocky outcropping at the summit, you can see Beetree Reservoir and a classic mountain view with layer upon layer of folding blue ridges. The tower in the distance sits atop Little Pisgah Mountain.

On the return you'll retrace your steps. Before reaching the Rattlesnake Lodge site, take an unmarked trail on the left, known colloquially as the cistern trail. Soon you'll reach a large walled-in area with water gushing out of a pipe. Past the cistern, the trail joins the MST at the main Lodge area. Continue back on the MST to finish the hike where you began it.

From atop Lane Pinnacle you'll view Beetree Reservoir and the source of much of Asheville's drinking water.

Folk Art Center

Starting at the Folk Art Center on the Blue Ridge Parkway, this short hike incorporates art and wilderness. It follows the Mountains-to-Sea Trail east to Lunch Rock overlooking the Haw Creek valley. This section of trail is maintained at a high standard. You'll meet dog walkers, joggers, and hikers doing a short section of this hike. While most city dwellers have a regular walking route in a park or on neighborhood streets, Asheville residents and their dogs are lucky enough to get their daily exercise in a national park.

Getting to the trailhead:
The Folk Art Center is on the Blue Ridge Parkway at milepost 382 and can also be reached from I-40 exit 55 just east of Asheville. Park in the Folk Art Center parking lot.

Type of hike: Out and back

Distance: 4.9 miles

Total ascent: 890 ft.

Highlights: Views, Folk Art Center

USGS map: Oteen

Trail map: *Trail Profiles: The Mountains to Sea Trail* by Walt Weber.

Land managed by: Blue Ridge Parkway

The Hike
Follow the white circle blazes of the Mountains-to-Sea Trail, which goes in front of the Folk Art Center. Here, several information boards detail the building of the Blue Ridge Parkway. This section of the MST begins on a graveled nature trail with interpretive signboards highlighting native trees and their traditional uses.

Passing a bench on the left, continue right on the descending path and follow the white circles into the woods. At 0.2 mile, the MST and the nature trail split; turn right on the MST.

The trail crosses Riceville Rd. on a bridge on the left side of the Blue Ridge Parkway. The paved road on your left is Bull Mountain Rd. You'll walk among sassafras, red maple, tulip poplar, remnants of American chestnut, and lots of poison ivy.

Now fully in the woods, you'll pass a bench at 0.4 mile and another one soon after. The trail begins to ascend. At 0.9 mile, a side trail shoots off to the left. Stay on the MST, which parallels the Parkway.

At 1.1 miles (2,480 ft. elev.), you'll cross the Blue Ridge

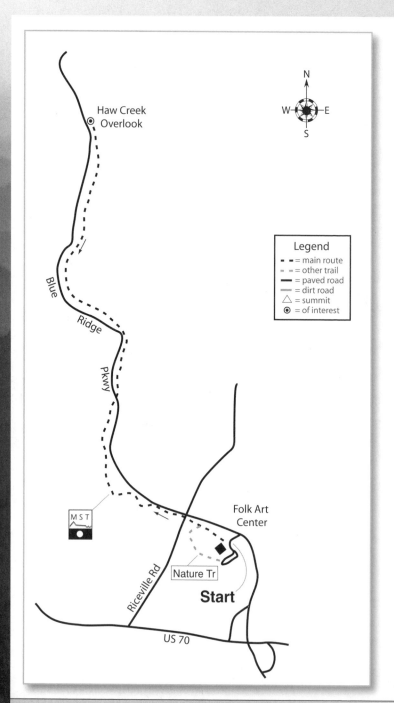

Legend
- - - = main route
- - = other trail
— = paved road
— = dirt road
△ = summit
◉ = of interest

Haw Creek Overlook

Blue Ridge Pkwy

MST

Folk Art Center

Nature Tr

Start

Riceville Rd

US 70

Parkway. The trail continues on the other side of the road with an MST post showing you the way. At 1.6 miles, the trail starts climbing steeply above the Parkway. On your left, at 1.8 miles (2,670 ft. elev.), you can see houses in the valley below. Pass a boulder on your right and continue up.

You'll reach a local top, and then the trail descends through white pine and rhododendron. Even in the summer it's a cool trail, well-shaded by trees. At 2.1 miles, note a large house straight ahead of you, built on the eastern side of the ridge. Here, land is developed right up to the Parkway boundaries. The trail turns sharply left.

After the last little climb, you'll reach a side trail to the left at 2.4 miles. The tree on the right side of the MST has a small red dot along with a white circle. Make a left and descend slightly to Lunch Rock/Haw Creek Overlook at 2,830 ft.elev. You're on a large rock outcropping surrounded by pitch pines and blueberry bushes, looking west onto the Haw Creek valley.

Haw Creek, now a neighborhood in east Asheville, was named for the creek which flows southwest into the Swannanoa River. Look down and to the left on the Parkway for the Haw Creek Valley Overlook at milepost 380. Return the way you came on the MST to end the hike.

The Folk Art Center

The Folk Art Center is the most popular attraction on the Blue Ridge Parkway. It is the centerpiece of the Southern Highland Craft Guild, founded in 1930. The Guild now has over 900 members, chosen by a jury of their craft peers.

Here you can watch craft demonstrations and stroll through exhibitions in three galleries. The Center also houses the Allanstand Craft Shop, the oldest continuously operating craft shop in the nation, which sells crafts by Guild members. The front of the building is a Parkway Visitor Center with water, restrooms, and Parkway information.

Upstairs, don't miss the engineering drawings from the construction of the Blue Ridge Parkway. Of special interest are old photos of the Parkway routes and explanations of the effort taken to give the Parkway a natural appearance.

Extra: When you get close to the Folk Art Center, you may want to finish the nature loop and learn more about native trees. Be sure to leave some time for visiting the Folk Art Center.

Dupont State Forest & Flat Rock

I'm an idealist. I don't know where I'm going,
but I'm on my way.

—Carl Sandburg, poet, biographer,
and owner of Connemara in Flat Rock, NC,
now a National Historic Site

Dupont State Forest & Flat Rock

Essential Facts for Dupont State Forest

Rules/fees:
Dogs must be on leash at all times. Pack in/pack out—this means there are no trash bins.

Facilities:
Portable toilets at some parking lots

Closest towns:
Brevard and Hendersonville, NC

Website:
www.dupontforest.com

Related movie:
The Last of the Mohicans (1992) with Daniel Day-Lewis.

Planning a hike in Dupont State Forest can be an expression of your philosophy of life. If you believe that life is uncertain and like to eat dessert first, then head for the waterfalls. If you believe you should work for your rewards and save the best for last, go for the woods and the views before coming down to the waterfalls toward the end of your walk.

Dupont State Forest is the most visited forest in North Carolina, which is not surprising since it contains Lake Julia and six outstanding waterfalls not far from the parking areas. Hikers, runners, cyclists, and horses share

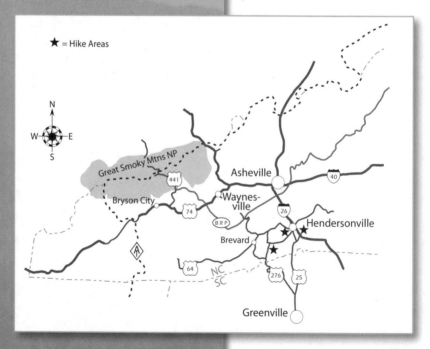

★ = Hike Areas

Bridal Veil Falls is one of Dupont State Forest's most popular destinations.

most of the 90-plus miles of trails and dirt roads.

The 10,000 acres which make up Dupont State Forest have a recent history which is still being played out in the news. In 1958, Dupont Corporation opened a plant in the center of what is now the State Forest, close to the community of Cedar Mountain between Brevard and Hendersonville. Dupont was attracted by the clean air and the clear water of the Little River which runs through the property. The plant manufactured two main items here: medical X-ray film and polyester film, used as a base for graphic arts film produced at other Dupont facilities worldwide. These products are now casualties of the digital imaging revolution.

Much of the land surrounding the plant was fashioned as a private corporate retreat with picnic shelters, barbecue pits, and wide dirt roads. Visitors from other Dupont corporate locations were taken on lunchtime picnics within view of High Falls. Later Dupont bought nearby Camp Summit, a private summer camp for children which operated from the 1960s to the mid-1980s. Lake Julia was its swimming and boating lake, complete with a boathouse. An airstrip was constructed for a development that was planned but never built. The airstrip, now off the Airstrip Trail, offers wonderful views of the Pisgah range, including Mt. Pisgah.

When Dupont decided to leave the area in 1996, they sold 7,600 acres to the state at a cut-rate price, forming the bulk of the state forest. Sterling Diagnostic bought the plant and the rest of the acreage, including three spectacular waterfalls: High Falls, Triple Falls, and Bridal Veil Falls. However, Sterling did not stay very long and sold its plant to Agfa, who did not want the surrounding land. The land went to Jim Anthony, an upscale housing developer, through a secret bidding process.

When the public woke up to the fact that the state was going to lose these outstanding waterfalls to a gated housing community, it petitioned the Governor to obtain the land, by eminent domain if needed, and enlarge the state forest. By this time, Anthony had improved a few roads, built a covered bridge, and started several houses.

A Friends of the Falls volunteer group was formed to lobby for saving the forest from developers. After lawsuits, editorials, and many letters and faxes to the Governor's office, the state paid the developer almost four times his purchase price. The waterfall tract was opened in December 2000, and the future of Dupont State Forest and its waterfalls was secured. Friends of Dupont Forest, the current volunteer

Fawn Lake in Dupont State Forest attracts fishermen as well as hikers.

Expect to see trail users of all stripes in Dupont.

organization, now maintains the trails. They have managed to correctly signpost over 90 trails and countless junctions.

But the drama may not be over. Now the Agfa plant in the center of Dupont State Forest has closed permanently and reverted back to Dupont, who has demolished the building and is cleaning up the site in preparation for turnover to the state. There has been a proposal to create a state park from the new land acquisition. North Carolina State Parks are better funded and more focused on recreation than state forests. Parks usually have better road access, which means that if the new land became a state park, visitors would be able to drive closer to the falls and Lake Julia. If the plant

building had been saved, it could have been turned into a visitor center, which the Forest does not have at this point.

However, the Friends of Dupont Forest wants to keep all the land as a forest and not build new roads, while still trying to get more funding. As a state forest, Dupont allows limited hunting by permit only for deer, turkey, and small game. A hunting safety zone has been delineated in the most popular part of the forest, which is clearly shown on the map. Only time will tell the outcome of these developments.

The parking lots and the trails to the first three waterfalls (Hooker, Triple, and High Falls) get plenty of visitors. Getting to these falls entails seeing just a small part of the forest; the rest of it is not very crowded. The trail map, available at the Pisgah National Forest Visitor Center on US 276 and at area outfitters, currently shows over 90 trails, most of them quite short. To explore the forest beyond the first three waterfalls, a map is absolutely necessary. Winter is a great time to hike the dirt roads and trails, which are generally well-marked and wide, with gentle grades.

Because of its easy, rolling trails and roads, Dupont State Forest is a hotbed for geocaching, a new sport for GPS users. Think of geocaching as a technical version of the

The Carl Sandburg Home today looks much the same as it did in Sandburg's lifetime.

old-fashioned treasure hunt. Caches are set up all over the world, and their locations are shared on the internet. GPS users can then use the location coordinates to find the caches. Once found, a cache may provide the visitor with a wide variety of rewards, usually small trinkets. Caches are rated by the difficulty of terrain and the challenge of finding the cache.

Dupont State Forest is young, and plenty of improvements are planned. Since Dupont opened to the public, trail numbers have changed, and some trails have been consolidated. Be sure to check the information boards located at the main entrances for the latest changes.

Carl Sandburg Home

Carl Sandburg was a poet, journalist, folk singer, and biographer who provided a unique American voice for working men and women. He is perhaps best known for his six-volume work chronicling the life of Abraham Lincoln. Twice he won the Pulitzer Prize. Though Sandburg is associated with the Midwest, he moved his family to Flat Rock, NC, in 1945, seeking privacy and a milder climate.

Since the early 1800s, Flat Rock had been a summer haven for rich Charlestonians who wanted to get away from the heat and malaria of the Low Country. The village of Flat Rock is considered a historic district, though most of the

en River Game Lands

Green River Game
ds, a relatively new
eation area, is located
he southwestern corner
orth Carolina, almost at
South Carolina border
just across interstate I-26
Hendersonville and Flat
. Currently the land is
sturbed wilderness with
and narrow ravines,
s, and some old growth
ts. The Green River runs
ugh a rugged gorge on
Blue Ridge Escarpment,
re at one point it drops
ft. in elevation in a
nce of 1.5 miles and runs
ugh a 6-ft.-wide crevice
vn as "the Narrows."
m Creek cuts a deep
e near the Green River,
ing several small cascades.
he 16 miles of trails
nanaged by ECO
onmental and
ervation Organization,
profit group based in
lersonville) and the N.C.
wildlife Resources Commission.
As the name implies, hunting,
trapping, and fishing are
allowed in the Game Lands.
The mix of trails and old roads
in the Game Lands are not
blazed. However, signs mark
the trails at intersections.

*Green River Game Lands boasts
large stands of huge hemlock.*

Dupont Five Falls Loop

This hike takes in five outstanding waterfalls in Dupont State Forest. The three most popular ones—Hooker Falls, High Falls, and Triple Falls—were sites for several scenes in The Last of the Mohicans. The other two, Wintergreen Falls and Grassy Creek Falls, offer more solitude and require a little more walking. On the way, you'll climb to a ridge in the northern part of the Forest which gets fewer visitors. Dupont's myriad of trails are all signposted.

Because Dupont is a multiple-use forest (hiking, biking, and horses), the trails look as if they are constantly under maintenance construction—you'll see new gravel patches on a section of trail and logs from freshly cut trees waiting to be collected. As a hiker, remember to yield to horses and watch out for bikers.

Getting to the trailhead:
From the community of Pisgah Forest, travel east on US 64 for 3.7 miles to Penrose. Turn right on Crab Creek Rd. for 4.3 miles. Turn right again on Dupont Rd. for 3.1 miles. Dupont Rd. turns into Staton Rd. The Hooker Falls parking lot is on the right.

Type of hike: Lollipop

Distance: 11.2 miles

Total ascent: 1,240 ft.

Highlights: Waterfalls, lake, covered bridge

USGS map: Standing Stone Mountain

Trail map: Dupont State Forest, published by Friends of Dupont Forest, 2005.

Land managed by: North Carolina State Forest

The Hike
At the Hooker Falls trailhead, take Hooker Falls Rd. [#38] at the back and to the left of the parking lot. Stay to the left on the trail; the right side has a view for wheelchair access. Passing a viewpoint of the falls on the left, continue to the base of Hooker Falls at 0.4 mile to get a closer look. The volume of water going over these falls is impressive, although the falls itself is not very high. Because of its proximity to the parking lot relative to other falls in Dupont State Forest, Hooker Falls attracts many visitors. Fishermen congregate along the Little River, which is stocked with trout.

Retrace your steps, but before you reach the parking lot, turn left on Hooker Ridge

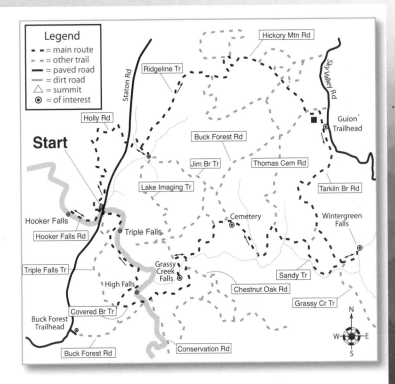

Legend
- = main route
- = other trail
— = paved road
— = dirt road
△ = summit
◉ = of interest

Staton Rd

Ridgeline Tr

Holly Rd

Start

Hooker Falls

Hooker Falls Rd

Triple Falls Tr

Triple Falls

Buck Forest Rd

Jim Br Tr

Lake Imaging Tr

Thomas Cem Rd

Cemetery

Grassy Creek Falls

High Falls

Covered Br Tr

Buck Forest Trailhead

Buck Forest Rd

Conservation Rd

Chestnut Oak Rd

Sandy Tr

Grassy Cr Tr

Wintergreen Falls

Tarkiln Br Rd

Guion Trailhead

Sky Valley Rd

Hickory Mtn Rd

N
W ✦ E
S

Rd. [#39]. Stay on Hooker Ridge Rd. as it bends to the right, and make a right on Holly Rd. [#36]. In this regenerated forest you'll see white pines, doghobble, Christmas fern, and club moss.

At 2.0 miles, cross Staton Rd. Take Lake Imaging Trail [#45] on the left and pass an information board. Soon after, you'll pass the Ridgeline Trail [#65] coming in on the left. You will come back to that trail, but for now continue straight on to Lake Imaging, a small man-made lake with a covered picnic shelter, benches, and bird feeders. Then turn back and take the Ridgeline

Trail [#65], now on the right, which represents the only real sustained climbing of the hike. It's a steep trail, but halfway up you'll start to see views of the surrounding mountains. Once on the ridge, turn right to stay on the Ridgeline Trail, which takes you away from the crowds to another section of the forest on the ridge. As the trail goes east and you head gently down and to the right, you can see good mountain views. It's a quiet part of the forest.

You'll reach a building with open sides, which used to be a place for target practice. Go straight across the field and

Triple Falls is one of the easiest waterfalls to get to in Dupont.

left. Go past the fields and head back into the woods on Tarkiln Branch Rd. [#80], which goes gently downhill. You'll see large boulders scattered on the hills to your left.

Make a left on Wintergreen Falls Trail [#90]. You'll hear the sound of the rushing creek before you can see anything. Stay left on Wintergreen Falls Trail. At the creek, turn left at the "foot traffic only" sign. The waterfall is at the top of a short but steep rock scramble at 6.4 miles. The rocks are slick when wet—and it is always wet, so proceed with care. Wintergreen Falls, named for the wintergreen growing in the area, is a photogenic cascade on the upper part of Grassy Creek.

Backtrack to Wintergreen Falls Trail and turn left on Grassy Creek Trail [#28]. When Grassy Creek Trail turns left and goes across the creek (there's no bridge), continue straight on Sandy Trail [#70], which parallels Grassy Creek on the left. Turn left and continue on Tarkiln Branch Rd. to cross a tributary of Grassy Creek.

Turn left on Thomas Cemetery Rd. [#81]. The cemetery is one of the first hints that there was a community here before Dupont. On Thomas Cemetery Rd. you can hear the constant sound of water, though you can't see it. At 8.1 miles, visit the cemetery on your left. The only legible grave markers are

make a left at 3.8 miles. You're now on Hickory Mountain Rd. [#33]. Look for the perfectly round holes high up in the trees, and you might see the woodpeckers that made them.

You'll pass a stand of white pine on the left. If you want to get the feel of a white pine forest, take the White Pine Trail which comes back to Hickory Mountain Rd.

At the intersection of Hickory Mountain Rd. and Buck Forest Rd., you can take Buck Forest Rd. right back to High Falls, but if you do you'll miss two waterfalls. Instead, go through the fields toward the Guion Farmhouse, public picnic shelter, horse tie-out, and gazebo. Stay on the trail with the parking lot on your for R.W.C. Thomas (1833-1908) and his wife, Harriet (1830-1906). The other grave markers are little stone stumps with no apparent dates. The cemetery is well-maintained and a new sign reads, "No pain, no grief, no anxious fear can reach our loved ones sleeping here."

Continue on Thomas Cemetery Rd . On the left, just before you reach Buck Forest Rd., look for a metal tube on a tree. The bark has now grown over the metal. The tube may have held early telephone or electrical wires.

Turn left on Buck Forest Rd. [#8], and then make a right on Lake Imaging Trail [#45] to see Grassy Creek Falls. Turn left on Grassy Creek Falls Trail [#27] and follow the arrow to the left to the falls. On the steep, narrow trail, you'll pass a large barbecue pit from the Dupont days. The trail goes down about 100 ft. to a side trail on the left which leads to a small lookout.

Grassy Creek Falls at 8.9 miles is broad and rocky. The dark brown water, stained with tannin, descends a long slide into a pool. Since you are looking at the falls at an angle, it may be difficult to photograph. The base of the falls is inaccessible, so just enjoy the stop.

Retrace your steps to the Lake Imaging Trail and make a right onto Buck Forest Rd., which was to have been the main road through a housing development. Note the substantial bridges. You are now entering the most popular part of the forest— popular primarily because of the falls and covered bridge.

Stay on Buck Forest Rd. as it makes a right and crosses the covered bridge at the top

Wintergreen Falls is found in a remote section of Dupont State Forest.

of High Falls. You'll see the picnic shelter and the steps on the other side—that's where you're heading. Turn right on Covered Bridge Trail [#20]. Further down on your left you can see the Dupont plant site which has been dismantled.

Turn right on High Falls Trail [#34] and pass a privy and shelter. To descend the

Hooker Falls and the huge plunge pool below are popular hangouts in the heat of summer.

steps to the base of High Falls at 10.2 miles, take the right fork to the new shelter with a barbecue pit and chimney. High Falls, about 120 ft. high, has been called perhaps the most impressive falls in the area. Make a left to continue on High Falls Trail and follow the Little River as it gathers momentum for the last waterfall on this hike.

Make a right onto Triple Falls Trail [#82]. Stay right through the wooden gate, signposted "foot traffic only" for the best view of Triple Falls at 10.8 miles. Despite the sign, watch out for bike traffic; the 150-ft. waterfall with three distinct cascades attracts a crowd almost all the time.

Continue down from Triple Falls as the trail parallels the rocky creek with several small cascades. Turn left on Galax Rd. [#26] and head up the steps. You'll cross Staton Rd. and go right to the Hooker Falls parking lot to finish the hike.

Bridal Veil Falls Loop

"It's not the destination; it's all about the journey." Most everyone has seen some version of this adage on bumper stickers and t-shirts. But in Dupont, sometimes the hike is about the destinations. Bridal Veil Falls Loop takes you to Bridal Veil Falls; to Lake Julia, a man-made lake with luxurious, half-finished houses; and to Fawn Lake. The journey, on trails and dirt roads, is pleasant and easy enough, but it's not wild—the highlights are what make the walk worthwhile. Walking allows for a sense of discovery and anticipation you just can't get riding in a car.

Getting to the trailhead:
From Brevard, take US 276S for 11.2 miles. Make a left turn onto Cascade Rd. at the Cedar Mountain Fire and Rescue Squad. After less than 0.1 mile, turn right onto Reasonover Rd. Go 2.8 miles and turn left into the Fawn Lake parking area.

Type of hike: Loop

Distance: 6.3 miles

Total ascent: 900 ft.

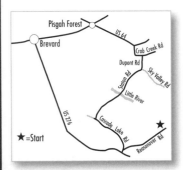

Highlights: Bridal Veil Falls, Lake Julia, Fawn Lake, brand-new abandoned houses

USGS map: Standing Stone Mountain

Trail map: Dupont State Forest, published by Friends of Dupont Forest, 2005

Land managed by: North Carolina State Forest

The Hike
From the parking lot, take a left on Fawn Lake Loop [#22]. Make a left on Mine Mountain Trail [#55] where, at the junction, you'll pass a small stone building. As you walk on Mine Mountain Trail, you can pick up a footpath on the left which later rejoins the main trail. The foot trails are meant to give hikers a break from bicycles and horses.

At 1.1 miles, take a left on Cart Trail [#14] and another left on Laurel Ridge Trail [#48] at 1.5 miles. Stay on Laurel Ridge Trail until you reach Corn Mill Shoals Trail [#19]. (There are several trail names with the word "shoals" in them, so pay attention to the exact trail name.) A right on Corn Mill Shoals Trail will take you to Bridal Veil Falls, the first highlight of the hike.

Corn Mill Shoals Trail is rockier than most trails in Dupont because it follows a limestone ridge, which can be slippery even when dry. The trail levels out a little and passes through

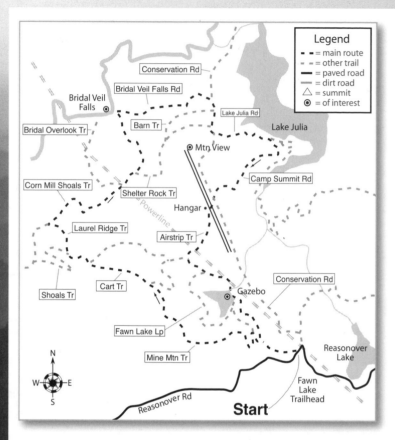

Legend
- ▪ ▪ = main route
- ▪ ▪ = other trail
- ▬ = paved road
- ▨ = dirt road
- △ = summit
- ◉ = of interest

Conservation Rd
Bridal Veil Falls Rd
Bridal Veil Falls ◉
Lake Julia Rd
Lake Julia
Bridal Overlook Tr
Barn Tr
◉ Mtn View
Corn Mill Shoals Tr
Camp Summit Rd
Shelter Rock Tr
Powerline
Hangar •
Laurel Ridge Tr
Airstrip Tr
Conservation Rd
Cart Tr
Gazebo ◉
Shoals Tr
Reasonover Lake
Fawn Lake Lp
Mine Mtn Tr
N W E S
Fawn Lake Trailhead
Reasonover Rd
Start

a rhododendron tunnel to parallel a tributary of the Little River on the right. Galax and mountain laurel abound, and you'll notice the trail maintainance workers have placed rocks to keep hikers from walking down off the trail. Long before you see them, you'll hear the thundering falls.

At 2.8 miles, the falls appear on the left. Note the sign warning of injury and possible death if you climb up the falls. The top part of the falls is a 4-ft. overhanging ledge and the lower section widens out into a shallow bridal veil, where water radiates over a jumble of rocks into a little lake. A dramatic scene in *The Last of the Mohicans* was filmed here. Sit on a log, have your lunch, and enjoy listening to the roar of the water.

Leaving the falls, walk to the intersection of Bridal Veil Falls Rd. [#6] and Corn Mill Shoals Trail and take Bridal Veil Falls Rd., which brings you quickly to a circular parking lot.

If this area were to become part of a state park, you would be able to drive to this point, only a few hundred feet from Bridal Veil Falls. The falls would be packed with people (not to mention law enforcement personnel), who now are unwilling to walk the two miles (via the shortest route) to Bridal Veil Falls. It's interesting to speculate about how this parking lot came to be. The road and a circular driveway may have been created during the Dupont days when employees were transported to all these sites and later upgraded when a film crew was brought in for *The Last of the Mohicans*.

Back on Bridal Veil Falls Rd., you'll pass a modern barn with paddocks. The barn is shut up and the curtains are drawn tightly to keep curious passersby from seeing inside. There is a picnic table and portable toilet next to the barn.

Take a right on Conservation Rd. [#18]. You'll pass a half-finished house on the left and a maintenance building on the right.

Make a left on Lake Julia Rd. [#46]. Driving is prohibited on all these roads now, but it is easy to imagine the gated community that could have developed here. The first building on the left with steps down to the dock and lake, known as the Lodge, was originally the boat house for an upscale summer camp and is now the Ranger Office.

At 3.8 miles, at the intersection of Lake Julia Rd. and Camp Summit Rd., continue a short distance to a peninsula with picnic tables on Lake Julia. One house, which looks finished— it even has an air conditioner unit—is under renovation to be used as a classroom. The other building on the right may have been intended as the clubhouse; it now has orange barriers to keep out curious onlookers. According to a ranger, this house is scheduled for demolition.

Back on Lake Julia Rd., make a left on Camp Summit Rd. [#12], which skirts the hill and goes up gently. You'll pass a modest house on the right, obviously occupied,

The view of Mt. Pisgah from the airstrip is amazing on a clear day.

It's the upper portion of Bridal Veil that gives the falls its name.

right at 5.8 miles. This tiny man-made lake can be used for fishing, swimming, or even boating, if you're willing to carry in a boat. By the most direct route, you are now less than 0.5 mile from your car. You can picnic at the table or in the gazebo on the lake. When you reach the other end of the Fawn Lake Loop, continue walking away from the lake. You'll soon be back at the intersection of Fawn Lake Loop and Mine Mountain Trail. Head down the hill and back to the Fawn Lake parking area to finish the hike.

with its propane tank, baby swing set, and barking dog.

If you made a left here on Conservation Rd., you would get back to your car faster, but you'd miss Fawn Lake. Past the house, looking across an airstrip, you'll see an airplane hangar with a sign "Summit 2,800 ft." To get the best view of the mountain ridges in the distance, including Mt. Pisgah, go right and walk out on the airstrip. Most of this hike focuses on what's on the ground, so take this view as a reminder that you're still in the Carolina mountains.

Head back to the hangar and take a right onto Airstrip Trail [#1]. Make a left on Fawn Lake Loop [#22], and Fawn Lake will sneak up on you on the

Stone Mountain Loop

This hike leads you to the northeast corner of Dupont State Forest and takes in two mountains: Stone Mountain, the highest in the Forest, and Hickory Mountain. It's in a quiet part of Dupont, away from the popular waterfalls and the crowds they sometimes attract. If you want to shorten the hike by about 1.7 miles, skip the rifle range and Hickory Mountain and take the Boundary Trail the first time you meet it.

Getting to the trailhead:
From the community of Pisgah Forest, travel east on US 64 for 3.7 miles to Penrose. Turn right on Crab Creek Rd. and continue for 4.3 miles. Turn right again on Dupont Rd. After 0.8 mile, turn left on Sky Valley Rd. Follow Sky Valley Rd. for 1.7 miles to the Guion Farm Access Area on the right. (The last 0.8 mile is gravel.)

Type of hike:
Double loop with an out-and-back extension

Distance: 9 miles

Total ascent: 1,620 ft.

Highlights: Mountain views, cool forest, history

USGS map: Standing Stone Mountain

Trail map: Dupont State Forest, published by the Friends of Dupont Forest, 2005

Land managed by: North Carolina State Forest

The Hike
The hike starts at the Guion Farm Access Area—a large parking area with portable toilets. Check the information board, which may have current news about trails and a current map. Walk north away from the information board past the picnic shelter, gazebo, and Guion Farm house on your right and a large field on your left.

You'll reach the corner of the field at the intersection of Buck Forest Rd. and Hickory Mountain Rd. The second house you see on the other side of Buck Forest Rd. is the ranger's house, a private residence. Follow Hickory Mountain Rd. [#33] into the woods. You'll be walking in a white pine forest with healthy poison ivy on the side of the trail.

Pass the first junction with White Pine Loop on the right, White Pine Trail on the left, and at 0.5 mile, the second junction of White Pine Loop on the right. An open field on the left at 0.8 mile is full of spring and summer

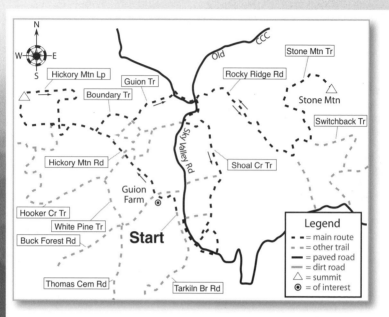

flowers. Pass the Boundary Trail on the right—you will come back to this intersection after returning from Hickory Mountain. If you want to shorten the hike, make a right and follow the instructions below from the Boundary Trail.

At 1.0 mile, reach an open field with a building on a hill to your right. The building at the end of the rifle range has open sides and a roof with a storage building on the end. The trail goes around the building and reaches the intersection of Hickory Mountain Loop [#32] and Ridge Line Trail at 1.1 miles. Take the loop clockwise, since it may be a little easier and less steep. The trail climbs through white pine, maple, oak, and hickory trees, reaching the top of Hickory Mountain at

1.5 miles (3,020 ft. elev.). The top of Hickory Mountain has winter views looking north out of the Forest.

The trail goes down immediately, descending gently through Fraser magnolia, oak, and sassafras. As you come out of the woods, look for the rifle range and a small building on your left. Looking back on your extreme left against the rocks, you can see the rusting target stands empty of their targets, like arms and legs without heads. Imagine men going out into the woods on a Sunday afternoon to practice target shooting before walking back to the Guion site for a picnic with the rest of the family.

When you get back to Hickory Mountain Loop

Trail and the junction of the Ridgeline Trail at 2.3 miles, go across the field, keeping the building to your right, and get back on Hickory Mountain Rd. toward the Guion farm site. At 2.5 miles, turn left on Boundary Trail [#4], which goes east and, as you can guess by the name, skirts the Forest boundary. This is where you'd pick up the directions if you skipped Hickory Mountain.

Make a left on the Guion Trail [#31], also bounded by private property on your left with paint on trees and huge signs littering the trail. At 3.0 miles, the Guion Trail goes down steeply on a wide, hard-packed trail, which is probably thrilling for mountain bikers. Toward the bottom of the trail, you're walking in a rocky trench. Go around a cable wire gate and turn right onto Sky Valley Rd. Make a left on Old CCC Rd. at 3.4 miles and look for a trail on the right. Almost immediately after you start on Old CCC Rd., turn right on Rocky Ridge Rd. [#69].

The climb is short and steep, but in about 0.2 miles the trail reaches a plateau and meanders pleasantly. Lined with rosebay rhododendron, it veers to the right and soon goes up again, but not with the same ferocity as before. You'll reach the intersection with the Stone Mountain Trail [#77] at 4.3 miles (3,000 ft. elev.) and make a left. Stone Mountain Trail starts as a wide flat road. This section was called W. Stone Mountain Rd. on older maps. At the intersection with the Switchback Trail, the Stone Mountain Trail makes a left and climbs, changing into a rocky, uneven trail under foot toward the end.

At 5.0 miles (3,400 ft. elev.), you'll reach a field. It's a wildlife clearing, filling in with grasses and flowers. The top of this clearing offers winter views

The Guion Farm area of Dupont is popular with the horse crowd.

of the Pisgah range Follow the trail through the clearing and go back into the woods. In the summer, the trail here can get overgrown, so you may need to just plow through a wall of bushes for a few feet. You'll see an old W. Stone Mountain Rd. sign, which may be confusing. The trail continues along the pleasant ridge line with smooth, rounded boulders on both sides; the trail climbs steeply at the end.

The top of Stone Mountain at 5.3 miles (3,620 ft. elev.) has rocky, angled granite cliffs with good southern views. In late July and early August you'll find plenty of blueberry bushes around the rocks, ripe for the picking. Take the time to explore the various outcroppings. Helpful cairns have been placed by other hikers, leading you to a lower outcropping through blueberry bushes with better views. In the winter, you'll be treated to mostly 360-degree views. Stone Mountain is a good place for lunch.

Retrace your steps back to Old CCC Rd. First, go down the Stone Mountain Trail. At the intersection of the Stone Mountain Trail with the Switchback Trail, make a right to continue on Stone Mountain Trail. Make a right on the Rocky Ridge Trail and reach Old CCC Rd. at 7.2 miles (2,600 ft. elev.). Make a left on Old CCC Rd. At the STOP sign, stay left on Sky Valley Rd., which here is a

Just off from the trailhead in a big field, the Guion Farm offers shaded picnic tables.

quiet gravel road with the occasional truck leaving you walking in a cloud of dust.

Sky Valley Rd. parallels Shoal Creek through the Dupont Forest. Pass the Rifle Trail on your right; turn left on the Shoal Creek Trail [#74] at 7.5 miles, and head back into the woods. The Shoal Creek Trail, a gentle trail enclosed by rhododendrons, parallels the bubbling creek almost all the way. Pass the Farmhouse Trail on your right and then at 8.2 miles, pass Flatwood Trail, also going off to the right. The trail then makes a left and doubles back on itself, heading north for a short distance before returning south again. You'll reach a wide, unpaved parking area at 8.6 miles and turn right on Sky Valley Rd., which will take you to the parking lot on your left.

Alternate hike ending: If you don't want to walk on the gravel, look for a broken post on your left at 8.8 miles, make a left there, and walk between two boulders. Turn right on the path toward the field to get back to the Guion Farm Access Area and your car to finish the hike.

Carl Sandburg Home

Before you visit the Carl Sandburg Home itself, this hike will give you a larger perspective of the Sandburg estate. Afterwards, you can shed your daypack, change out of your boots, and return to the house itself for a tour. The property is well signposted, so if you want, you can head for the house from almost any trail intersection.

Getting to the trailhead:
From I-26, take exit 53. Turn right onto Upward Rd. if traveling east; turn left onto Upward Rd. if traveling west. At the intersection with Rt. 176 continue straight; Upward Rd. becomes North Highland Lake Rd. At the light, turn left onto US 225/Greenville Hwy. S. At the next light take a right onto Little River Rd. and go about 0.2 mile. Visitor parking is on the left.

Type of hike: Out and back, with several intermediate loops

Distance: 4.4 miles, plus another mile to see the house and outbuildings

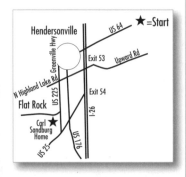

Total ascent/descent: 1,000 ft., including the walk to the house and outbuildings

Highlights: views of mountain ridges, house, and grounds with goats

USGS map: Hendersonville, NC

Trail map: Available on the web only; see website

Land managed by: Carl Sandburg Home National Historic Site (National Park Service)

Rules/fees: Open daily 9 am to 5 pm all year except for Christmas Day. Dogs must be on a leash. There is a $5 fee for adults to tour the house. Admission to the grounds and other buildings is free.

Facilities: Restrooms at the visitor center

Closest town: Flat Rock, NC

Website: www.nps.gov/carl

Related books: *Zoro's Field* by Thomas Rain Crow; *A Great and Glorious Romance: The Story of Carl Sandburg and Lillian Steichen* by Helga Sandburg

The Hike
From the parking lot, follow the paved path and take the trail to the left of Front Lake. At the end of the lake (0.4 mile), turn left at the Sandburg Home sign and climb to the top of the hill where there is a bench. You can see several other houses from here. At the

four-way intersection, turn left toward Little Glassy Mountain. The trails are well-manicured. A nice feature is a wooden walkway to help you negotiate a rock face. Turn right and go up to Little Glassy Mountain.

At 1.0 mile, the top of Little Glassy Mountain has a bench where you can admire the easterly view through trees. Continuing on down the other side, take a left at the T toward Big Glassy Mountain. As you come down, you'll see the back of the house, gardens and barn of Connemara. Take a left away from the buildings toward Big Glassy.

At the four-way intersection, go straight across to the beginning of the loop trail up to Big Glassy Mountain, and take the left-hand trail which goes up steadily. You'll pass a pond and several benches as the trail keeps climbing. At 2.5 miles, you'll reach the rocky Big Glassy Overlook (2,770 ft. elev.), looking southwest into the valley and to the ridges beyond. From this view, Sandburg was inspired to write:

> *It is necessary now and then for a man to go away by himself and experience loneliness; to sit on a rock in the forest and to ask of himself, 'Who am I, and where have I been, and where am I going?*

Retrace your steps and note how close the trail comes to private property. Carl Sandburg was not isolated;

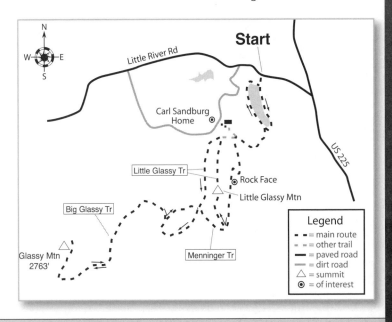

he could see his neighbors' houses when the trees were bare. Be on the lookout for a bench on the left with a hiker sign in the back. This trail, steeper and shorter than the way up, goes straight down the mountain.

At 3.5 miles, you'll be back at the four-way intersection. Take a right on Menninger Trail, skip Little Glassy Mountain Trail, and continue. You are now retracing your steps.

At the next four-way intersection, go straight. When you reach the lake, bear left to go around the south side of the lake and back to the parking lot. Now leave your pack in the car, go back up to the house and barn, and see the estate like a tourist. Don't miss the goats!

A quiet trail circles the small lake below the Sandburg's home.

Green River Game Lands

This hike creates an outer clockwise loop in the Game Lands, descending into the gorge and down to the Green River. The trail then parallels the river and goes to a sandy beach which makes a good lunch spot. You'll make a gentle ascent on the return, following Pulliam Creek.

Getting to the trailhead:
Take I-26 to exit 53 (Upward Rd). Go east (away from Hendersonville) on Upward Rd. for 1.8 miles. Turn right on Big Hungry Rd. (SR 1802). Stay on Big Hungry Rd. as it turns left and then right; it's 4.8 miles to the end of the pavement. Continue 0.6 mile past the point where the road turns to gravel (a total of 5.4 miles) and park just before the road fords the creek.

Getting to the alternate
trailhead: From I-26, take exit 59 at Saluda. Go east, away from Saluda, and turn left onto Green River Cove Rd. Drive 3.9 miles on a narrow, twisty road, cross the bridge, and park on the right. The

access trailhead is across the road. It goes uphill 100 ft. and meets the main trail at the intersection with the Bluff Trail.

Type of hike: Loop

Distance: 9.4 miles

Total ascent: 1,650 ft.

Highlights: Remote, river, boulders

Rules/fees: None

Facilities: None

Closest towns:
Hendersonville and Saluda, NC

Website:
www.ncwildlife.org and
www.eco-wnc.org
to get a map

USGS map: Cliffield Mountain

Trail map: Green River Game Lands map available from ECO (Environmental and Conservation Organization, a nonprofit group based in Hendersonville)

Land managed by: N.C. Wildlife Resources Commission

Related book: *Zoro's Field* by Thomas Rain Crow

The Hike
After parking, walk back on Big Hungry Rd. for a few hundred feet. Make a left on the unmarked Long Ridge Trail and walk around the gate and along the road bed. At 0.75 mile, make a left on Turkey Gut Trail. Stairstep Falls Trail comes in from the right; continue on Turkey Gut Trail. As you go

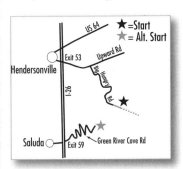

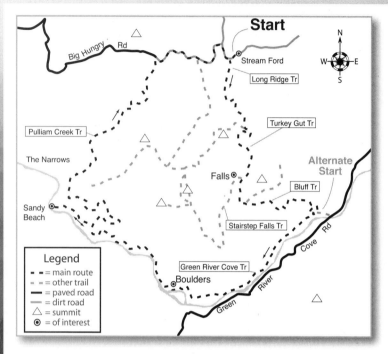

Legend
- – = main route
- – = other trail
- — = paved road
- ⁓ = dirt road
- △ = summit
- ◉ = of interest

down on the south side of the ridge, watch for blowdowns. Make a right on Bluff Trail. By the time you reach this intersection, you will have already descended 700 to 800 ft. in elevation. The trail climbs down a boulder-strewn slope with switchbacks and stairs. To avoid slipping on sections covered with fallen leaves, you may want to sit down and slide, or walk on the rocks on the side of the trail.

At the river, make a right on the Green River Cove Trail. Across the river is Green River Cove Rd., a quiet road with cabins, trailers, and houses. The trail parallels the north bank of the river with several good fishing spots. You are

at the lowest spot on the hike—about 1,000 ft. elev., where wildflowers bloom early. In late March, Little Sweet Betsy trilliums with maroon petals, bloodroot, chickweed, and violets line the first section of the trail. If you are lucky, you might see a great blue heron on the riverbank.

Wooden steps lead away from the river onto boulders which continue to provide good views. Here the river picks up speed and rages through a narrow rocky passage. You'll pass a horseshoe-shaped waterfall. Up a little ridge, continue straight on past a faint trail coming in from the right. Though you'll lose sight of the river in spots, you can always hear it. At the intersection with the Pulliam Creek Trail, turn left to stay on the Green River Cove Trail. It's a steep 0.75 mile and 130 ft. down to the river. Closer to the bottom, you'll climb up and around some low boulders to get to the river at 5.5 miles. The little sandy beach is a good place to snack and hang out for a while. Rocks are good for sunning, but the water is too swift and dangerous to even think about swimming.

Climb back up to the intersection and take the Pulliam Creek Trail. Ignore the Bear Branch Trail on the right and continue walking up on an eroded hillside. After about 1.0 mile, look to your left through the trees for views of the steep rapids known as "Gorilla." The best kayakers in the country paddle this section of the Green River.

The trail ascends more gradually and passes a beautiful little pool to the left, which requires a little rock hopping. Pulliam Creek comes in from the right in gentle cascades. Closer to the top, walk up well-maintained steps and look for a large cracked boulder overhanging the trail, good for a rest break. You can now see the road. Make a right onto the road and walk about 0.75 miles back to your car to end the hike.

Alternate route: If you would rather do your climbing in the morning, an alternate plan is to park at the Green River and start the loop at the Green River Cove Trail, the lowest point.

Just upstream of this spot is the Green River Gorge, where whitewater kayakers test their skills.

Upstate South Carolina

The gorges of the Blue Ridge Escarpment...you
hear gouged, edged, cut, and carved, scooped,
scoured, and scalloped.

—James Kilgo, essayist and novelist

Upstate South Carolina

Essential Facts

The hiking areas of upstate South Carolina are spread across the top of the state and comprise several state parks as well as a few wilderness areas. For those that are off by themselves, you'll find essential facts listed on the hike page. Information for the Mountain Bridge Wilderness appears on pages 112-114.

The mountains of South Carolina have always played second fiddle to the higher peaks of North Carolina. Sassafras Mountain, the highest point in South Carolina, is more than 3,000 ft. lower than Mt. Mitchell which, at 6,684 ft., is the highest point in North Carolina and also the highest east of the Mississippi. However, in the winter when the Blue Ridge Parkway is closed and other high altitude areas are snow-covered, South Carolina is a great place to hike. Upstate South Carolina is not totally ice-free, but its weather is much milder. Gorgeous views, amazing rock outcroppings, and

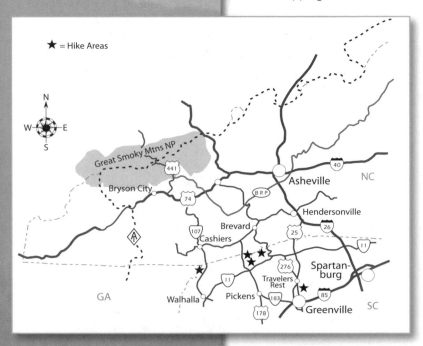

outstanding waterfalls make it a good place to explore just about any time of year except the very height of summer.

The northwest corner of South Carolina is part of the Blue Ridge Escarpment, a meeting place of two tectonic plates where the Blue Ridge Mountains end and the land drops 2,000 ft. in elevation into the foothills. The Cherokees referred to the area as the Blue Wall. The result is sculpted boulders that you have to maneuver over, under, around, and sometimes between.

The topography also means that a tremendous amount of water falls in various ways. Raven Cliff Falls is a major destination for families and photographers—every nature photographer in the area seems to have a picture of this 420-ft. waterfall on display. On other trails, you will follow, cross, and walk through small cascades and creeks. All that water is heading for the Piedmont.

The 76-mile Foothills Trail follows the Blue Ridge Escarpment through several steep gorges, including the Jocassee Gorge, home of the Oconee bell flower, and up Sassafras Mountain. Much of the Blue Ridge ruggedness is preserved in several state parks clustered along the South Carolina/ North Carolina border, offering hiking, campgrounds, cabins, and backcountry

One word describes the trails in upstate South Carolina—dramatic.

campsites. Indeed, the area is so beautiful, it's a wonder it has not been subsumed into a national forest or park.

State parks in South Carolina are managed by the S.C. Department of Parks, Recreation and Tourism, while state parks in many other states are under a department of environment and natural resources. This may seem like a bureaucratic detail to hikers, but it means that South Carolina state parks are treated as a tourist draw and income producer, not just a cost to taxpayers. The result is impeccably maintained and well-signed trails. And though the trails are well-marked, they are not any less strenuous.

Then there is the Chattooga, designated a Wild and Scenic River in 1974, the first east of the Mississippi to be so designated. The purpose of the Wild and Scenic River Act is in part to "preserve...selected rivers or sections thereof in their free-flowing condition to protect the water quality of such rivers and to fulfill other vital national conservation purposes." The Chattooga starts in Cashiers, NC and flows down to Lake Tugaloo in north Georgia, forming the South Carolina/Georgia border for much of its length.

The lower sections of the river gained fame as a filming location for the 1972 movie *Deliverance,* and have seen an influx of kayakers, fishing families, and rafting companies since the early 1970s. *Deliverance* did not depict north Georgia kindly, and its title became a code word for Appalachian stereotypes. Nonetheless, active and adventurous tourists now head for the river in droves.

About ten miles below its headwaters, the Chattooga flows through the Ellicott Rock Wilderness Area at the point where North Carolina, South Carolina, and Georgia meet. Unlike the sections used in the film, this upper stretch of river is too narrow to be negotiated in a canoe or kayak.

Mountain Bridge Wilderness

Rules/fees:
$2 entrance fee per person. This is a pack in/pack out park, so you won't find any trash bins. Pets must be leashed.

Facilities:
The visitor center at Caesars Head State Park is open during normal business hours. The visitor center at Jones Gap State Park is open only from 11 am to noon. Restrooms are open when the park is open.

Closest towns:
Brevard, NC for Caesars Head State Park. Greenville, SC for Jones Gap State Park

Website:
www.southcarolinaparks.com

Raven Cliffs Falls is spectacular.

Like its northern cousin Looking Glass Rock, Table Rock is a monadnock—a giant hunk of stone that remained after the surrounding mountains weathered away.

Related books:
Gap Creek by Robert Morgan;
The Pleasure was Mine
by Tommy Hays

Caesars Head State Park and Jones Gap State Park form the Mountain Bridge Wilderness and Recreation Area. Together the two parks create a bridge of protected land between Table Rock and Poinsett watersheds, the latter named for Joel Poinsett, who shall forever be remembered for bringing the poinsettia flower from Mexico. With over 50 miles of trails and many primitive campsites, the Wilderness offers hikers myriad day hiking and backpacking combinations. This area was designated as an "important bird area" by the Audubon Society because it provides essential habitat for one or more species of bird.

In 1972, Tom Wyche, a real estate lawyer and photographer, formed the Naturaland Trust to protect the Blue Ridge escarpment. The Trust approached each property owner within the Mountain Bridge area to discuss the acquisition or permanent protection of the owner's tract. Almost everyone was enthusiastic and sold their land at below market value, and the Mountain Bridge was created in 1980.

The Mountain Bridge Wilderness is part of the South Carolina State Park system and not a Federal Wilderness area.

Originally, distinctive Mountain Bridge black metal markers with orange circles were placed high on trees to label the trails; some can still be seen. These days painted blazes mark the trails. In general, the trails in the Wilderness are well marked and maintained.

The Mountain Bridge has a visitor center in each park where you can buy a trail map. The Caesars Head State Park Visitor Center is on US 276 south of the North Carolina/South Carolina border. See the individual hikes for specific directions to Caesars Head State Park.

To the right of the visitor center, past the restrooms, take the walkway to a panoramic view of the area, including the Greenville reservoir and Table Rock in the distance. If you follow the sign to Devil's Kitchen, you'll go down a staircase and between two boulders. Descend about 50 ft. to a view of the profile of Caesars Head.

The Caesars Head Hotel, one of many hotels attracting those who could afford to get away from the summer heat, was located south of here on US 276. The original hotel was built in the 1860s; the most recent building burned in 1954.

The second visitor center is Jones Gap State Park, north of Greenville. There you'll find the old Cleveland Fish Hatchery, the first state-owned fish hatchery in South Carolina.

Children will get a kick out of the large trout in the pond. The area has a bathroom, an environmental learning center with nature exhibits, and a park office with erratic hours. If you do catch it open, buy a trail map of the Mountain Bridge Wilderness Area; these maps are hard to come by.

Ellicott Rock Wilderness

This wilderness area maintained by the Sumter National Forest straddles the Wild and Scenic Chattooga River where Georgia, South Carolina, and North Carolina meet. Here you will find the Chattooga River Trail as well as a number of others which make for a pleasant day's outing. The area gets its name from the state boundary marker—a boulder near the headwaters of the Chattooga—between the three states.

Jones Gap Loop

This loop has a Jekyll-and-Hyde quality—easy for the first half and challenging for the second half. The Jones Gap Trail is a historic road which parallels the Middle Saluda River, South Carolina's first designated State Scenic River, to its headwaters at the Gap. On the return, the hike takes you to the base of a majestic perpendicular rock face over 300 ft. high. You really have to watch your footing on this stretch, particularly when the rock is wet—and it is always wet. You can also hike the loop clockwise and walk up through the rocks and stroll down the Jones Gap Trail. Either way, you'll want to stop at Jones Gap Falls, a short detour off the Jones Gap Trail.

Getting to the trailhead:
From I-26, exit 54, take US 25 for 10.4 miles and turn right on Gap Creek Rd. where there is a sign to Jones Gap State Park. After 5.7 miles, turn right on River Falls Rd. and follow signs to Jones Gap State Park. The Park is 2.1 miles further on. Park in the lot on the right-hand side. *From Greenville,* take US 276N to where it meets SC 11S. After 1.5 miles, turn right on River Falls Rd. and take it for 3.5 miles to the intersection with Gap Creek Rd. Then follow the instructions above.

Type of hike: Lollipop

Distance: 10.2 miles

Total ascent: 2,250 ft.

Highlights: views, waterfall, rocky cliffs, river walk

USGS map: Cleveland, SC

Trail map: Mountain Bridge Wilderness Area, available at Caesars Head and Jones Gap State Parks Visitor Centers

Land managed by: Mountain Bridge Wilderness Area, a South Carolina State Park

Special challenge: At this writing, the bridge over Cold Spring Branch is washed out.

The Hike
From the parking area, cross a small bridge over the Middle Saluda River and follow the paved path to the start of the Jones Gap Trail [#1 – blue blazes]. This trailhead is also the eastern end of the Foothills Trail, a 76-mile trail which follows the Blue Ridge Escarpment and ends at Oconee State Park. Cross a second bridge over the Middle Saluda and sign in at the information board.

★ =Start

Hendersonville
US 64
Exit 53
Exit 54
US 25
I-26
NC
SC
Jones Gap State Park
★
River Falls Rd. Gap Creek Rd.

Almost immediately after you start on the Jones Gap Trail, you'll reach the intersection with the Rim of the Gap Trail to your left, a loop possibility for another day. Though the Jones Gap Trail goes uphill and away from the Middle Saluda for short stretches, it always comes back to the river. Cross the river on the John Reid Clonts Bridge and make a sharp left.

On this trail, the river provides the entertainment with its cascades, waterfalls, rock formations, and occasional beaches. (A shorter version of this hike, 3.0 miles round trip, is to Ben's Sluice, a cascade with a sandy beach.) At 2.1 miles, you'll reach the junction with the Coldspring Branch Trail. You will come out here later when you close the loop.

The trail follows the old Jones Gap Toll Rd. built by Solomon Jones between 1840 and 1848. One of the first routes cut into the rugged mountains between North and South Carolina, it went from River Falls, SC to Cedar Mountain, NC and remained a toll road until 1910. Jones used neither dynamite nor surveyor's equipment when he built the road, just his feel for the contour of the land. The route was considered so superior that it was a candidate for the present-day US 276.

At 3.9 miles, Dargan's Cascade makes a good lunch stop; then the trail turns right and uphill. Because of the sharp zigzags, this section is known as the Winds (and rhymes with "finds").

At 4.5 miles, turn left on Tom Miller Trail [#2 – blue

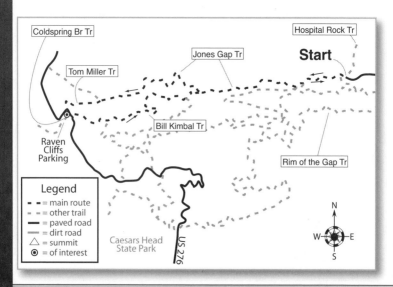

Coldspring Br Tr

Hospital Rock Tr

Tom Miller Tr

Jones Gap Tr

Start

Bill Kimbal Tr

Raven Cliffs Parking

Rim of the Gap Tr

Legend
- ▪ ▪ = main route
- ▪ ▪ = other trail
- —— = paved road
- —— = dirt road
- △ = summit
- ◉ = of interest

Caesars Head State Park

US 276

N
W E
S

The Middle Saluda River's course is chock full of boulders.

blazes] while the Jones Gap Trail continues across the river. Located close to the stream, Campsite #17 on the Tom Miller Trail is an idyllic stop for a short backpacking trip.

The trail now gets steep with steps cut into the hillside, and you start to see views of the whole gap. The trail ends at Raven Cliff Parking Area on US 276 at 5.2 miles.

Walk through the parking lot (do not cross the road) and take the Coldspring Branch Trail [#3 – orange blazes] on the left. Walking on the Coldspring Branch Trail, look left (west) for a view of Mt. Pisgah with its unmistakable tower. Take a left on Bill Kimball Trail [#5 – pink blazes]; the sign says "2.2 miles to Jones Gap Trail." Coldspring Branch Trail continues on the right.

The Bill Kimball Trail, which skirts the base of a spectacular sheer granite cliff, is challenging. (Known as "El Lieutenant," this rock face reminded people of a small version of "El Capitan" in Yosemite National Park. However, rock climbing is not allowed in South Carolina state parks.) As you pick your way through the rocks and bog, hold on to the chain along the trail. At one point the trail goes right, away from the rock face, to avoid a slick spot. Take that section slowly; it's wet and slippery all year.

Leaving the rock face for the last time, the trail turns right; farther down, it levels out as it approaches the creek. At 7.9 miles, turn left on the Coldspring Branch Trail at a campsite, and cross a tributary of the Middle Saluda Trail. Until the bridge is rebuilt, you must hold to a log hand railing or plow through the shallow water. You'll cross a second stream on a plank bridge.

Make a right on the Jones Gap Trail at 8.1 miles. On the way back, take a short diversion to the Jones Gap Falls, signposted on your left. The trail to the waterfall is about three minutes off the main trail and worth the detour.

Raven Cliff Falls Loop

If you want to experience the original meaning of "awesome"—a mixture of reverence, wonder, and dread—take the Raven Cliff Falls Loop. This hike delivers an outstanding distant view of Raven Cliff Falls, one of the most photographed waterfalls in the Blue Ridge Escarpment, and later crosses above the waterfall on a wide suspension bridge. In between the two waterfall views, a huge rock wall towering over 120 ft. called the Cathedral inspires reverence. In addition, you'll cross Matthews Creek on a pair of cables, generating either smiles or fear.

Getting to the trailhead:
From the center of Brevard, at the junction of US 276 and US 64, take US 276 south for 14.4 miles to the Raven Cliff Parking Area on the left. Park here; the visitor center at Caesars Head State Park is another 1.2 miles farther south on the right.

Type of hike: Loop

Distance: 8.4 miles

Total ascent: 1,950 ft.

★ =Start

Highlights: Waterfall, gorge views, cable crossing, suspension bridge, rock wall

USGS map: Table Rock

Trail map: Mountain Bridge Wilderness Area, available at Caesars Head and Jones Gap State Parks Visitor Centers

Land managed by: Mountain Bridge Wilderness Area, a South Carolina State Park

Fee: $2

The Hike
To start the hike, cross US 276 and take the Raven Cliff Falls Trail [#11–red blazes] at the registration station. Make sure to pay your fee; you're going to get your money's worth on this hike. The gentle gravel trail follows the route of an old carriage road, built to take resort guests to view the waterfall at the beginning of the 20th century. This section of the Raven Cliff Falls Trail is also part of the Foothills Trail spur, so you'll see blue blazes periodically. The trail turns right through wild hydrangea, fern, and hemlock after passing a maintenance building. Follow the signs to Raven Cliffs Falls.

At 0.8 miles, you'll reach a flat spot with a tree holding a branch at a right angle. Turn left off the trail for good winter views of the gorge from a two-level boulder.

Coming back from this little diversion, if you make a left before the main trail, you can stand on another rock for a different view into the Blue Ridge Escarpment. Go back to the main trail, which turns sharply right, and continue among rhododendron bushes, mountain laurel, and white pine, then come down a set of wooden stairsteps.

As the trail turns left at 1.3 miles, it changes to a flat, sandy road. At 1.5 miles, reach the intersection with the Gum Gap Trail. This is where you'll come back to close the loop. Make a left to continue on the Raven Cliff Falls Trail (3,090 ft. elev.), which has left the Foothills Trail. The trail goes down steeply now. Look left into the gorge (south) for winter views. On clear days, the transmission towers on Paris Mountain may be visible.

At 1.9 miles, you'll reach a three-way junction. Go straight to continue on the Raven Cliff Falls Trail; the trail on the far right was closed permanently in 2006. Reach the Raven Cliff Falls viewpoint in less than 0.2 miles. Here, Matthews Creek drops 420 ft. elev. in several levels to create this outstanding waterfall, one of the highest in the Southeast. Look at the top of the waterfall for the suspension bridge, which you'll cross in a few hours. At this writing, only the upper falls are visible, but the Park plans to build an observation deck for better views.

This is as far as most trail tourists go. At this point, if you decide to return the same way, you have about

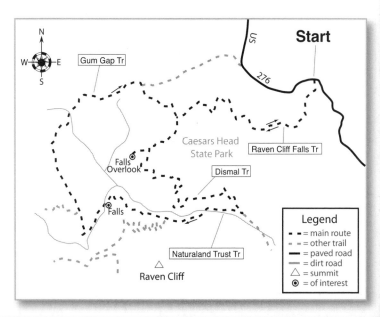

Imposing rock cliffs line the trail to Raven Cliff Falls.

You'll pass a thick patch of poison ivy lining an enclosed section of trail, and you'll start hearing Matthews Creek.

The trail turns right as it reaches 1,900 ft. elev. and continues down for another 0.1 mile to intersect the Naturaland Trust Trail at 3.7 miles. At 1,830 ft. elev., this is the lowest point on the loop. Make a right here on the Naturaland Trust Trail [#14 – pink blazes], which immediately starts uphill.

Cross a small stream coming in from the right to meet Matthews Creek, and walk through a flat hemlock grove peppered with boulders. At 3.9 miles, cross the creek on two heavy parallel cables. The bottom cable is for your feet; you hold the top cable with your hands as you sidle across the creek. If you want your mates to take pictures of you on the cable, make sure to give them your camera and show them how to use it before you begin the crossing.

The trail climbs gently at first and then relentlessly up Raven Cliff Mountain. This is the most challenging part of the loop because you are regaining the altitude you lost going down the Dismal Trail. You'll pass a huge boulder on the left as you switchback through Christmas fern, mountain laurel, hemlock, and poison ivy.

At 4.5 miles, the trail reaches the Cathedral, a

400 ft. in elevation and two miles of ascent to retrace your path back to the trailhead.

Return to the three-way intersection at 2.3 miles and make a right on the Dismal Trail[#12 – purple blazes], a conventional narrow trail. The Dismal is a thick, mature forest lying beneath Caesars Head. The trail drops 1,200 ft. in elevation on a steep grade through nettle, blackberry cane, spiderwort, and black-eyed susans. At 2.4 miles, as the trail veers left, look straight ahead for a striated rock that you can scramble up on to get another view of the falls.

At 2.9 miles, a metal chain has been placed to the left of the trail to help hikers with the descent.

spectacular 120-ft.-high semicircular rock wall. The water coming down from the many ledges encourages plants to grow in the cracks and is refreshing on hot days. Continue climbing on a ladder and then on rough, rocky steps. At 2,620 ft. elev., on a short rocky side trail where a cable has been pulled out of its support, you begin hearing the waterfall. Look out into the gorge and note the dead hemlocks across the abyss.

Make a left turn to continue up the trail on rocks and a metal ladder as the creek gets louder. You may feel like you're above the falls and that somehow you missed them, particularly when you begin to descend. At 4.8 miles (2,720 ft. elev.) you'll reach the suspension bridge which crosses Matthew Creek—the bridge you could barely see at the waterfall viewpoint on the other side of the gorge. The roar of the water is deafening as it cascades down into the gorge.

At the end of the bridge, turn left as the trail parallels the creek going upstream. As you leave the bridge, you are also leaving your solitude behind; trail tourists come directly down here to see the waterfall. The trail turns right and climbs away from the creek. Reach the crest of the ridge on an old road bed.

At 5.4 miles (3,030 ft. elev.), make a right on the Gum Gap Trail [#13 – blue blazes], which runs concurrently with the Foothills Trail, and head uphill. You're walking in a rocky, red clay trench which soon moderates and changes to a jeep road. At 6.6 miles, the trail makes a sharp right; a sign says it's 1.7 miles to the parking lot. Continue straight on as the trail intersects other old roads and trails. At 6.9 miles, you have closed the loop. Make a left onto Raven Cliff Falls Trail to return to the trailhead and end the hike.

Hospital Rock

Don't let the low mileage fool you; this is a full-day hike and quite strenuous. With its rocks, boulders, and cables, it requires a style of climbing that's more common in New Hampshire than in South Carolina. Though it is a shuttle hike that can be done from either direction, do the challenging rocky climb first thing in the morning.

Getting to the trailhead:
This hike starts at the Jones Gap State Park trailhead and ends near Palmetto Bible Camp. Place a car at Palmetto Bible Camp first. To get there: *From I-26*, exit 54, take US 25 south for 10.4 miles and turn right on Gap Creek Rd., where there is a sign to Jones Gap State Park. Drive 5.7 miles and turn right on River Falls Rd. Continue 0.4 mile and turn right on Duckworth Rd. (there is a sign here for the Palmetto Bible Camp). Drive 0.5 mile, turn right on Falls Creek Rd., and then drive another 0.5 miles to the trailhead on the left, where there is a signboard and space for a few cars.

Next drive the remaining car to the start by travelling back to the intersection of River Falls Rd. and Duckworth Rd. the way you came. Turn right on Falls Creek Rd and drive 1.7 miles to Jones Gap State Park. Park in the lot on the right-hand side.

From Greenville, take US 276 north to where it meets SC 11S. Drive 1.5 miles on SC 11S. Turn right on River Falls Rd. and take it for 3.5 miles to the intersection with Gap Creek Rd. Then follow the directions above.

Type of hike: Shuttle

Distance: 6.5 miles

Total ascent/descent: 2,390 ft. /2,430 ft.

Highlights: Waterfall, rock formations

USGS map: Cleveland, SC

Trail map: Mountain Bridge Wilderness Area, available at Caesars Head and Jones Gap State Parks Visitor Centers

Land managed by: Mountain Bridge Wilderness Area, a South Carolina State Park

The Hike
From the Cleveland Hatchery at Jones Gap State Park Visitor Center (see the introduction to the Mountain Bridge Wilderness, p. 112), the Hospital Rock Trail [#30

★ =Start

Hendersonville

US 64
Exit 53
Exit 54
US 25
I-26
NC
SC
Jones Gap State Park
River Falls Rd
Gap Creek Rd

– orange blazes] starts on the paved path which goes north and up, passing the restrooms on your left, and enters the woods. Register your hike and go up several rock steps. Chickweed, rue anemone, and bloodroot line the trail in early spring. Pass a campsite and a concrete structure, which was the old water filtration system for the fish hatchery. Stay to the left as you climb on log waterbar steps with a minor creek to your right.

The trail generally goes north/northeast, though it zigzags considerably on its way to the Cleveland Connector. You'll pass a flat rock on your right which looks like a tent site. At 0.8 mile, turn right and cross at the base of a smooth, angled rock that could be a child's slide, and continue climbing.

The trail is drier now and lined with mountain laurels. At 0.9 mile (1,760 ft. elev.), enjoy your first view to the right, looking northeast. Ignore a short side trail coming in from the left and continue right and up through boulders that seem to grow as you go. The trail switchbacks and slabs around the escarpment. Enjoy the respites of the flat stretches because you're going to be climbing soon. The trail goes sharply down for a few hundred feet, but then goes back up again. Blueberry dots the trail at 1,890 ft. elev. In

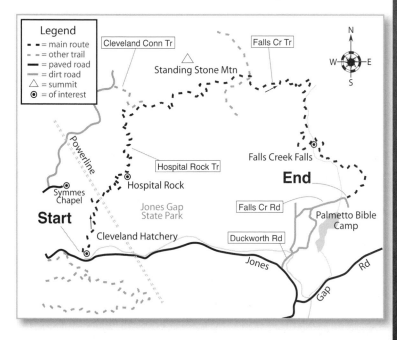

Sections of the trail are littered with boulders and rocks.

The trail continues up and to the left, hugging the cave. The trail is no longer as rocky as it has been—as if Hospital Rock was the grand finale of all these boulders—but it is still very steep. At 1.8 miles, you'll pass a drippy rock face. Don't miss a view to your right (southwest). Cross several creeks bordered by trillium and Solomons plume as the trail flattens out. At 2.1 miles, the trail makes a sharp right and zigzags almost flat through blackberry bushes.

At 2.6 miles (2,900 ft. elev.), reach the junction with the Cleveland Connector [#32]. The Cleveland Connector connects with the old CCC road, which goes to Symmes Chapel, also known as Pretty Place, in the YMCA Camp Greenville. Camp Greenville welcomes visitors to the Chapel when there are no scheduled private functions.

Turn right to stay on the Hospital Rock Trail, now an old road which descends gently through a mature, hardwood cove forest. The road narrows to a trail and veers left. At 3.4 miles, you'll cross a tributary of Headforemost Creek on wet rocks. Follow the creek upstream in an enclosed tunnel of doghobble, rhododendron, and vines as the trail meanders up and down.

At 3.8 miles, the Hospital Rock Trail ends. Make a right onto the Falls Creek Trail [#31 – orange blazes] at the signpost.

several places you'll have to use your hands to hold on to boulders. At 1.3 miles, a cable has been set to assist hikers— you may not need it going up, but it will be convenient for those going down.

On your right, huge boulders have tumbled and look like they've been abruptly arrested in place. At 1.5 miles (1,990 ft. elev.), you'll approach a huge rock on your right. This is the back of Hospital Rock, a house-sized boulder. The trail comes around to the front of Hospital Rock where there is a huge cave with a large overhang. According to legend, Confederate deserters hid out in this cave during the Civil War.

Purple violets, dwarf crested iris, and a few pink lady slippers live under the mountain laurel. At 4.4 miles, a rock face on the left comes down almost to the trail, and you can hear Little Falls Creek above the waterfall. The trail is dark and enclosed as the creek becomes wider through mountain laurel and rhododendron thickets. Several tributaries gather their waters for the falls.

The trail makes an unmarked left turn at 4.9 miles. There is a blaze and Mountain Bridge metal marker, but only after the turn. The water speeds up, gathers in pools, and then rushes down. At 5.1 miles, step off the trail on a boulder to the left for views of Friddle Lake, a field, and a house.

The trail veers away from the water, and you may feel as if you missed the waterfall, but the trail comes back toward the water again. A few fire pinks hang onto the

The cave underneath Hospital Rock stays dry no matter what the weather.

stony slope, and hemlocks with bent roots adhere to rocks.

Descend to Falls Creek Falls, and at 5.4 miles cross using a cable. Water tumbles over the flat ledges of the wide and spectacular falls. Several little falls at the bottom add to the complexity and interest of this waterfall. You are most likely to meet tourists at this spot as they come up from the Bible camp trailhead to admire the waterfall.

Once across the falls, the trail goes sharply left and up, with a cable to assist hikers. At the top of the cable, the trail turns right and away from the waterfall, then into the woods and straight down. The sound of the waterfall stays with you on the dry, eroded path.

Cross a wide creek at 5.8 miles and then walk a wide road that switchbacks up and down to the trailhead, close to the Palmetto Bible Camp. This ends the hike for those who set a vehicle here. If your car is at the starting trailhead, it is a 2.7-mile, mostly flat road-walk back to Jones Gap State Park.

Rim of the Gap

If you want to truly experience the physical definition of an escarpment—a long steep slope or cliff at the edge of a plateau or ridge—hike the Rim of the Gap Trail. As the trail winds its way around rock walls hugging the south rim of the Gap, it seems that falling boulders stopped all at once in a line. The views into the Gap are amazing. The western end of the Rim of the Gap Trail is slow going for about two miles as you pick your way through wet, slippery rocks; watch your footing carefully.

Getting to the trailhead:
From I-26, exit 54, take US 25 for 10.4 miles and turn right on Gap Creek Rd. where there is a sign to Jones Gap State Park. After 5.7 miles, turn right on River Falls Rd. and follow signs to Jones Gap State Park. The park is 2.1 miles farther. Park in the lot on the right-hand side. *From Greenville,* take US 276 north to where it meets SC 11S. After 1.5 miles, turn right on River Falls Rd. and take it for 3.5 miles to the intersection with Gap Creek Rd. Then follow the directions above.

Type of hike: Loop

Distance: 9.9 miles

Total ascent: 2,540 ft.

Highlights: Rocky cliffs, waterfalls and cascades, ridge views

USGS map: Cleveland, SC

Trail map: Mountain Bridge Wilderness Area, available at Caesars Head and Jones Gap State Parks Visitor Centers

Land managed by: Mountain Bridge Wilderness Area, a South Carolina State Park

Special challenge: In winter, check the condition of the Rim of the Gap Trail, which may be closed if icy.

The Hike
From the parking area, cross a small bridge over the Middle Saluda River and follow the paved path to the start of the Jones Gap Trail. Cross a second bridge across the Middle Saluda and turn right on the Jones Gap Trail [#1 – blue blazes]. Be sure to register your hike here, as it lets officials know that these park trails are being used.

At 0.4 mile, turn left on the Rim of the Gap Trail [#6 – yellow blazes]. The trail leaves the Middle Saluda River as it climbs gently through hemlock, rhododendron,

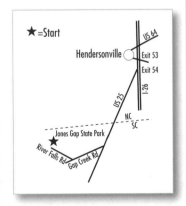

★ =Start

Hendersonville

US 64

Exit 53

Exit 54

I-26

US 25

NC
SC

Jones Gap State Park

River Falls Rd

Gap Creek Rd

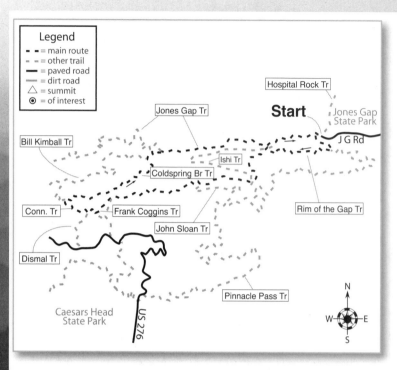

Legend
- ▪ ▪ = main route
- ▪ ▪ = other trail
- ▬ = paved road
- ▬ = dirt road
- △ = summit
- ◉ = of interest

Hospital Rock Tr

Jones Gap Tr

Start

Jones Gap State Park

J G Rd

Bill Kimball Tr

Ishi Tr

Coldspring Br Tr

Conn. Tr

Frank Coggins Tr

Rim of the Gap Tr

John Sloan Tr

Dismal Tr

Pinnacle Pass Tr

Caesars Head State Park

US 276

N
W ✦ E
S

and poison ivy. A huge rock on the right is an indication of things to come as you switchback up and around the boulders. The presence of these rocks lets you know you're on an escarpment. On the left, at 0.7 mile, you'll pass a rock that looks like a face of a statue in a Mayan ruin.

Soon after, the Pinnacle Pass Trail [#20] comes in on the left. Make a right turn here to stay on the Rim of the Gap Trail. Trillium, bloodroot, and ferns line the trail as it climbs steadily. You'll cross a small stream; the trail then climbs up a little more steeply on an old roadbed of eroded, packed, solid red clay—slippery when

wet. The trail goes generally west with outstanding winter views across Jones Gap on the right, then hunkers down into a hemlock forest, crosses a creek, and continues climbing with more views across Jones Gap at 1.7 miles.

At 2.4 miles, the Ishi Trail [#8], a connector trail to the Jones Gap Trail, comes in from the right. Continue straight on. A few feet later, the 6 & 20 Connector Trail (yes, that's its name) [#22] is a short trail which connects to the Pinnacle Pass Trail for another loop possibility. Ignore these connector trails and continue uphill through a forested area with limited view.

At 3.0 miles, the John Sloan Trail [#21] takes off to the left. Soon, Rim of the Gap Trail changes character. You'll descend some steps—you can hear the Middle Saluda below on the right. The rest of Rim of the Gap Trail follows the base of the escarpment, with water spilling from granite rocks onto the trail, passing tree roots holding onto huge boulders. Most of the time, you can't see down into the gap, but you can feel the void as the trail wiggles and zigzags up and down.

At 3.4 miles the trail passes through a keyhole structure called Weight Watchers Rock, formed from stacked slabs of rock with a horizontal piece sitting across the other boulders, creating a rectangular opening. Take your pack off to go through the hole. Otherwise, negotiate around the rock—you may need to sit and slide down.

Come through a crevice as you slowly leave the wall. The trail is no longer hugging the boulders, and walking may seem to be a little easier. However, just when you think you're finished with the boulders, they reappear. Continue to pick your way through wet rocks, and watch your footing.

At 3.8 miles, the trail makes a sharp left turn. You'll go up a wooden ladder; look for a good high-level view of the Gap. Pass a drippy rock and climb down a metal ladder. Cross the slippery rocks below the waterfall. Don't try to keep your boots dry; just forge ahead into the water.

You'll climb another metal ladder as the trail appears to curve around the rock face. The trail turns sharply right at 4.1 miles and soon passes a cascade on your left, climbs gently among mountain laurel, and at 4.4 miles crosses at the bottom of a waterfall—use the rope here, if it is available. Cross another waterfall on two wooden planks and admire the stream coming down in several cascades. Then cross at the bottom of Cliff Falls, a multi-step waterfall, as the trail doubles back on itself.

At 4.9 miles, at the top of Cliff Falls, Rim of the Gap Trail ends. Make a right on the Frank Coggins Trail [#15 – purple blazes]. The left fork,

Blazes of all shapes and sizes mark the trails. This one is unique to the Mountain Bridge Wilderness.

the Naturaland Trust Trail [#14], goes to US 276. The Frank Coggins Trail, shown as a road on some maps, goes up through the forest, away from the rocks. In this section, you can finally stretch your legs. Stay right as Frank Coggins Trail appears to go both ways.

At 5.2 miles, make a right on the Coldspring Connector [#7 – blue blazes]. The trail descends steadily through the forest as Coldspring Branch gets louder, zigzags down to a little creek which it crosses on rocks, and then goes uphill steeply on log steps.

Make a right on the Coldspring Branch Trail [#3 – orange blazes] at 5.9 miles. Solomon's plume, wake robin trillium, mayapple, and Christmas ferns border the trail as it bobs up and down, crossing several tributaries while you hear the main stream rippling below. As the trail fords Coldspring Branch a few times, the stream gets wider, and the sound of water obscures the sound of birds. Enjoy all the ways water can play on rocks.

At 7.0 miles the trail reaches a flat area and crosses the Bill Kimball Trail [#5] coming from the left. Soon you'll cross a tributary of the Middle Saluda. At this writing, the bridge is out and you must hold onto a log for a banister or plow through the shallow water. The trail crosses a second stream on a plank bridge and then goes straight up.

Make a right on the Jones Gap Trail, a wide trail which offers comfortable walking. As you parallel the Middle Saluda downstream, you'll pass several riverside campsites. At 8.1 miles, turn left on a short side trail to Jones Gap Falls. The waterfall flows over many granite ledges for about 50 ft.

At 8.4 miles, cross the river on John Reid Clonts bridge. On the right is the other end of the Ishi Trail, which goes to Rim of the Gap Trail. Continue down on the Jones Gap Trail and back to your car to end the hike.

Paris Mountain State Park

In the winter, when other trails are cold and icy, Paris Mountain State Park is the place to come. In early spring, when brown is still the dominant color in the Carolina mountains, you can see the first dogwood and rhododendrons in bloom here. Autumn brings spectacular reds and golds. Two trails, the Sulphur Springs Loop and the Brissy Ridge Loop, can be done as one hike. The altitude ranges from 1,070 ft. at the trailhead to 1,800 ft.

Paris Mountain is a monadnock, an immense rock that remained when the mountains around it weathered away. One of the oldest protected areas in South Carolina, Paris Mountain State Park has large stands of old-growth forests. The lakes were originally built to provide drinking water to the city of Greenville. In most places, the walking is easy and pleasant. The 1,540-acre park has only 12 miles of trail, most of which are also bicycle trails. The trails are well-marked and well-groomed.

Getting to the trailhead: From US 25 in Travelers Rest, SC, north of Greenville, turn east on State Park Rd. The turn should be signposted. Drive 8.0 miles (the road name changes to East Mountain Creek Rd.). Take a right on State Park Rd. The entrance is 0.8 mile on the left. Drive into the Park past Lake Placid and several picnic shelters, and park at the Sulphur Springs Picnic Area.

Type of hike: Two loops

Distance: 6.6 miles

Total ascent: 1,380 ft.

Highlights: Early flowers, lake, mountain ridges, stream

USGS map: Paris Mountain

Trail map: Available at entrance

Land managed by: South Carolina State Parks

Rules/fees: $2 entrance fee per person. Dogs must be on a leash.

Facilities: Picnic shelters, campground, restrooms, seasonal swimming, and boat rental

Closest town: Greenville, SC

Website: www. southcarolinaparks.com

The Hike

Cross the road and take the left fork of the Sulfur Springs Trail, marked with white blazes. You'll cross a bridge over a small creek. The trail is

Legend
- ‑ ‑ = main route
- ‑ ‑ = other trail
- ▬ = paved road
- ▬ = dirt road
- △ = summit
- ◉ = of interest

Start

manicured as it passes through club moss, fern, and mountain laurel.

The creek attracts cardinals and juncos. After a second creek crossing, pass a gazebo at 0.4 mile. The trail climbs up a little, and the stream on the left is down below the trail. At 0.6 mile, at the runoff below Mountain Lake, a bizarre stone turret seems to stand guard to protect the lake. The trail turns sharply right and goes up the steps to the lake. You can walk on the dam to see the runoff and the top of the turret. Continue left on the trail. You are now on a foot-traffic-only trail which gets a little rougher. Following the stream that feeds the lake, the trail is banked with rhododendron and mountain laurel.

Cross the creek at 0.8 mile and climb briefly above the stream. When you come back to the stream, the trail seems freshly cut from a bramble of rhododendron and downed trees. In the spring, halbert-leaved violets, yellow violets, robin's plantain, unfurled ferns, and crested dwarf iris line the trail. Look across to see two small waterfalls hugging a rock at 1.1 miles.

The trail follows the creek upstream as it contours up the mountain. At 1.3 miles, cross the creek again on a rock, and follow the stone steps. Before crossing, look for a rock cave formation on the left and a little cascade as you cross.

As you go up, the trail gets a little rocky and feels dry, though you can still hear the creek. A wire fence separates the Park from a private house on the left. At 1.7 miles, the Sulphur Springs Trail continues on the left toward the ruins of a fire tower. (The right-hand trail is the Fire Tower Trail, which goes back down more steeply.) A brick and stone chimney and a brick column are all that remain of what must have been a substantial fire tower. The trail goes through scrubby white pines, and more houses can be seen in the distance as trail reaches its top at 1,800 ft.

Ignore faint side trails on the left, and stay on the main trail which goes down. The trail changes character, back to a smoother bike trail, and offers valley views through the trees. Continue down past the signboard. Due south, you can see Greenville.

At 2.8 miles, at the second junction with the Fire Tower Trail, stay left on the Sulphur Springs Trail. Continuing down, look on the right for a group of transmission towers on top of Paris Mountain, outside the park.

The next parking area, at 3.1 miles, is the junction with the Brissy Ridge Trail. Turn left at the information board onto the yellow-blazed Brissy Ridge Trail, a well-maintained multi-use trail with eastern views through the trees.

On the left, several incongruous cacti are all that's left of a former house site. At 4.2 miles, at the intersection of Brissy Ridge and Pipsissewa Trails, stay right on the Brissy Ridge Trail. The trail goes down a little more steeply through the pine forest and heads south. Cross the power line

Within the first mile you'll come to what looks like a stone turret.

Mountain Lake offers a serene setting and a good place to take a break before continuing your hike.

at 4.5 miles and, soon after, cross the main park road.

The park road at this point is restricted to guests of Camp Buckhorn. The trail again becomes a hiking trail, crosses a small creek, and goes up wooden steps. Here you're walking on the side of a ridge as the trail stays in the woods, going up and down—sometimes steeply—with only minor glances through the trees to the ridge on the right. This is the wildest part of the hike.

At 5.5 miles, you're back at the upper parking lot; take Sulphur Springs Trail. Here the dry and open trail crosses a muddy creek twice and reaches a split. The right turn leads to a parking area.

Make a left to continue on the Sulphur Springs Trail. You'll cross a third bridge. At 6.5 miles and the intersection with the Mountain Creek Trail, the trail makes a sharp left to emerge from the woods across the road from the parking area to finish the hike.

Table Rock State Park

This hike, a clockwise loop with two tails, climbs to Pinnacle Mountain, passing the outstanding panorama on Bald Rock Overlook. At Pinnacle Mountain, you'll pick up the Ridge Trail to Panther Gap. Once there, you'll climb up the Table Rock Trail, a designated National Recreation Trail, to the top of Table Rock's imposing granite dome.

The return takes you down to three ledges on the back side of the mountain. Retracing your steps back to Panther Gap, you'll follow Table Rock Trail back to the nature center. This hike will take longer than most trails of equal distance and ascent because you'll find yourself stopping to admire the many views.

Getting to the trailhead:
From I-26, Exit 54, take US 25 south for 17 miles. Turn left on SC 11 (Greer Hwy.) and drive 17.5 miles to the turnoff for Table Rock State Park's West Gate on the right. Follow the signs to the nature center. *From Greenville*, take US 276 North where it meets SC 11 South. Drive for about 13 miles to the turnoff for Table Rock State Park's west gate on the right, and follow the signs to the nature center.

Type of hike: Lollipop with two tails

Distance: 11.2 miles

Total ascent: 3,900 ft.

Highlights: Outstanding views of mountain ridges and valleys, lakes

USGS map: Table Rock

Trail map: Hand-drawn map available at the nature center

Land managed by: Table Rock State Park, a South Carolina State Park

Rules/fees: $2 entrance fee per person

Facilities: Nature center at the west gate entrance; full-service visitor center at the east gate entrance; cabins.

Closest town: Pickens, SC

Website: www.southcarolinaparks.com

The Hike
The hike starts at the rear of the nature center on the wooden walkway. Cross the bridge and register at the kiosk. The first short section is on a paved trail which parallels a cascading creek. At the junction with the Carrick Creek Nature Trail (0.8 miles), continue left on the Pinnacle Mountain Trail [yellow blazes]. After leaving the creek, go up a gentle incline heading

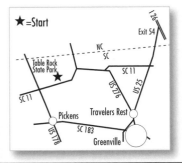

★=Start

I-26
Exit 54
NC
SC
Table Rock State Park ★
SC 11
US 276
US 25
SC 11
Pickens
Travelers Rest
US 178
SC 183
Greenville

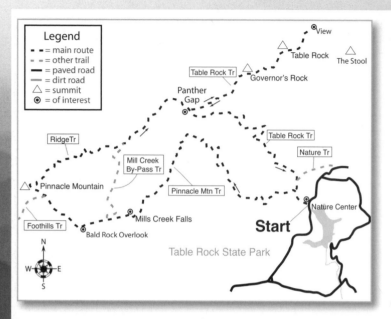

Legend
- ▪ ▪ ▪ = main route
- ▪ ▪ ▪ = other trail
- ▬▬ = paved road
- ▬▬ = dirt road
- △ = summit
- ◉ = of interest

View

Table Rock

The Stool

Table Rock Tr

Governor's Rock

Panther Gap

Table Rock Tr

Nature Tr

RidgeTr

Mill Creek By-Pass Tr

Pinnacle Mountain

Pinnacle Mtn Tr

Nature Center

Mills Creek Falls

Start

Foothills Tr

Bald Rock Overlook

Table Rock State Park

N W E S

west. The trail passes huge boulders, some fringed with trees on top, making you really feel you are on the Blue Ridge Escarpment.

At 2.3 miles, you'll pass an unnamed waterfall (which may be dry in summer) and go under a rocky ledge. Continue past Mill Creek Falls, a high, thin waterfall with straight ledges on each side, and cross a wooden bridge at 2.9 miles. At this point, the trail conditions deteriorate for a stretch because of the terrain. If you decide this is your turnaround point, be sure to cross the bridge and follow the arrow left to the top of the waterfall before turning back.

Continuing on, the trail climbs and contours around Pinnacle Mountain. At 3.1 miles you'll pass the intersection with the Mill Creek ByPass Trail [blue blazes] which bypasses Bald Rock Overlook, one of the highlights of this hike, and Pinnacle Mountain. Stay left on Pinnacle Mountain Trail. Beyond this intersection the trail goes up at a more reasonable grade, but there's still plenty of climbing to do.

At 3.5 miles, you'll reach Bald Rock Overlook. This huge sloping rock, which can be slippery when wet, affords views of Greenville and beyond. For a more relaxed stop, go out to the left where you can see the Greenville reservoir and, in the distance, the tower on Paris Mountain.

Head back to the main trail. Where the ledges end the trail continues to the right at a gentle grade. The rock you'll see on your right is Governor's Rock, located between Panther Gap and Table Rock. From here, it looks very far away.

At 3.9 miles, you'll pass the junction with the eastern terminus of the Foothills Trail [white blazes], a 76-mile trail which goes west to Oconee State Park. Continue straight on; the trail goes steeply up for a while.

At 4.1 miles you'll reach Pinnacle Mountain, which at 3,430 ft. is the highest mountain entirely in South Carolina. The top has no view; just a lot of metal and wood debris.

From Pinnacle Mountain, gradually descend on the Ridge Trail [orange blazes] which connects Pinnacle Mountain to the Table Rock Trail at Panther Gap. If you're hiking before the trees have leafed out, you'll see the lake below. You'll reach the other side of the Mills Creek Bypass at 5.1 miles (the length of the entire Ridge Trail is 1.9 miles). You can see Governor's Rock in front of you. When you reach Panther Gap at 6.1 miles, make a left on Table Rock Trail [red blazes].

You will notice more people on Table Rock Trail, and the trail is gentler than what you've hiked so far. Climb to Governor's Rock on steps chiseled into the rock. The trail hugs the rock ledge on the left and follows the carved steps. Once on

Table Rock State Park

Table Rock State Park takes its name from its most dominant geological feature. Table Rock is a monadnock—a mountain that has resisted erosion and stands isolated in a level area. Besides hiking, at Table Rock State Park visitors can fish in two lakes, boat on Lake Oolenoythe, picnic in a shelter, or stay in cabins. When you are on top of Pinnacle Mountain and Table Rock, you really get the full experience of being at the edge of the Blue Ridge Escarpment.

The first white people came to the Table Rock area after the 1785 Hopewell Treaty with the Cherokee Indians. Tourists followed, and in 1840 a hotel was built. By the beginning of the 20th century, several farming families were living in the area.

Table Rock State Park was acquired by the State of South Carolina in 1935 from the City of Greenville and Pickens County. The Civilian Conservation Corps built the dam for Pinnacle Lake, the superintendent's residence, the lodge, cabins, and hiking trails, including the trails to Pinnacle Mountain and Table Rock in use today.

The Park has just one spectacular and steep full-day hike—with several cut-offs to make for an easier day, if desired. But what a hike! It's every bit worth the visit.

Governor's Rock at 6.7 miles, turn back for a moment to look at Pinnacle Mountain.

Follow the rock up and to the right, and you're back into the woods. The top of Table Rock (7.2 miles, 3,120 ft. elev.) has no view. Continue downward for three views—each one worth the effort—for a total of 250 ft. descent in elevation. You can see the Greenville Reservoir, a golf course, and the valley laid out in front of you below.

Retrace your steps to Panther Gap, and continue left downhill onto Table Rock Trail. You'll pass a Civilian Conservation Corps trailside shelter where people have stopped to rest on the way up to Table Rock. Pass the intersection with the Carrick Creek Nature Trail, and head back to the nature center to end the hike.

Extra: If it's open, the nature center is worth a visit.

Seen from the highway on your drive in, Table Rock is an impressive sight.

Sassafras Mountain

This hike is in the Jocassee Gorge, now managed by the S.C. Department of Natural Resources Wildlife Management Area. The Oconee bell, a rare plant first collected in the late 18th century by French botanist André Michaux, can be found in the Gorge's shaded mountain streams. According to Native American legend, the word Jocassee means "place of the lost one." However, there should be little fear of getting lost now that the trail is so well-marked with white blazes. This section will take you from the Laurel Valley to the top of Sassafras Mountain.

Getting to the trailhead:
From I-26, exit 54, take US 25 south for 17 miles. Turn left on SC 11S (Greer Hwy.) and drive for 21.7 miles. Turn right on US 178W and continue for 8.3 miles. The road crosses a highway bridge over Eastatoe Creek.

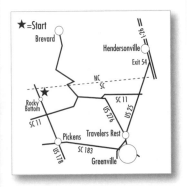

★ =Start
Brevard
Hendersonville
Exit 54
I-26
NC
SC
Rocky Bottom
SC 11
US 276
US 25
SC 11
Pickens
Travelers Rest
US 178
SC 183
Greenville

Immediately after the crossing, turn left into a parking area. From Greenville, take US 276 north where it meets SC 11S. Stay on SC 11 for 16.8 miles. Turn right on US 178W and continue for 8.3 miles. The road crosses a highway bridge over Eastatoe Creek. Immediately after the crossing, turn left into a parking area.

Type of hike: Out and back

Distance: 9 miles

Total ascent: 2,380 ft.

Highlights: Highest point in South Carolina, house-sized boulders, winter views

USGS map: Eastatoe Gap

Trail map: Foothills Trail, published by the Foothills Trail Conference

Land managed by: S.C. Natural Resources Wiildlife Management Area

Related book:
One Foot in Eden by Ron Rash

The Hike
From the parking area, cross Eastatoe Creek on the car bridge. The trail starts on your left; look for a wooden railing, after which it climbs up a series of wooden steps and soon flattens.

The first wooden bridge you cross is a good indication of the high level of trail maintenance on this section. Note the logs bordering the trail, lined with

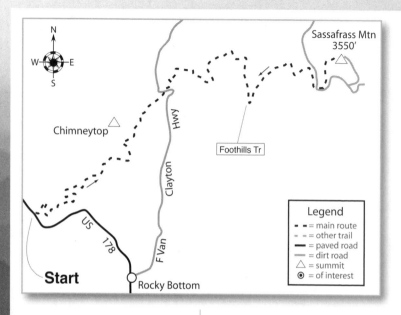

Rosebay rhododendrons, Christmas fern, and hemlock.

At 0.3 mile, a waterbar was constructed with a step to make it easier to walk over the log bar. The purpose of these bars and the trenches behind them is to divert water off the trail. The logs also hinder mountain bikes from coming onto the trail. At 1,940 ft. elev., you'll reach a ridge line and descend, with rocky ledges to the left and obstructed winter views on the right. The shorter rhododendron bushes with small leaves are the Carolina or Piedmont rhododendron. At 0.5 mile, after going up steeply on rocks, the trail levels out in a maple and Fraser magnolia forest, along with spiderwort and poison ivy.

At 1.0 mile, a bridge goes up and under a large fallen log that missed destroying the bridge. On the left at 1.2 miles, a rock formation stands like a large house on a ridge and extends down to the trail. Note the dry cave under the rocks. Fire marks above the cave indicate that people may have taken shelter here. You'll walk up a bridge at 1.5 miles as the trail makes its way around Chimneytop, and reach a wide spot on a flat road at 1.8 miles.

At Chimneytop Gap (1.9 miles), the trail crosses F. Van Clayton Hwy. A narrow, abandoned trail takes off on the right, circles around, and comes back to the main trail. Solomon's seal and Solomon's plume, blue-bead lily, trillium, bloodroot, crested dwarf iris, and trout lily line the trail as it gently ascends.

At 2.5 miles, a short side trail takes you to Balancing Rock, where there are excellent southwestern views. The trail turns on an old, grassy road at 3.4 miles and heads due north to reach White Pine Point, a reforested area that was harvested in 1971. A large sign explains that the area was reseeded in 1972. White pine trees share the forest here with tulip trees, maple, oak, and rhododendron.

The trail goes down, and at 3.7 miles, you'll pass a wooden barrier. The trail turns right, and shortly you'll reach a multi-level rock formation on the right at 3.9 miles.

Cross F. Van Clayton Hwy. again at 4.1 miles (3,290 ft. elev.). On the road, a sign reads "Sassafras Mountain on the right - 0.3 miles and Chimneytop - 2.2 miles going left." Turn right here and cross the road. In about 150 ft., the trail goes back into the woods. Look for log steps with a banister on the left. Now the trail goes up steeply among fern and fire pinks.

As you approach the top, at 4.4 miles, a side trail to the left leads to an overhanging rock offering good winter views, and soon a second side trail takes off also on the left. Both outcrops are good, flat spots for a break, with winter views to the northwest.

Continue straight to the top of Sassafras Mountain at 3,550 ft. elev. The flat top once had a tower; look for a benchmark marking the top of the mountain. Congratulations – you're at the highest point of South Carolina and have bagged another high point.

In 2004, the S.C. Department of Natural Resources bought the top of the mountain from Duke Energy, guaranteeing public access to the peak. If you want to see how most other people get to the top of Sassafras Mountain, follow the Foothills Trail down 0.1 mile to a gate and a parking area. On your left, you'll see a blue-blazed trail; that's the spur going off to Jones Gap State Park. Immediately after, white blazes of the main Foothills Trail lead off to the left, heading for Table Rock State Park.

Retrace your steps to get back to your car and finish the hike.

Balancing Rock makes a nice place to sit and take in the scenery.

Ellicott Rock

Ellicott Rock Wilderness is located where North Carolina, South Carolina, and Georgia meet. Congress established the 3,300-acre Wilderness in 1975 and made additions in 1984; it now contains 9,012 acres in the three states. Ellicott Rock Wilderness straddles the 15,432-acre Chattooga Wild and Scenic River Corridor, and though it is not virgin forest, some old-growth trees escaped the saw. Made famous by the movie, *Deliverance*, the Chattooga in 1974 became the first river east of the Mississippi to be added to the National Wild and Scenic River System.

The hike starts at the picnic shelter at the Walhalla Fish Hatchery and goes west on the East Fork Trail, paralleling the East Fork Branch. It then picks up the Chattooga River Trail, heading north to Ellicott Rock at the tri-state border.

Getting to the trailhead:
From Cashiers, NC, take NC 107S and then SC 107 for 12 miles. Turn right into the Walhalla Fish Hatchery and drive 2.2 miles to the trailhead. (At the split, take the left fork over the river.)

Type of hike: Out and back

Distance: 8.7 miles

Total ascent: 960 ft.

Highlights: Chattooga River, Ellicott Rock, history

USGS map: Tamassee

Trail map: Nantahala & Cullasaja Gorges, National Geographic Trails Illustrated (#785)

Land managed by: Sumter National Forest, Andrew Pickens Ranger District, Ellicott Rock Wilderness

Rules/fees: Group size limited to 12 people

Facilities: Bathrooms, picnic shelter at the trailhead

Closest town: Cashiers, NC

Website: www.fs.fed.us/r8/fms/forest/aboutus/AP.html

Related books & film:
Saints at the River by Ron Rash; *Deliverance* by James Dickey (novel and film with Burt Reynolds).

The Hike
From the parking lot, follow the paved path and turn left toward the picnic shelter. The area around the picnic shelter has a small number of old-growth hemlocks and white pine. Past the shelter, make a sharp left on the signed

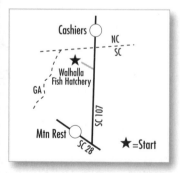

East Fork Trail. You have now entered the Wilderness Area.

At 0.3 miles, you'll cross the East Fork of the Chattooga on a wooden bridge. The East Fork stays on your left, south of the trail, which goes generally downhill. White trillium, foam flower, violets, and robin's plantain dot the trail in spring. Poison ivy is also present.

At 0.9 miles, cross a creek and small cascade on stepping-stones. The East Fork is visible even through thick foliage, and you can always hear the water. The trail narrows as it gets closer to the stream. At about 1.4 miles, pass a large striated rock formation on the right.

You are in the proverbial temperate rainforest jungle with tangled rhododendron and doghobble and tree roots growing halfway out of the soil. Water drips off moss-covered rocks. At 1.8 miles, look down for a view of a cascade on the East Fork. You'll pass several old-growth hemlocks as the trail continues downward and narrows. Farther along, you'll see a rock piling that was left on the river.

At 2.2 miles, the East Fork Trail ends. Turn right to

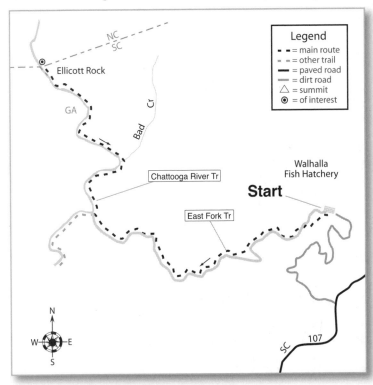

go north on the Chattooga River Trail, following the river upstream. A left at the bridge leads to Burrells Falls Road and campground. This wide junction appears to be a favorite for anglers. The river is calm here. Small sandy beaches edge both sides of the river at 2.6 miles.

At 2.8 miles, cross Bad Creek on your left after going through a camping area. Rocks across the usually shallow Bad Creek will help you to the other side. On the far bank, go up steps and turn left onto an old roadbed. The trail stays close to the river and passes several sandy and rocky beaches. At 3.8 miles, a huge dome-shaped rock

A sign beside the Chattooga River points the way to Ellicott Rock.

stands across the river from a little beach on the trail side.

When you reach the end of the Chattooga River Trail and the spot above Ellicott Rock, pieces of colored flagging tape and a sign point to Ellicott Rock below the trail.

At the sign, carefully scramble down the riverbank. The ground is muddy and slippery here. If you expected Ellicott Rock to be a large monument with a plaque commemorating a heritage group, you'll be disappointed. The rock, located just below the sign on the trail, is inscribed simply N G, presumably standing for North Carolina and Georgia. Surveyor Andrew Ellicott, who established the state boundary in 1811, was a man of few words.

But don't climb back up just yet. A few feet downstream is Commissioner Rock, which established the North Carolina-South Carolina border in 1813 with the following inscription:

LAT 35
AD 1813
NC + SC

To find the Georgia-South Carolina border, look in the middle of the river for a large rock island, designated Chattooga Rock. The inscription on the survey marker visible from shore atop the downstream side

War in the Carolinas

Nothing proclaims the state boundary when you cross into another state on small back roads or trails. That doesn't diminish the importance of the state line. Sometimes the border is so important that states literally battle over it with guns.

This quiet section of the Chattooga was the site of the Walton War in 1810, brought about by a border dispute between Georgia and North Carolina, with South Carolina also getting into the act. The 35th parallel was accepted as the northern border of Georgia, but exactly where was that? In the late 18th century, Georgia and North Carolina could not agree on which one owned a 12-mile tract of land on the state border. This orphan strip was home to 50 white families, but because neither state was policing it, it was also a haven for outlaws and criminals. In 1803, Georgia laid claim to the section and called it Walton County. Both Georgia and North Carolina referred the boundary problem to the U.S. Congress which, not surprisingly, did nothing about it. In 1810, North Carolina sent out its state militia to displace the Georgia government, resulting in a battle near present-day Brevard. North Carolina won and took back the area.

Nevertheless, Georgia remained unsatisfied and hired Andrew Ellicott, a noted surveyor from Pennsylvania, to establish the border. In 1811, Ellicott and his team of men bushwhacked through rhododendron and mountain laurel thickets to determine the location of the 35th parallel. He engraved the state boundary on a rock on the east side of the Chattooga River, which gave the orphan strip to North Carolina. Ellicott Rock now marks the location.

of Chattooga Rock says "SC 1996" where the three states come together. The water is swift and deep here; it is inadvisable to wade out into the river to get a closer look.

Return on the Chattooga River Trail. The way back looks different as you're hiking downstream and anticipating all the cascades. Most of the gentle climbing comes as you near the trailhead to the end of the hike.

Extra: If you have time, stop at the Walhalla Fish Hatchery, which produces more than 200,000 pounds of brown and rainbow trout to stock the Chattooga River and other waters in upstate South Carolina.

Pisgah District–East

Mr. Vanderbilt was the first of the large forest owners in America to adopt the practice of forestry. He has conserved Pisgah Forest from the time he bought it up to his death, a period of nearly twenty-five years, under the firm conviction that every forest owner owes it to those who follow him, to hand down his forest property to them unimpaired by wasteful use....

—Edith Vanderbilt in a letter to the U.S. Secretary of Agriculture dated May 1, 1914, offering to sell much of what is now Pisgah National Forest to the Forest Service.

Pisgah District—East

Essential Facts

Rules/fees:
None outside the wilderness area and outside Blue Ridge Parkway land

Facilities:
The Pisgah Inn, on the Blue Ridge Parkway, offers rooms and meals. For October, the prime tourist season, rooms are booked up a year in advance (www.pisgahinn.com). Restrooms, shops, and snack bars are located off US 276. Limited services are available on NC 215.

Trail map:
Pisgah Ranger District, Pisgah National Forest, National Geographic Trails Illustrated #780

Closest towns:
Asheville, Brevard, and Waynesville, NC

Website:
www.cs.unca.edu/nfsnc

Related film:
The Clearing (2004) with Robert Redford and Helen Mirren.

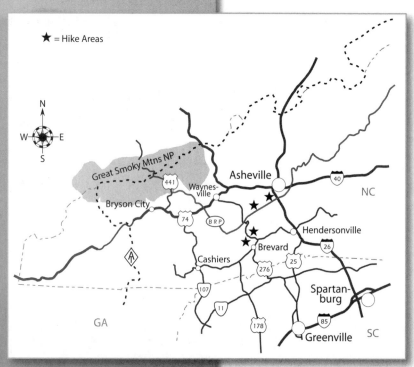

★ = Hike Areas

According to the Bible (Deuteronomy 3:27), Moses could not enter the Promised Land but could only see it from Mt. Pisgah in present-day Jordan. Legend has it that in 1776 James Hall, a chaplain who accompanied General Griffith Rutherford on his mission to destroy the Cherokees in what is now western North Carolina, saw a high mountain from the French Broad River valley. Impressed with the rich green land, Hall named the mountain Pisgah, since it overlooked North Carolina's "promised land." Mt. Pisgah is one of the first mountains newcomers to western North Carolina climb in Pisgah National Forest to get oriented and identify other peaks in the Blue Ridge.

The Pisgah Ranger District of Pisgah National Forest, ranging from the Bent Creek Experimental Forest west of Asheville to the Nantahala National Forest just west of NC 215, has over 400 miles of trails and might be the most popular hiking area in the Carolina mountains. Both the Mountains-to-Sea Trail and the Blue Ridge Parkway run east-west through the Pisgah District.

The best way to introduce yourself to the eastern Pisgah Ranger District is a drive up US 276, followed by a hike up Mt. Pisgah. Both the drive and the hike are included in

Looking Glass Falls is one of the Pisgah District's main attractions.

this section, which lists hikes east of US 276. The next section describes hikes west of US 276, including two in the Shining Rock Wilderness.

James Hall and his companions were not the only ones who saw a rich land of milk and honey in the mountains of western North Carolina. After the railroad arrived in the Blue Ridge Mountains, wealthy Northerners and Midwesterners were attracted by the scenery, climate, and cheap land.

George Vanderbilt, grandson of the railroad magnate Cornelius "Commodore" Vanderbilt, first came to Asheville with his mother in 1888 to get away from New York winters. The next year, he started buying land and planning his country estate. Eventually Vanderbilt bought 125,000 acres extending from the present-day Biltmore Estate in Asheville to Mt. Pisgah, which he bought from Thomas Lanier Clingman of Clingmans Dome fame.

In addition to the Biltmore Estate, in the early 1900s Vanderbilt built Buck Spring Lodge, a hunting lodge located a few hundred feet from the current Mt. Pisgah parking area. Though the lodge was dismantled in 1961, there are still some fascinating remains, including the springhouse. (see the *Mt. Pisgah* hike, p.158).

Vanderbilt also constructed a system of trails, including the 18-mile Shut-In Trail, which originally went from the Biltmore House to the lodge, enabling him and his hunting companions to ride their horses there. Now the Shut-In Trail, part of the Mountains-to-Sea Trail, goes from the Arboretum to the Pisgah Inn. Each fall, runners challenge each other in the Shut-In Race, considered one of the most grueling foot races in the country. Competing means climbing over 5,000 ft. in elevation while dealing with roots, rocks, and other runners on a narrow path—for 18 miles.

Vanderbilt hired Frederick Law Olmstead, designer of New York's Central Park, to landscape his property. Vanderbilt had wanted to plant elaborate gardens from his estate all the way out to Mt. Pisgah. His landscape designer politely told him that even he did not have enough money for that project. Instead, Olmstead encouraged Vanderbilt to think about forest preservation—because even in the land of milk and honey, forests need management.

At the time, the prevalent thinking in the United States was that forests were an infinite resource, because nature would always generate new trees. Loggers just took out the trees they wanted, sometimes dragging them down steep mountain slopes and killing everything in the way. Forest fires were left to burn themselves out. Erosion then made the land too poor to cultivate.

Scientific forestry in this country started with George Vanderbilt; he financed it all. Vanderbilt hired Gifford Pinchot, an American forester trained in Europe, to manage his forests and turn them into an asset which would pay for itself. Pinchot worked on selective harvesting of trees and reforestation and turned a profit his first year on the job. Pinchot did not stay long; he had bigger ambitions. He became President Theodore Roosevelt's chief forester, and in 1905 was appointed

Many trails lead you to amazing views of Pisgah's rugged terrain.

the first head of the newly created U.S. Forest Service.

Pinchot recommended Dr. Carl Schenck, a German national, to take over his job with Vanderbilt. Schenck believed that the only way to preserve forests on private land was to make a profit. Schenck started the first school of forestry in the United States; the original school buildings and equipment are preserved in the Cradle of Forestry on US 276. The curriculum in Schenck's forestry school consisted of lectures in the morning and horseback trips into the woods in the afternoon. The school lasted in various forms until 1913. By that time, Vanderbilt had fired Schenck and the school had lost its pool of

students to new, university-based schools of forestry.

Schenck recalled his Biltmore days in a book, *Cradle of Forestry in America*, which he wrote in a direct and charming style many years after returning to Germany. In his memoir he sums up his accomplishments, including building over 200 miles of rough trails through the forest—trails that we still hike and bike today.

In 1911, Congress passed the Weeks Act, which allowed the Federal Government to purchase land to protect flowing streams; the land could then be managed as national forests. The next year, Congress authorized the first land purchase east of the Mississippi in Curtis

Creek, and Pisgah National Forest was created.

George Vanderbilt died in 1914 at the age of 52 following an appendectomy. Within three months of his death, his widow Edith Vanderbilt sold 86,700 acres of land for $5 an acre. She continued to sell most of her land to the Federal Government, and it became the core of Pisgah National Forest. As Schenck recalls, she could have sold it in parcel lots to lumbermen and speculators; she would have made more money. Today, only about 8,000 acres remain as part of the Biltmore Estate.

Bent Creek Experimental Forest

Rules/fees: In the NC Arboretum, dogs must be leashed.

Facilities: Restrooms at some trailheads

Closest town: Asheville, NC

Websites: www.srs.fs.usda. gov/bentcreek; www.ncarboretum.org

Every great city has a great park: London has Hyde Park, Paris has the Bois de Boulogne, Vancouver has Stanley Park, and New York City has Central Park. Asheville has Bent Creek. A great park includes a manicured section, designed for flowers and planted trees (Asheville's North Carolina Arboretum) and a more natural section (Pisgah National Forest). A great park has water as its center and focus (Lake Powhatan). A great park allows for various types of activities such as hiking, biking, horseback riding, dog walking, and birding.

These days most parks claim an environmental purpose as well. Bent Creek is also an experimental site for forest management. The Experimental Forest houses the headquarters and research laboratory for the care of Southern Appalachian hardwoods. Since 1925, it has studied acorn production, regeneration of chestnuts, ground water quality, and tree thinning.

Though research is the primary purpose of the Bent Creek Forest, the 6,300 acre area is also Asheville's playground. Most trails are shared with cyclists, horseback riders, and others. Because Bent Creek both logs its forests and improves its roads, individual trails are occasionally closed. Be sure to check the information board before you head out. At Hardtimes trailhead, on weekends, you need to arrive early (before 9 am) to get a good parking space. Otherwise, be prepared to turn around and go back to the overflow parking on the road coming in. In this respect, Bent Creek is like New York City—tough parking.

US 276—Short Hikes

The best introduction to hiking in Pisgah National Forest may be a drive on US 276, the spine of the Pisgah district of Pisgah National Forest. Most of the forest's accessible attractions, which lie off this road between the forest entrance at Pisgah Forest, NC, and the Blue Ridge Parkway, are worth a visit. Once on the Parkway, you should also see Looking Glass Rock at the overlook at milepost 417. Several stops on this drive deserve their own day.

Getting to the trailhead: From NC 280 in the community of Pisgah Forest, go north on US 276 to enter Pisgah National Forest.

Type of hikes: Out and back

Distance: varies; all are short

Total ascent: varies; all gentle

Highlights: waterfalls, history, understanding the layout of the Pisgah District

USGS map: Shining Rock

★=General Area

Trail map: Pisgah Ranger District, Pisgah National Forest, National Geographic Trails Illustrated #780

Land managed by: Pisgah National Forest, Pisgah District

The Hikes & Attractions
The mileages for all the attractions are given from the intersection of NC 280 and US 276.

Entrance to Pisgah National Forest
• 0.3 miles
   The entrance to Pisgah National Forest has two stone columns to honor the residents of Transylvania County who served in World War I.

Davidson River Campground
• 1.3 miles on left
   The campground offers overnight camping for trailers and tents. Restroom facilities, drinking water, tent pads, grills, and even hot showers are available.

Pisgah Visitor Center and Ranger Station
• 1.7 miles on the right
   The Visitor Center has books, maps, exhibits, and up-to-date information on road conditions in the forest.

English Chapel
• 2.0 miles on the left
   The English Chapel, established in 1860 by A.F. English, is still a working

United Methodist church with Sunday services. The original building served as both church and school house for the 50 families of the Davidson River Community. A gate bars vehicles from entering via US 276. The easiest way

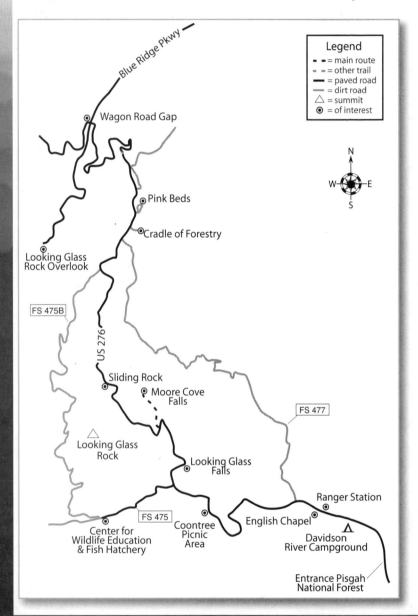

The thin veil of Moore Cove Falls has a vertical drop of about 50 ft.

the trailhead and turn left for the Wildlife Education Center and Fish Hatchery.

This site was first a logging camp, then Camp John Rock, a Civilian Conservation Corps camp. A statue commemorates the contributions of the young men who worked to improve America's federal and state lands. Later a Boy Scout camp was located on this site.

The fish hatchery raises trout to stock North Carolina streams. Three types of trout are bred: brown trout, native to Europe; rainbow trout from the waters of the Pacific Northwest; and brook trout, the only trout species native to North Carolina. You can buy fish food from a dispenser and watch a true feeding frenzy in the raceways.

The Pisgah Center for Wildlife Education has a gift shop in the front of the building; farther back are exhibits on the diverse ecosystems in North Carolina. You can watch a 20-minute film on the North Carolina mountains and then tour outdoor wildlife management exhibits on a quarter-mile loop of paved pathway. The walkway ends in a native flower garden, a great place to learn how to incorporate indigenous plants in your flower beds.

to see the chapel is to walk from the Visitor Center.

Coontree Picnic Area
• 5.0 miles on the left

This is a large picnic area by the Davidson River with outhouse facilities. In the summer, children wade in the shallow section of the creek.

FS 475
• 5.5 miles on the left

The road leads to the Looking Glass Rock Trailhead and the Pisgah Center for Wildlife Education and Fish Hatchery.

From the turn, it is 0.4 mile to the Looking Glass Rock Trailhead on the right. Drive one mile past

Looking Glass Falls
• 5.6 miles on the right

Looking Glass Falls, with a 60-ft. drop, may be the

most popular falls in western North Carolina. A steep staircase leads down to a more intimate view of the falls, making it very accessible.

Moore Cove Falls
- 6.7 miles on the right

Distance: 1.3 miles
Total ascent: 430 ft.

The walk to Moore Cove Falls is an easy walk to an obvious destination which makes it perfect for young children. The Moore Cove Trail [#318 – yellow blazes] starts at a parking area on the right just before a stone bridge. Walk past an information board, and cross Looking Glass Creek on a large footbridge. The wide and well-maintained trail climbs gently, crossing Moore Cove Creek several times.

The waterfall is a thin, broad veil with a perpendicular drop of about 50 ft. A huge overhang creates a cave so you can stand under the rock without getting wet. It is cooler here, looking out through the falling water, as if you were behind a picture window. The waterfall is captivating in winter when the base partially freezes and icicles hang from rocks.

Sliding Rock Recreation Area
- 8 miles on the left; fee area

The Sliding Rock Recreation Area is a natural amusement park, complete with a bathhouse. The paved path leads to a 60-ft. stone water slide on Looking Glass Creek with an 8-ft. pool at the bottom. Shrieking children and adults stand at the top of the slide trying to decide on their take-off point. In the summer, when there are changing rooms and

The giant water-covered slab that is Sliding Rock is irresistable.

life guards, the line to the top of the slide resembles a bus queue at rush hour.

Sliding Rock is so popular that there is a parking fee during the swimming season. Spectators, who usually outnumber the sliders, can choose between an upper and a lower observation point. The less adventurous cool off in a wading area to the side. No picnicking or alcohol is allowed.

Cradle of Forestry

• 11.6 miles on the right; fee area (www.cradleofforestry.org)

The Cradle of Forestry is a 6,500-acre historic site set aside by Congress to commemorate the beginning of forestry conservation in the United States. It features an 18-minute movie explaining how George Vanderbilt came to understand that his vast holdings needed to be managed scientifically. The character of Prussian forester Dr. Carl Schenck is so funny and over the top that it alone is worth the price of admission.

Children will love the helicopter simulator, computer games, and scavenger hunt. You can walk through two interpretive one-mile loops. The Biltmore Campus Trail [#006] has reconstructed buildings depicting how Dr. Schenck and his students lived and worked. On the Forest Festival Trail [#319] are logging equipment and a locomotive.

Pink Beds Picnic Area

• 11.9 miles on the right

The area is a mountain bog with an average elevation of 3,200 ft. The name may have come from the dense growth of rhododendron and mountain laurel which in the late spring blankets the area in pink flowers. The large picnic area with toilets, barbecue grill, and picnic shelter attracts many groups and families.

At this writing, some of the trails emanating from the picnic area are being rerouted due to recent flooding, and many bridges have been removed. Trail signs are limited, and according to posted signs, "hiking the Pink Beds is not suggested at this time." Do check the status of the Pink Beds trails at the Visitor Center.

Wagon Road Gap/Cold Mountain Overlook

• 16 miles

Turn left on the Blue Ridge Parkway. This is the classic view of Cold Mountain at milepost 411.8. The view varies with the season and the tree leaves, which obstruct it at some times of the year.

Looking Glass Rock Overlook

• 21.8 miles

Continue south on the Blue Ridge Parkway to the Looking Glass Rock Overlook at milepost 417. This mountain gets its name from the way its ice-coated rock face glistens in the winter. When water freezes on the rock, it shimmers in the sunlight like a mirror or looking glass. The hike to Looking Glass Rock is one of the most popular in the Pisgah Forest. See the *Looking Glass Rock* hike, p. 184.

Mount Pisgah

Mt. Pisgah is like the Eiffel tower. It's probably one of the most recognized high points in western North Carolina, and it's a destination to return to often. It's also the first mountain to climb if you want to orient yourself to the landmarks in the area—Cold Mountain, Frying Pan Mountain, and Looking Glass Rock. Bring a compass to understand how they all relate to each other from the observation platform. After you see the iconic transmission tower up close and personal, you'll recognize it from other vantage points. Just like the Eiffel Tower, it is popular and crowded, especially on sunny weekend afternoons. However, the analogy isn't perfect. Unlike the Eiffel Tower, you can't buy a drink atop Mt. Pisgah, and you can't take an elevator to the summit.

Getting to the trailhead:
At milepost 407.6 on the Blue Ridge Parkway west of Asheville, turn into the Mt. Pisgah Parking Area.

Type of hike: Out and back

Distance: 5.0 miles

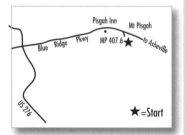

Total ascent: 1,190 ft.

Highlights: views, history

USGS map: Cruso, Dunsmore Mountain

Trail map: Pisgah Ranger District, Pisgah National Forest, National Geographic Trails Illustrated #780

Land managed by: Pisgah National Forest, Pisgah District

The Hike

The Mt. Pisgah Trail [#355 – no blaze] starts behind the large Mt. Pisgah information board. The trail is flat and rocky through rhododendron and mountain laurel. You'll pass a striated boulder on your left as the trail goes slightly up at 0.5 mile. Then the trail veers left, narrows, and goes up on log steps. At 0.8 mile (5,240 ft. elev.), a short side trail on the right allows for good views to the north, with layer upon layer of blue mountain ridges.

The trail climbs on good rock steps through countless varieties of spring and summer flowers including star chickweed, violet, bee balm, jewel weed, and galax. This section, slippery when wet, may slow you down on the way back. Before the trail turns right at 1.1 miles (5,510 ft. elev.), you have another good southwestern view. The prominent tower is on Frying Pan Mountain.

The trail turns right to continue more steeply. As

you get closer to the top, the trail switchbacks on log steps and you can see the tower in front of you.

You'll reach the observation platform at 1.3 miles (5,720 ft. elev.). On a clear day, you can see Cold

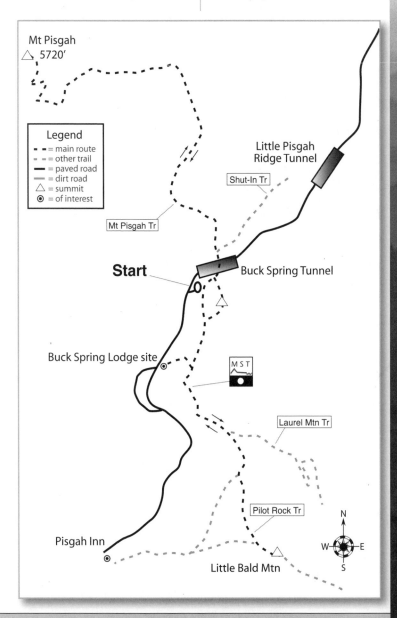

Mt Pisgah
△ 5720'

Legend
- ▪ ▪ = main route
- ▪ ▪ = other trail
- ▬ = paved road
- ▬ = dirt road
- △ = summit
- ◉ = of interest

Little Pisgah
Ridge Tunnel

Shut-In Tr

Mt Pisgah Tr

Start

Buck Spring Tunnel

Buck Spring Lodge site

MST

Laurel Mtn Tr

Pilot Rock Tr

N
W ✦ E
S

Pisgah Inn

Little Bald Mtn

You'll have a 360-degree view from the tower atop Mt. Pisgah.

The trail goes up and into the woods. When it splits into a high road and low road at 2.8 miles, take the left (the right-hand is the MST) and then another left to an obstructed view from a flat spot.

Go back and make a left on the "high road" through spruce and fern, and another left as you join the MST again. You'll reach Buck Spring Gap Overlook (4,980 ft. elev. on the sign) where you have a good view of Mt. Pisgah. At 3.1 miles there is a wooden sign to "Buck Spring Overlook 500 ft." and "Mt. Pisgah lodge, 1.0 mile."

With its wide steps and good grade, this section is the most manicured part of the MST, perhaps because it is close to the Pisgah Inn. The Buck Spring Overlook is oriented southeast, offering three benches and an information board. You're looking at the same view George Vanderbilt's guests might have had when they came to Buck Spring Lodge to hunt and breathe the fresh mountain air.

The lodge could have been considered rustic only in comparison to the Biltmore Estate. It had hot and cold running water, not easily found in any home in the late 19th century; indoor plumbing; electric lights; and an army of servants to make sure that guests did not have to rough it.

Mountain to the west; Pisgah Inn, Looking Glass Rock, and Frying Pan Mountain and its tower to the southwest. Behind you to the north, the most prominent feature is the transmission tower for the local ABC television affiliate. A recent movement to remove the 271-ft. tower did not succeed. The observation tower you're standing on was built by the Youth Conservation Corps in 1979.

Retrace your steps to go back to the parking area. At 2.6 miles, walk on the pavement and find a signpost for the Mountains-to-Sea Trail on your left. Take the MST going trail west, away from the Shut-In Trail sign, and follow the white circle blazes.

Edith Vanderbilt, George Vanderbilt's widow, who died in 1957, spent much of her later life at Buck Spring Lodge. When she died, the family sold the land to the Blue Ridge Parkway, and the buildings were demolished. However, several signs of the Vanderbilt's opulent life on top of the mountain are still evident. At the signboard, turn right on a narrow trail which leads through a clearing and into the woods, where you'll find stone steps and the remnants of a retaining wall. Beyond the steps, stay to the left and continue down the path for a few hundred feet to a wooden springhouse still in good condition. The springhouse was used to keep perishable foods cool. On the far wall, water flows through a pipe into the springhouse.

Return to the MST at 3.3 miles. Almost immediately as you continue on the trail, you'll pass the foundation of a root cellar. The numbers on a wooden post are from an old nature loop abandoned over ten years ago. The trail here is very shut-in, in a rhododendron tunnel.

George Vanderbilt's Buck Spring Lodge in its heyday. (Photo courtesy North Carolina Collection, Pack Memorial Public Library, Asheville, NC)

This springhouse is the only building left of Vanderbilt's Buck Spring Lodge compound.

You'll each a split where Laurel Mountain Trail takes off to the left at 3.6 miles. At the next intersection, take the left on the Pilot Rock Trail [#321 – orange blazes], heading to the summit of Little Bald Mountain. Here you're on a more typical Pisgah trail, which climbs steeply.

When Pilot Rock Trail starts to descend at 3.9 miles, look for a short side trail on the left to Little Bald Mountain. Little Bald Mountain is not so bald anymore; it's a flat grassy spot being filled in by new trees.

Retrace your steps to return to the Pilot Rock Trail intersection and head back down to the MST. From here, turn right to go back to the car and end the hike.

Extra–Pisgah Inn: At the intersection of the Pilot Rock Trail and the MST, you are just about 0.5 mile from Pisgah Inn and its convenience store, where you can get a cold drink. You may find it worth your while to turn left and add the extra 1.0 mile round-trip on the MST to your hike before returning to the start.

Hardtimes Loop

This easy six-mile loop shows off the northern area of Bent Creek and gets you into the North Carolina Arboretum. In the summer, Lake Powhatan offers swimming, camping, and easy walking.

In the 1800s, Bent Creek was divided up, logged, and—by today's standards—abused; by 1900, more than 100 homes and 200 businesses stood on 73 different tracts ranging from five to 100 acres each. It became an experimental forest in 1925, and little of that earlier history is evident now for those who just want to have fun here. Along with hikers, the area attracts mountain bikers from all over the Southeast.

Note that mountain biking is not allowed on the Mountains-to-Sea Trail (MST), which converges with Hardtimes Rd. for a very short stretch of this hike.

Getting to the trailhead: Take I-26 to exit 33, NC 191. Turn left onto NC 191S and drive two miles. Turn right at the stoplight on Bent Creek Ranch Rd. and follow the brown signs to the Lake Powhatan Recreation Area. After 0.2 mile, bear left onto Wesley Branch Rd. The Hardtimes Trailhead parking area is just over 2.0 miles down this road on the left.

Type of hike: Loop

Distance: 6 miles

Total ascent: 600 ft.

Highlights: views of mountain ridges and the Biltmore Estate, river

USGS map: Dunsmore Mountain

Trail map: A map displayed on the trailhead information board shows all the trails. A smaller version of that map is sometimes available at the trailhead to take away, or at area bicycle shops.

Land managed by: Bent Creek Experimental Station. The recreational aspect is managed by Pisgah National Forest. The North Carolina Arboretum is also a manager.

The Hike

From the trailhead, walk down the road. At the first intersection, turn right where you walk along a canal on your left. If you continued on the road, it would take you to Lake Powhatan.

Take a left across the canal on a concrete bridge and continue up to Hardtimes Rd. The Homestead Trail [orange blazes] veers off to the right. Continue on Hardtimes Rd. as it climbs up gently. This road is one of several old Forest Service roads which

★ =Start

Bent Creek Rd

FS 479

NC 191

Lake Powhatan Campground

NC Arboretum

Blue Ridge Pkwy

have been turned into trails, though the map still labels them as roads. As you walk up, you'll notice mysterious-looking, unsigned roads going downhill and trees blazed with various colors of paint. At one point, you'll notice the Biltmore Estate and Asheville skyline visible in the distance through trees on the left.

You can tell this has been a managed forest for a long time because the trees are all the same height. After gently climbing several hundred feet, Hardtimes Rd. reaches the MST and the Blue Ridge Parkway (at about milepost 395) on the right at 2,500 ft. elev. At 2.5 miles, the MST and Hardtimes Rd. converge for a very short while, and then the MST veers off to the right. As the road starts down, you can feel yourself descending into the watershed.

When the road reaches the back fence of the Arboretum, go through the

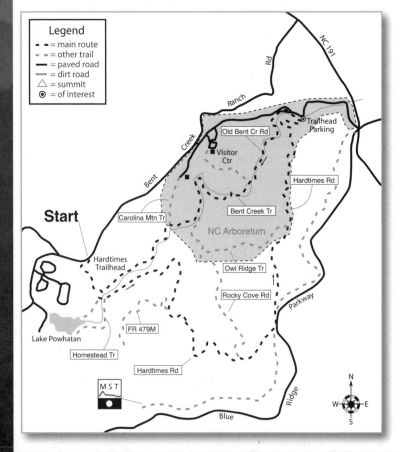

Hardtimes Trailhead in Bent Creek Experimental Forest.

to get into the heart of the Arboretum for a longer hike. The best is just before you come out of the Arboretum. Take the Carolina Mountain Trail, which goes up to the greenhouses and eventually to the Visitor Education Center in 1.2 miles.

To go back to the trailhead directly, exit the Arboretum through the gap in the fence, and soon you are back at your car and the end of the hike.

gap in the fence and you'll soon see the parking area.

Just before the parking area at 4.1 miles, take the Old Mill Trail, clearly signposted, on the left which will take you through the Arboretum. Turn left onto Bent Creek Rd. This area looks more manicured than your walk through the forest; the flat road follows the creek. On the left, you'll see the Natural Azalea Demonstration Plot, which is closed due to storm damage and at this writing has not yet been repaired. Take the Bent Creek Trail, which parallels the road. The trail allows you a closer look at the creek and gets you away from cyclists.

On Bent Creek Rd., there are at least two opportunities

Interpretive signs are found throughout the Bent Creek Forest.

Stradley Mountain

This hike follows a combination of trails and forest roads in a quiet section of the Bent Creek forest. The elevation on this hike goes from about 2,230 ft. to a little over 3,000 ft. on the Stradley Mountain Ridge, making it a gentle hike suitable year round. In winter when the Blue Ridge Parkway is closed, this is an easy all-day hike with good views. Because the hike is in the forest under tree cover, you will stay cool in the summer. Few other walkers use these trails.

Getting to the trailhead:
Take I-26 to exit 33, NC 191. Turn left onto NC 191S and drive two miles. Turn right at the stoplight onto Bent Creek Ranch Rd. and follow the brown signs to the Lake Powhatan Recreation Area. After 0.2 mile, bear left onto Wesley Branch Rd. After 1.2 miles, turn right on FS 491B (Rice Pinnacle Rd.). Bear left into the Rice Pinnacle parking lot, labeled FS 419B.

Type of hike: Loop

Distance: 8.3 miles

Total ascent: 940 ft.

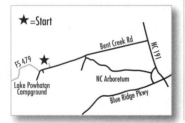

Highlights: Gentle trails suitable year-round, experimental forest

USGS map: Dunsmore, Enka, Skyland

Trail map: A map, displayed on the information board, shows all the trails. A smaller version of that map is sometimes available to take away at the signboard, or at area bicycle shops.

Land managed by:
Bent Creek Experimental Station. The recreation aspect is managed by Pisgah National Forest.

The Hike
Walk toward the information board, away from the restrooms to the Deer Lake Lodge Trail [#664 – orange blazes], a paved trail at this point. Plaques along the way with titles like "From Field to Forest" explain the history of forest management here. The paved trail goes downhill and at 0.2 miles crosses a creek on a large wooden bridge. The Hardtimes Connector Trail comes in from the left followed by a tributary of Wolf Branch on your right.

Pass a flat field on your right, the site of a lake and Deer Lake Lodge. According to old-timers, it was a beautiful lodge with a large stone fireplace, first privately owned, and then taken over by the U.S. Forest

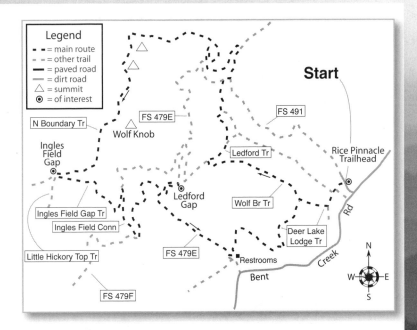

Legend
- ▪ ▪ = main route
- ▪ ▪ ▪ = other trail
- ▬▬ = paved road
- ▭▭ = dirt road
- △ = summit
- ◉ = of interest

Start

FS 479E

Wolf Knob

N Boundary Tr

Ingles Field Gap ◉

Ledford Tr

Rice Pinnacle Trailhead ◉

FS 491

Ledford Gap ◉

Wolf Br Tr

Ingles Field Gap Tr

Ingles Field Conn

Deer Lake Lodge Tr

Little Hickory Top Tr

FS 479E

Restrooms

Bent Creek Rd

FS 479F

N W E S

Service. Eventually it fell into disrepair and was dismantled.

At 0.4 mile, a rough, unmarked road comes in from the left. Continue straight on the Deer Lake Lodge Trail, now unpaved, through hemlock, ferns, white pine, oak, and poison ivy.

At 0.5 mile, turn left on Wolf Branch Trail [#666 – yellow blazes], a wide, almost flat trail. The trail crosses minor creeks through club moss and rhododendron. At 1.1 miles, you'll reach a T junction. Make a right on the Ledford Trail [#660 – blue blazes]. The forest is thickly wooded but the trees are all the same height, the classic sign of a logged forest. When the trail splits at 1.2 miles, follow the left fork with the blue blazes. Wolf Branch parallels the trail on your right. Cross the creek at 1.5 miles over a drainage pipe; the trail then switchbacks right and crosses Wolf Creek. At the T, turn left; the trail on the right has no blazes.

The trail ascends gently to reach FS 479E. Make a right on FS 479E, a gravel road. Soon after, at 1.8 miles, make a left on FS 491, Rice Pinnacle Rd., which is lush with spiderwort and wild hydrangea.

In another 0.1 mile, FS 491 goes right. Continue straight on FS 485—North Boundary Rd., a gravel road which is also designated as a trail [#135 – blue blazes]. The trail switchbacks gently as it climbs to Stradley Mountain with winter views. On the left, the high point is Wolf Knob.

The paint markings (yellow on this stretch) on trees are for those designated to be cut. On any road in Bent Creek, you might see a Forest Service truck with a crew surveying the land for possible road improvement or potential timber cut. Sometimes the Forest Service wants to "daylight" a road to dry it out.

The trail snakes south, reaches a high point at 3.9

miles (3,060 ft.), and descends to cross the ridge. You'll have winter views to the left. At 4.4 miles, four trails connect at Ingles Field Gap, also known as "4-Corners." FS 485 continues straight. Little Hickory Top Trail makes a wide left to go down to the western end of Bent Creek. Take the extreme left, Ingles Fields Gap Trail [#150 – blue blazes], which goes down steeply, heading southeast.

Make a sharp right on Ingles Fields Connector [#150A – blue on the map, but the trees have orange blazes] at 5.1 miles. Ignore a bullet-riddled sign marked 145A. At 5.4 miles, make a left at the T onto a wide gravel road. The current map shows it as Sidehill Trail, but was renamed as part of 479F Boyd Branch Rd. when the Forest Service widened the Sidehill Trail into a road. The road, lined with rosebay rhododendrons, crosses a stream at 5.7 miles. You're walking on loose stones, which is hard going sometimes, especially downhill.

At 6.2 miles you'll reach Ledford Gap with picnic tables (and no other facilities) and turn right on 479E, Ledford Branch Rd., lined with black-eyed-susans and lavender phlox. Pass another picnic table on the left on a gravel side road and later a sign, also on the left, which invites walkers to "Walk up this road. Old field on left. Hardwood forest on the right."

About Bent Creek Trails

Most hiking trails in Bent Creek are also mountain bike trails, marked as such on the Bent Creek map. Outdoor enthusiasts can all share the trail. Though hikers technically have the right-of-way when meeting bikers, it's just as easy to step off the trail and wave the bikers past.

Bent creek is quiet—that is, when the Forest Service is not logging or building roads. In this section, recent road construction has created a change from the map by turning one of the trails into a road—not a paved road for the general public, but still a wide gravel road to accommodate 15-passenger vans on tours. This particular construction has angered and organized the outdoor community (bikers, hikers, and runners) who typically stay out of the fray.

Without upkeep and maintenance, the Carolina mountains environment will reclaim most buildings. This is Deer Lake Lodge in 2001. (Photo courtesy Bent Creek Experimental Station, Asheville, NC)

At 6.9 miles, you'll arrive at a parking area at the intersection of Ledford Branch Rd. and Bent Creek Rd. Take the Deer Lake Lodge Trail, located left of the restrooms and trash cans. On this trail, you'll find several metal interpretive signs which explain tree growth and the forest cycle. At the T junction, make a left to continue on Deer Lake Lodge Trail, and at 7.9 miles, you have closed the circle. Make a right (at the beginning of the hike you went straight) to go back to the Deer Lake Lodge site and the paved trail leading to the trailhead.

Extra: If you have a little more time, walk out to the road and turn left on Rice Pinnacle Rd. Take the 0.6-mile Bent Creek Centennial Trail, a self-guided interpretive loop. The trail is flat and soft underfoot, perfect for young children.

Avery Creek Loop

The Avery Creek Valley, south of Club Gap, is reached by Forest Service roads east of US 276. On this hike, you'll follow water much of the time as you go up, generally following Henry Branch, and come down beside Avery Creek, which flows southeast into the Davidson River. Like so much of Pisgah National Forest, this valley was logged over and the timber taken out by rail. You can see evidence of the path taken by the logging railroads if you are attuned to the wide, gentle grades of some sections of trail. Twin Falls is a major attraction and can be the destination for a short hike.

Type of hike: Loop

Distance: 9.5 miles

Total ascent: 1,680 ft

Highlights: Views, creeks, twin waterfalls

USGS map: Shining Rock

Trail map: Pisgah Ranger District, Pisgah National Forest, National Geographic Trails Illustrated #780

Land managed by: Pisgah National Forest, Pisgah District

The Hike

The well-maintained Buckhorn Gap Trail [#103 – orange blazes] starts gently downhill through a rhododendron tunnel and then flattens out. Stay left at the junction, while the right branch goes across the river without a bridge. At this point, orange and blue blazes indicate that you are following both the Buckhorn Gap Trail and Avery Creek Trail [#327 – blue blazes].

Cross the three-log bridge and turn left to parallel the creek. At 1.0 mile, turn right to stay on Buckhorn Gap Trail. Cross Henry Branch several times within a 0.5 mile; the Branch generally flows southwest into Avery Creek. Ferns, doghobble, violets, and poison ivy line the trail. The trail follows Henry Branch upstream through a hemlock forest.

At 1.6 miles, turn left on the Twin Falls Trail [#604 – yellow blazes], a diversion of

Getting to the trailhead:

From NC 280 in the community of Pisgah Forest, go north on US 276 to enter Pisgah National Forest. Drive 2.3 miles and turn right at the Horse Rental sign (FS 477). Drive 2.4 miles, passing the Avery Creek Trailhead, and another 0.3 mile to the Buckhorn Gap Trailhead.

★ = Start

Horse Stables

FS 477

US 276

Ranger Station

Davidson River Campground

NC 280

Pisgah Forest

Brevard

US 64

about 0.6 mile which should not be missed. When you get to the base of the falls, climb up a narrow trail to get closer. The two falls are not parallel or even close together, and if you want pictures, you'll need to photograph them separately. The first waterfall is higher than the second and has more water. Cross the creek below the falls and follow a trail to the second waterfall, wispy and partly obscured by trees and debris. The two waterfalls mark the beginning of Henry Branch.

Return the same way on Twin Falls Trail back to Buckhorn Gap Trail. Make a left turn on Buckhorn Gap and start climbing. The trail goes up in long switchbacks, away from the creek; it feels drier here.

At 2.9 miles, turn left to stay on Buckhorn Gap Trail, which at this point is also FS 5058. The road changes back to a trail at 3.4 miles and reaches Buckhorn Gap at 3.7 miles. The gentle grade of Buckhorn Gap Trail, as it goes off to the right, indicates

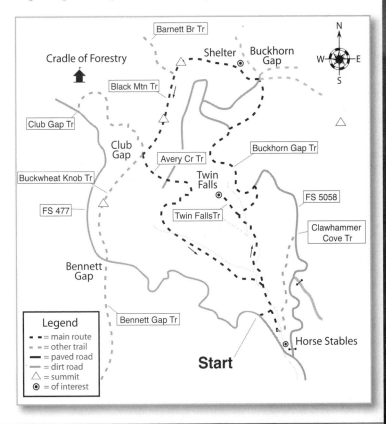

Hiking around waterfalls is a thrilling experience. These hikers are traversing just below the left falls of Twin Falls.

an old railroad grade right-of-way. Cross the road to pick up the Black Mountain Trail [#127 – white blazes].

Black Mountain Trail climbs moderately through mountain laurel. You can see the Buckhorn Gap Shelter on a side trail to the right at 4.1 miles. This old shelter with built-in bunks and two outside cooking shelves is a good destination for a short backpacking trip. The trail keeps climbing gently on Soapstone Ridge. Speckled wood lilies, bluets, and rue anemone abound. On your left, don't miss the iconic Looking Glass Rock. The Barnett Branch Trail [#618] comes in from the right. As the Black Mountain Trail veers southwest and gently descends, Clawhammer Mountain and Black Mountain come into view.

Looking southwest, you may be able to pick out Pilot Mountain, which stands taller than other mountains in that direction. You'll reach the high point of the hike at 4,090 ft. elev. with excellent ridge views. The wide and rocky trail goes down to Club Gap at 4.9 miles. At the gap, the Club Gap Trail [#343] takes off on the right to the Cradle of Forestry. The Buckwheat Knob Trail [#122] goes straight and up. Make a left on Avery Creek Trailwith its blue blazes.

The trail goes down gently through a patch of flame azaleas. Cross a dirt road and soon you'll hear Avery Creek as you continue down on the dry and rocky trail. After crossing Avery Creek a couple of times, the terrain becomes lush with hemlock and doghobble. At 8.2 miles, the Buckhorn Gap Trail meets the Avery Creek Trail, and the two run together for a short while. Turn left to stay on the Avery Creek Trail.

A wide series of cascades can be seen to the right through the trees. At 9.0 miles, the Clawhammer Cove Trail [#342] comes in from the left. Stay right and cross a three-log bridge.

On your left, notice where Avery Creek has been dammed up by beavers creating a swamp. Several bird feeders have been installed here. In summer, congregations of butterflies may hover over wet earth as you reach the end of the trail.

Turn right on the road and walk 0.3 mile to the Buckhorn Gap Trail parking area, where the hike ends.

Coontree/Buckwheat Knob

This hike has all the classic elements of the Pisgah woodland: a variety of trees, several creeks, rhododendron tunnels, and good views. It also offers more solitude than the "top of the pops" hikes in western North Carolina. It takes you up Coontree Mountain and through Saddle Gap, passing three outstanding views of the mountains and valleys. It then proceeds to Bennett Gap before climbing Buckwheat Knob. On your return, it takes you around the eastern side of the Coontree Loop as you head back down to the trailhead.

Getting to the trailhead:

From NC 280 in the community of Pisgah Forest, go north on US 276 to enter Pisgah National Forest. Drive 5.0 miles to the Coontree Picnic Area on your left. The Coontree Trail starts on US 276 across from the picnic area.

Type of hike: Lollipop

Distance: 8.4 miles

Total ascent: 2,130 ft.

Highlights: Views of mountain ridges, creeks, spring flowers

USGS map: Shining Rock

Trail map: Pisgah Ranger District, Pisgah National Forest, National Geographic Trails Illustrated #780

Land managed by: Pisgah National Forest, Pisgah District

The Hike

The Coontree Loop Trail (#144 – blue blazes) starts on the right side of Coontree Creek. You'll cross the creek on a wooden bridge. At the split, take the left fork and climb up the gently sloping valley. In early spring, this is a good place to see the first yellow and halberd-leaved violets.

Pass a rock cave on the right, large enough for children to stand in. At 0.9 mile, make a sharp left to follow the trail as it veers up and away from the main creek to climb Coontree Mountain. Cross several small tributaries as you go through large rhododendrons. The switchbacks alternate between strenuous uphills and almost flat sections around the bends. As you climb, you see other creeks across the hollow.

At 1.8 miles—having climbed 1,100 ft.—turn left onto Bennett Gap Trail (#138 – red blazes). The Coontree Loop Trail continues on the right. You'll climb the side of Coontree Mountain and pass a huge fallen tree on

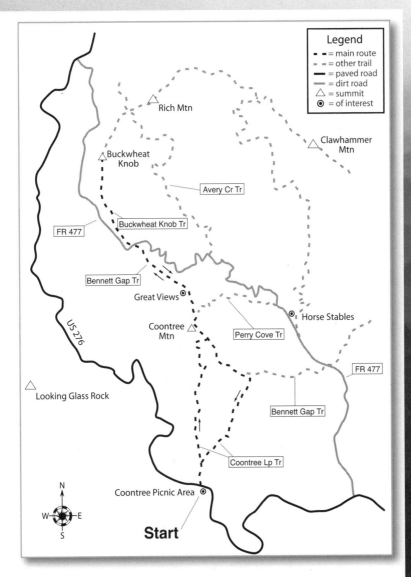

Legend
- - - = main route
- - - - = other trail
━━━ = paved road
──── = dirt road
△ = summit
◉ = of interest

Rich Mtn

Clawhammer Mtn

Buckwheat Knob

Avery Cr Tr

FR 477

Buckwheat Knob Tr

Bennett Gap Tr

Great Views ◉

Coontree Mtn

Perry Cove Tr

Horse Stables ◉

US 276

FR 477

Looking Glass Rock

Bennett Gap Tr

Coontree Lp Tr

N
W · E
S

Coontree Picnic Area ◉

Start

the left. The trail goes down through a mountain laurel tunnel and on the left, you get your first good view of Looking Glass Rock. At this point, though, there are too many trees to get a picture-postcard photo of Looking Glass Rock, so don't get your camera out of your pack yet.

At Saddle Gap, the Perry Cove Trail (#151) takes off on the right from the Bennett Gap Trail to go to the Horse Rental

Area. Stay left on Bennett Gap Trail. The trail gets steeper as you climb over rocks and large tree roots. Farther on, it flattens out to a ridge walk, and in early spring you may find some trailing arbutus hidden under the leaf litter.

At 2.4 miles, reach a rocky local summit with good views on both sides of the trail. The view to the left beneath white and pitch pines is the Davidson River Valley. On the right, you are looking at the Avery Creek Valley.

A little farther on up the trail, take the short spur on the left for an outstanding panorama of the three plutons (see box, p. 187) in the area. On the right, you can see Looking Glass Rock, and

this view of it rivals the one from the Blue Ridge Parkway. Straight ahead is Cedar Rock. John Rock, about 800 ft. lower than the other two, is in front of Cedar Rock.

Pass through a field that looks as if it's been mowed. This is a Wildlife Management Area, kept clear by the Forest Service to attract wildlife. Reach Bennett Gap at 3.1 miles. Cross FR 477 and take a right on the Buckwheat Knob Trail (#122 – yellow blazes). The trail goes straight up on log steps. Note the shaggy bark hickory trees.

Go over several false tops before reaching the crest of Buckwheat Knob at 4.1 miles and 4,000 ft. elev. A large downed tree on the left is a

Some overhanging rocks along the trail almost qualify as caves.

good place for lunch. There is a partial view on the right.

At this point, retrace your steps and go back to Bennett Gap at 5.1 miles. When you reach the Coontree Trail at 6.5 miles, continue straight up on Coontree Trail/Bennett Gap Trail (red and blue blazes). This south-facing section is typically much drier than the rest of the hike. The trail heads downhill with drop-offs on both sides.

At Coontree Gap, (7.0 miles), turn right to stay on the Coontree Trail, which continues steeply downward. A tributary of Coontree Creek comes in from the right, and the trail goes down more gently. There are several pleasant flat camping areas along the creek. Cross the creek on a three-log bridge. You'll reach the bottom junction of the Coontree Loop at 8.1 miles, and the road soon after, to end the hike.

Alternative: For a shorter hike, you can walk the Coontree Loop, which is 3.7 miles.

Pisgah District–West

...To assure that an increasing population,
accompanied by expanding settlement and growing
mechanization, does not occupy and modify all areas
within the United States and its possessions, leaving
no lands designated for preservation and protection
in their natural conditions, it is hereby declared to be
the policy of the Congress to secure for the American
people of present and future generations the benefits
of an enduring resource of wilderness.

—From *The Wilderness Act of 1964*, Sec. (2)

Pisgah District—West

Essential Facts

Rules/fees:
In the Shining Rock Wilderness Area, wood fires are prohibited; only camp stoves are permitted. Group size is limited to ten hikers. Trails are not blazed, so hikers must know how to use a map and compass.

Facilities:
None

Closest towns:
Asheville, Brevard, and Waynesville, NC

Website:
www.cs.unca.edu/nfsnc

For some, wilderness means walking alone or with a partner under a stand of trees that have never seen a saw blade, or along an unspoiled stream without seeing another soul. Others picture wilderness as a place with savage animals where they will need to rub two sticks together to start a fire and somehow survive until they get rescued.

The Shining Rock Wilderness Area does not fit either picture. Rather, it is a land ravaged over the decades

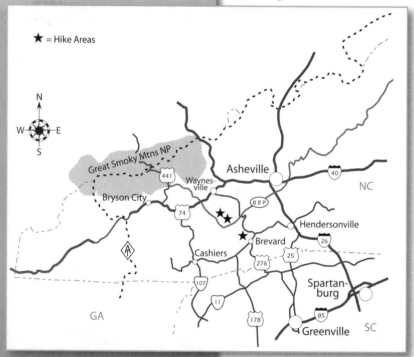

by logging, fire, and exotic insects, which has been turned into one of the favorite hiking areas in the Southeast. The Cherokees burned strategically to create new plant growth which attracted game. Then loggers came into the area and cut down stands of fir, hemlock, spruce, chestnut, and other hardwoods between 1906 and 1925. They would have continued longer but in 1925, after a severe drought, a wildfire started that was so hot that in some places the soil burned to below the root level. The U.S. Forest Service then bought most of the Shining Rock land, and another fire in 1942 decimated the young trees that had grown back. After that, there was not much left to log, and the land was nicknamed "the land that nobody wanted."

The Shining Rock Wilderness is named for the white quartz outcropping atop Shining Rock Mountain, the magnet that draws so many hikers and backpackers. It is one of the original tracts declared wilderness area by the Wilderness Act of 1964. The Wilderness Act was intended to protect "undeveloped Federal land retaining its primeval character and influence." However, if the Forest Service applied the phrase literally, it would mean untouched woods with no trails, no pipe springs, and no emergency rescue. The land would be

The Art Loeb Trail over Black Balsam is wide open and offers great views.

impenetrable; no one would ever go there, including Forest Service employees.

While the Wilderness Act of 1964 specifies land that is "untrammeled by man," according to Mark Woods in *Federal Wilderness Preservation in the United States* (1998), most places east of the Mississippi have been "roaded, logged, farmed, and otherwise impacted by humans at one time or another." That certainly includes Shining Rock. With the Eastern Wilderness Act of 1975, Congress introduced modifications based on managing wilderness lands so they would be untrammeled in the future. Without these modifications, no area in the Eastern United States would have met the original standard for "wilderness."

Another clause of the Act reads, "where man himself is a visitor who does not remain." "Man as a visitor" is a charming sentiment, but it's also a practical one. No one lives in a wilderness area, and there are no active roads, but plenty of people visit Shining Rock.

You can get into the Shining Rock Wilderness Area from FS 816 off the Blue Ridge Parkway, from NC 215 (Big East Fork Trailhead), or from Camp Daniel Boone heading toward Cold Mountain. The Art Loeb Trail, going north from the Blue Ridge Parkway, is the backbone of the Wilderness Area, with several trails shooting off from it in different directions.

Shining Rock and Cold Mountain are the only 6,000-footers in the Wilderness accessible by trails. On the Art Loeb Trail, a ridge walk north from FS 816 offers an incredible panorama as you bob from mountain top to mountain top, staying above 5,000 ft. elev. the whole time. Though technically you are not in the Wilderness until you reach Ivestor Gap, it feels wild. Logging and fires created the grassy balds that make the views so remarkable.

Hikers from all over the Southeast who may not know any other destination in western North Carolina come to the Shining Rock Wilderness. In August, the blueberries are at their peak, drawing even more visitors.

Wilderness areas have been designated as special areas that should be left, well—wild. Each wilderness area is created by an act of Congress and comes with its own rules. If there were any old roads, they are now gated. Logging is not permitted, and only hand tools can be used to maintain the trails, so trails are not maintained to the same level as outside the wilderness areas. It is much harder to saw a large blown-down tree with a handsaw than with a chainsaw, and trail maintainers cannot bring in weed whackers to cut down the mid-summer growth.

Though people may camp in wilderness areas, they must cook on stoves because wood fires are banned. Mountain bikes are prohibited; foot travel

Behind this sign is Wilderness.

Quiet streams with gentle waterfalls offer solitude at many places within Pisgah.

is allowed only in groups of ten or fewer. Hikers can bring dogs as long as they are always under control. According to a long-time Pisgah Forest volunteer, hunters had great influence in campaigning for a wilderness area; banning dogs would have effectively banned hunters.

The most troublesome rule is the one prohibiting trail markers and signage. When the Forest Service created guidelines for the Shining Rock Wilderness, they thought that leaving out blazes would decrease the number of hikers in the area and create the possibility of solitude. That did not happen. Instead, hikers create extra herd paths and confusion by wandering about looking for the real trail. Why not blaze the official trail and expect people to stay on it?

This is a recreational issue hotly debated in hiking groups. You can decide to "sacrifice" a trail by clear signposting and keeping it good condition, thereby encouraging and leading the bulk of hikers down that path. Some areas have taken this to extremes by paving trails that get a lot of use. Alternatively, you can try to spread out hikers by having few signs and no blazes, hoping that only the few experienced hikers who feel comfortable with a topo map and compass will use the area.

Of the hikes in this section, only the Cold Mountain hike is completely within the Wilderness Area.

Looking Glass Rock

A hike to the top of Looking Glass Rock is one of the most popular in western North Carolina. It is on every "must-hike" list, because the trailhead is located in the heart of the popular attractions of Pisgah National Forest and easy to find. Though the route does go uphill, it is a well-switchbacked, moderate climb on a well-maintained trail. At the end, sheer granite cliffs a few hundred feet from the top of the mountain offer outstanding views of the forest.

USGS map: Shining Rock

Trail map: Pisgah Ranger District, Pisgah National Forest, National Geographic Trails Illustrated #780

Land managed by: Pisgah National Forest, Pisgah District

The Hike

The hike starts on Looking Glass Rock Trail [#114 – yellow blazes] on log steps and passes an information board on your right. As you walk through a majestic forest on a wide trail with tall hemlock and maple, you cross a minor stream at 0.1 mile. This is a well-traveled trail that requires and receives a great deal of maintenance. Please do not take shortcuts—they create erosion and encourage others to do the same until the whole hike becomes a confusing maze of herd paths, making it impossible to find the official trail.

After the initial uphill, the trail is flat for a short while as it contours around Looking Glass Rock. Climb above a small creek on your right; you're in a lush forest with a wealth of wildflowers, including spring beauty, bloodroot, trillium, and countless other species. At 1.0 mile (2,710 ft. elev.), you'll reach a laurel and rhododendron tunnel as the trail heads for a rock outcropping, offering winter views before turning right on a beautifully constructed plank retaining wall.

Getting to the trailhead:
From NC 280 in the community of Pisgah Forest, go north on US 276 to enter Pisgah National Forest. Drive 5.5 miles and turn left on FS 475 (Fish Hatchery Rd.). The trailhead is located 0.4 mile on the right.

Type of hike: Out and back

Distance: 6.2 miles

Total ascent: 1,530 ft.

Highlights: Views galore

At 1.4 miles (2,950 ft. elev.) at the end of a switchback, a tree supported by a rock bends into a comfortable seat—a "love seat pine." This spot offers partial northern views.

At 1.6 miles the trail opens to a winter view to your left, making you feel like you've made progress on your climb—in fact, you've ascended over 900 ft. at this point. You'll pass a wide spot on the left at 1.8 miles with several downed logs, good for sitting and enjoying a break.

The trail then moderates, but this is not the end of the climb.

At 2.3 miles (3,500 ft. elev.), a trail wand on the left directs you to a helipad used by the Transylvania County Rescue Squad. The H painted on the ground of a large, flat, rocky clearing can stand for both helipad and hospital. Either way, it'll remind you that Looking Glass Rock is most famous as a place to rock climb. People as far away as Florida come to climb the granite face on

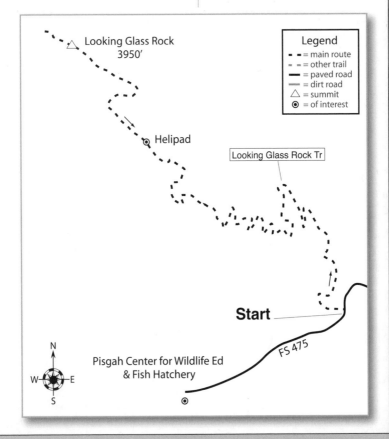

Looking Glass Rock
3950'

Helipad

Looking Glass Rock Tr

Legend
- ▪ = main route
- ▪ = other trail
━ = paved road
▨ = dirt road
△ = summit
◉ = of interest

Start

FS 475

Pisgah Center for Wildlife Ed
& Fish Hatchery

N
W E
S

This view of Looking Glass rock from the Blue Ridge Parkway is one of the most famous.

the other side of Looking Glass Rock; the hikers and the rock climbers rarely meet.

Continue climbing and note a huge rock face on your right through trees. The trail is rockier here. After a double blaze, a faint side trail veers off to the right and should be ignored. The Looking Glass Rock Trail turns sharply left at this point.

You'll reach a wide, flat spot at the top of the rock at 3.0 miles (3,950 ft. elev.) enclosed by hemlock, maple, and oak. Don't be disappointed by the top— there are no views—it's not your ultimate destination. The trail descends through a mountain laurel tunnel for about 0.1 mile, dropping 80 ft. in elevation to arrive at the

rock cliffs and excellent views. The outcropping is bordered by hemlocks, blueberry bushes, and table mountain pine that seem to cling to bare rock.

You must literally watch your step here; the slope of the rocks goes from horizontal

The slabs on top of Looking Glass are big enough for helicopters to land on.

to vertical very quickly. There is no fence or barrier of any kind, so don't get close to the edge. Hikers have been known to slide down to a very unhappy ending.

From your vantage point at the rock cliffs, walk left for a view of Cedar Rock to the south. On a clear day, you can also see Pilot Mountain, Shining Rock, and Mt. Pisgah in the 180-degree panorama. Cars on the Blue Ridge Parkway look like the proverbial ants.

If you look down at the verdant forest below you may notice the gaping streaks of shorter, lighter green stands of trees that have been described as giants' footprints pressed into the forest canopy.

Through the early 1990s, the U.S. Forest Service used clearcuts as the primary method of logging, and these are the scars that remain.

When you've had your fill of the great views, return to the trailhead the way you came to end the hike.

Looking Glass Rock

Describing Looking Glass Rock as a big rock is like calling the Grand Canyon a big hole in the ground. Yes, it's a rock—but it's also an icon in western North Carolina. The name derives from the way water freezes on its massive exposed granite face in winter and reflects the sun like a mirror. If you have stopped in any gift shop in this area, you've probably seen pictures of it taken from the Blue Ridge Parkway. However, until you've climbed it, you have not really experienced the Looking Glass.

From Looking Glass Rock Overlook at milepost 417 on the Parkway, the rock looks like a chiseled piece of sculpture on which nature did the carving. The rock is a pluton formed by a big ball of molten magma, similar to lava, that did not reach the surface. This magma solidified into rock much harder than rocks that later overlaid it. After millions of years, erosion wore down the soft outer rock, and the Looking Glass Rock we see today is the exposed magma body that's left, accounting for its domed appearance.

Cat Gap Loop

In the heart of the Davidson River valley, this hike meanders along the bottom of Cedar Rock, a huge pluton, and includes two named waterfalls. It passes several good campsites and a shelter, and crosses many creeks. Picklesimer Fields reminds us that people lived and farmed in the area. The Picklesimer family name is still prominent in Transylvania County.

After your hike, there will still be daylight hours left to check out the Wildlife Education Center and North Carolina's largest fish hatchery.

Type of hike: Loop

Distance: 8.3 miles

Total ascent: 1,720 ft.

Highlights: Views, Cedar Rock, waterfalls, shelter, good campsites

USGS map: Shining Rock

Trail map: Pisgah Ranger District, Pisgah National Forest, National Geographic Trails Illustrated #780

Land managed by: Pisgah National Forest, Pisgah District

Getting to the trailhead:

From NC 280 in the community of Pisgah Forest, go north on US 276 to enter Pisgah National Forest. Drive 5.5 miles and turn left onto FS 475. The parking area for the Pisgah Center for Wildlife Education and Fish Hatchery is 1.5 miles down on your left, just before the paved road ends.

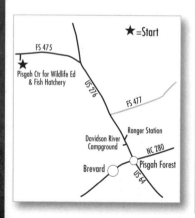

The Hike

The Cat Gap Loop Trail [#120 – orange blazes] starts at the eastern end of the parking lot opposite the Wildlife Education Center. At this end, it's an old roadbed which crosses the bridge over Cedar Rock Creek. The trail turns left and soon begins climbing. Club moss, fern, and poison ivy line the trail. Follow Horse Cove Creek upstream, and at 0.9 miles, rock hop across; dwarf crested iris, foam flower and violets grow alongside. Cross the road (FS 475C), which is an alternate though less pleasant way to get to this point.

The John Rock Trail [#365] comes in from the right at 1.25 miles. Stay on the Cat Gap Loop Trail which now starts climbing seriously. At Horse Cove Gap (1.8 miles), three trails come together. The other end of the John Rock Trail comes in from the right. The Cat Gap Bypass [#120A] begins straight ahead. Make a left to stay on the Cat Gap Loop Trail, which continues to climb steeply.

The trail curves and slabs the ridge until it reaches Cat Gap at 2.2 miles (3,380 ft. elev.), where it overlaps the Art Loeb Trail for a few feet. Take the Art Loeb Trail [#146 – white blazes] left, going southwest. Along with the white blazes of the Art Loeb Trail, you may see old blue circles of the old Alternate MST.

The 30.7-mile Art Loeb Trail starts at Daniel Boone Scout Camp, crosses the Shining Rock Wilderness, and ends at Davidson River Campground near the Pisgah Visitor Center. It was named in 1969, a year after his death, for Art Loeb, the general manager of Ecusta Paper and a leader of the Carolina Mountain Club.

You'll reach the high point of the trail (3,710 ft.) at 2.5 miles, where it begins a gentle descent. At a split in the trail, stay left on the Art Loeb Trail. Coming around, you'll have your first view of Cedar Rock on your right. The Rock seems to follow you for a long time as the trail goes around the long, wider part of the rock. In fact, as you come down, Cedar Rock appears to get closer.

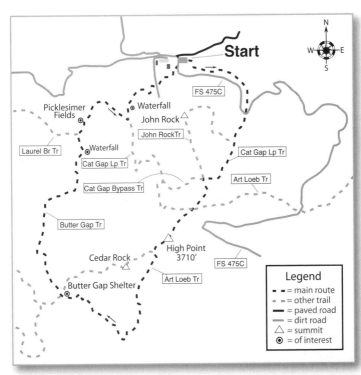

After a steep and slightly rocky descent, the trail veers left, away from Cedar Rock.

Cross Kuykendall Creek at 3.5 miles. Look left (northwest) to see Pilot Mountain. At 4.5 miles, you'll reach the A-frame Butter Gap Shelter, which has a piped spring and bear pole. Past the shelter, the Art Loeb Trail turns right and then quickly veers left and up to wooden steps leading to Butter Gap at 4.7 miles. Butter Gap is the intersection of several trails, some unmarked. Take the Butter Gap Trail [#123 – blue blazes] straight ahead, going downhill. Soon you'll find the beginning of Grogan Creek, which follows the trail most of the way down to Picklesimer Fields.

At 5.6 miles, cross a tributary of Grogan Creek and you'll pass flat areas on both sides of the trail—good for camping spots if you want to make this hike into an easy backpacking trip. Here the trail flattens out and zigzags northeast and northwest. At 6.4 miles, you can hear Grogan Creek Falls on your right. This cascading waterfall is so perfect that it looks artificial. No path leads down to the waterfall, but you can scramble a short way, holding on to trees.

At 6.8 miles, you'll reach an intersection with Long Branch Trail [#116], which goes off to the left. Turn right to stay on Butter Gap Trail, and head toward the Fish Hatchery. As you approach Picklesimer Fields, named after the family who lived here in the mid-19th century, note that there is not much open field left. At this point, Grogan Creek is flat and marshy because beavers have been at work creating a swamp. The middle of the field, at 7.3 miles, is still open. It's interesting to speculate whether the knoll to the left might have been the location of the farmhouse.

Turn left on the Cat Gap Loop Trail as Grogan Creek feeds into Cedar Rock Creek and supplies water to the fish hatchery. Listen for a waterfall on your right—Cedar Rock Creek

Butter Gap Shelter looks like a big wooden tent.

Grogan Creek Falls is just a short scramble off the trail.

Falls—at 7.4 miles. A short, steep path leads down to the falls. The waterfall is not high, but it's very photogenic and well worth the diversion. When you see the fish hatchery dam to the right, you know you're getting close to the hike's end. Cross a service road and veer left onto the bridge to continue on the Cat Gap Loop Trail. The fenced-in fish hatchery research area is on your left.

Take a left on FS 475C and head back to the parking lot to finish.

Extra: After the hike, take a look at the displays at the Pisgah Center for Wildlife Education and the Fish Hatchery.

Graveyard Fields

Graveyard Fields includes two outstanding waterfalls within a short distance—Upper Falls and Second Falls (sometimes called Lower Falls) of the Yellowstone Prong—in addition to a meadow full of berries. To make your visit worth a whole day out, this hike adds a side trip to a third waterfall, Skinny Dip Falls, reached after an 800-ft. descent.

Start this hike early or you may end up having to drive to the next overlook to find a parking place.

Getting to the trailhead: Blue Ridge Parkway, milepost 418.8, west of Asheville. If the parking lot is too crowded, go 0.5 mile to the next overlook on the left and park there.

Type of hike: Loop

Distance: 7.9 miles

Total ascent: 1,470 ft.

Highlights: Waterfalls, high-altitude meadows

USGS map: Shining Rock

Trail map: Pisgah Ranger District, Pisgah National Forest, National Geographic Trails Illustrated #780

Land managed by: Pisgah National Forest, Pisgah District

The Hike

The trailhead is at 5,140 ft. elev., almost as high as you'll be all day. Two staircases go down to Graveyard Fields. To start the hike, take the left-hand staircase down and turn left at the arrow. The hike will end at the right-hand staircase.

The Upper Falls Trail [#358A – orange on the map, blue blazes on the trail] goes into a rhododendron tunnel on wooden steps with trillium, galax, and Indian cucumber lining the trail; a wooden boardwalk protects the soil and plants underneath.

The trail initially heads due west, then turns right at 0.5 mile, doubling back to go east. You'll cross the stream on several well-placed rocks and make a left turn at the "Upper Falls" sign. A slow-moving creek winds around on your left as you walk through a meadow gradually filling in with blackberry and blueberry bushes.

At 1.0 mile, you'll pass a second sign pointing to the left, which says "Graveyard Ridge Connector and Trailhead." The trail starts to climb a little on rock steps. You're back in the trees as you begin to hear the waterfall, and you'll reach the Upper Falls

★ =Start

at 1.6 miles (5,240 ft. elev.). In the summer, a thin stream of water flows down through rock cracks, creating pools below. On sunny afternoons, people are on every rocky bank dipping their feet in the water.

Retrace your steps to go back to the Graveyard Ridge Connector and Trailhead sign at 2.2 miles (5,090 ft. elev.). When you reach a signpost at 2.6 miles (5,080 ft. elev.) which says "Trailhead" with an arrow pointing left and "Upper Falls" with an arrow pointing right, make a left turn on the Graveyard Ridge Connector [#356A – yellow on map, no blazes on the trail].

When you come out of the trees into an open area, you can see the Blue Ridge Parkway and parking area above and to your right. At the next intersection, with the sign "Graveyard Ridge" at

2.8 miles, make a left. There are no trail markers here; just follow the trail north, uphill.

Climb through a meadow of mountain St. John's-wort and blueberries, which are at their best in mid-to-late August. While you may see a wand with an orange circle, you won't find see a trail name. Continue switchbacking on the main trail, and pass another orange wand as you go through the meadow. At 3.3 miles, the trail intersects the Graveyard Ridge Trail, going both ways at a T-junction. Make a right on the Graveyard Ridge Trail [#356 – orange blazes].

Graveyard Ridge Trail may be overgrown, and you may feel you're just bushwhacking —but notice the stepping-stones, an encouraging sign that you're on a maintained trail. The area is thick with

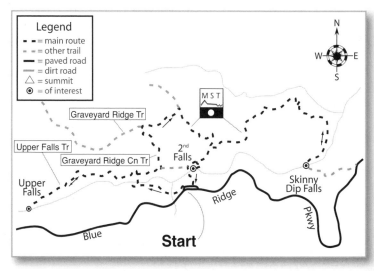

Origins of Graveyard Fields

Graveyard Fields is not a spooky, dark place. Its name comes from the extensive logging done there in the early part of the 20th century, leaving behind stumps and roots which looked like gravestones. Then in 1925 a fire swept through the area, burning over 25,000 acres of forest. Bushes and grasses are filling in the meadows, but for now, the wide expanse of flat emptiness still reminds visitors of the American West. Even the name of the river, Yellowstone Prong, conjures up the Rocky Mountains. If Mt. Pisgah is the Eiffel Tower of Pisgah National Forest, Graveyard Fields is like the Louvre—an icon you should see at least once, doing bits and pieces of it, as much or as little as you want—and in the middle of a weekend day, it's just as crowded as the museum.

The Forest Service has tried to deal with erosion by relocating some sections of trail to higher ground, upgrading other sections, and building boardwalks in many places to encourage visitors to stay on the trail. Because of the new trail system, the blaze colors have changed from the current National Geographic map. The Graveyard Fields area is still a maze of trails—some old, some relocated, many cut by people's feet walking off the beaten path. Though you can wander around and create more paths, the route listed here will take you to waterfalls on official, maintained trails.

raspberry bushes and mint. An occasional cable from the old railroad days still remains across the trail.

At 3.5 miles (5,210 ft. elev.), make a right on the Mountains-to-Sea Trail [#44 – white circle blazes], going trail east. The MST wanders gently down in a mature forest and passes a huge balsam tree with dead bottom branches and roots spreading over several feet. At 4.0 miles, the trail makes a left and goes into a dark tunnel of laurel and rhododendron. The trail has changed character; you're no longer in the meadow. Continue downhill in a sunless rhododendron tunnel with

the occasional spruce—you can hear the Yellowstone Prong on your left. At 5.0 miles and 4,470 ft. elev., the trail flattens out a little on good log steps. Sounds of the waterfall lure you as you pass a huge boulder at 5.4 miles. Now you can see Skinny Dip Falls and hear voices. At 5.6 miles (4,370 ft. elev.), you'll reach Skinny Dip Falls.

By now you've probably figured out that most people do not hike down to Skinny Dip Falls the way you did. In fact, most take a side trail from Looking Glass Overlook on the Blue Ridge Parkway which leads to the MST. From here, the MST continues east across the bridge and up the wooden steps. Skinny Dip is a multi-level falls that curves around through rocks and under the bridge to create several pools. In spite of the waterfall's name, everyone is fully clothed around the water.

Retrace your steps by heading away from the wooden steps and bridge to climb over 800 ft. in

Second Falls is easy to get to and attracts a lot of people.

elevation. As you go up, when you start seeing opening in the trees, you know you're getting close to the top. Two wands at 6.9 miles point to the right to stay on the MST, marked "To Graveyard Fields parking."

Back at the intersection at 7.2 miles, take a left on the MST Access Trail [# 358B – yellow on the map, blue blazes on the trail]. The plaque here says, "Graveyard Parking Lot – 0.4 mile." On the left, you'll pass several attractive (but waterless) campsites.

As you get closer to the Blue Ridge Parkway, you can hear Second Falls. The trail makes a right turn, passes a huge boulder, and continues west. You can hear people below to your left. There are many side trails and cut-throughs which the Forest Service is trying to mask with piles of brush to close them off and let the area regenerate. Please stay on the main trail to prevent yet more erosion—you'll also get to the bottom of Second Falls more easily.

At the T junction (7.4 miles), go left on Lower Falls Trail [#358C] to a huge wooden staircase system. Halfway down, there is an observation platform with a plaque. As you walk down to Second Falls (7.5 miles; 4,960 ft. elev.), listen to the kids and dogs in the water. From the sound of it, you could be in the inner city swimming pool in the summer—except they don't allow dogs in city pools.

To return to the trailhead, climb up the steps and continue straight on a boardwalk. At the end of the boardwalk, the trail turns left and continues toward the sign "To the trailhead." The trail crosses over the top of Second Falls on two bridges. Head up the stone steps and then up a paved path, back to the Graveyard Fields Overlook to end the hike.

Cold Mountain

The hike starts at the northern end of the Art Loeb Trail. At Deep Gap, it heads north on the Cold Mountain Trail to the top of the mountain. On this hike, you will travel from 3,200 ft. elev. at the trailhead to 6,030 ft. at the top, through several zones of vegetation.

Your hike up is like going back to an earlier season. In spring, flowers past their prime at lower elevations are still waiting to bloom up top. In early autumn, trees at the summit have already changed color, while foliage is still green at the trailhead.

Since this hike is in a Wilderness Area, the trails are not blazed. However, because of the increased fame of Cold Mountain brought on by the book and movie, there is now a wand and sign at the Forest Service information board.

Getting to the trailhead:
From Waynesville, take US 276 south for 6.5 miles. Turn right onto NC 215 south in Bethel. Drive 5.3 miles and turn left on Little East Fork

Rd. (SR 1129) and proceed 4 miles until it deadends into Camp Daniel Boone. Once in the camp stay to the left, drive past the buildings and onto the forest road, and park on the right side of the road. The trail starts at the Forest Service sign on the left.

Type of hike: Out and back

Distance: 9.8 miles

Total ascent: 3,500 ft.

Highlights: Views, flowers, literary reference, SB6K in the Wilderness Area

USGS map: Waynesville, Cruso, NC

Trail map: Pisgah Ranger District, Pisgah National Forest, National Geographic Trails Illustrated #780

Land managed by: Pisgah National Forest, Pisgah District

Related book & movie: *Cold Mountain* by Charles Frazier and the 2003 film of the same name, with Nicole Kidman

The Hike
The Art Loeb Trail [#146 – no trail blazes in this section] starts out rocky and steep. Umbrella leaf, mayapple, trillium, ferns, bluet-like houstonia, Vasey trillium, bloodroot, and squaw root are plentiful at the start—and so is poison ivy. You'll pass a large boulder with rock tripe on your left as the trail switchbacks. Shortly after, the trail flattens among

rhododendron, mountain laurel, hemlock, and oak, and crosses a creek at 0.3 mile.

As you go up, bellwort, speckled wood lilies, and yellow mandarin appear along with flame azalea. You'll reach an old road bed at 0.9 mile; make a left turn to stay on the Art Loeb Trail. At 1.1 miles, go down a wooden step ladder. You may see some Jack-in-the-pulpit. At 1.4 miles, the trail makes a left as an overgrown road comes in from the right.

At 1.7 miles and 4,080 ft. elev., you'll cross Sorrel Creek, whose water cascades down to Sorrel Creek Rd. You may see an almond millipede, so named because of the almond smell it emits when it feels threatened, crawling across a trail. Pass two large chestnut oaks on the right and another one close by. Cross a minor creek at 1.9 miles among Carolina silverbells.

At 4,100 ft. elev., the trail turns north and changes

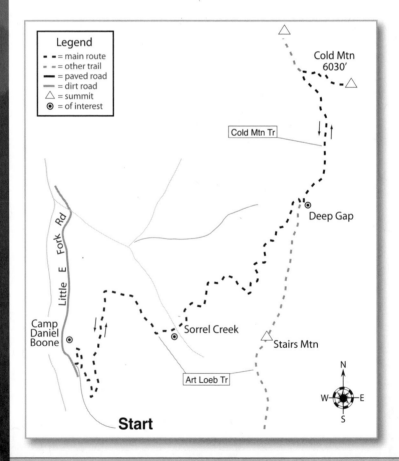

The upper reaches of Cold Mountain are rugged, with many unusual rock outcroppings.

direction. The wildflowers seem to have left the trail for a moment as you walk through a galax, rhododendron, and mountain laurel thicket.

Soon you have an obstructed eastern view of one end of Cold Mountain. At 2.3 miles, you'll cross a minor creek. The trail meanders, then climbs steeply, heading north as the vegetation decreases. Before you turn right, there are good but obstructed views to the west. At 4,700 ft. elev., striped maples and ramps grow close to a muddy and rocky spot.

As you get close to Deep Gap, mint and blackberry cane abound. You'll reach Deep Gap at 3.4 miles (5,010 ft. elev.)—a large flat area, once a grassy bald where cattle grazed in the summer. It has not been kept cleared for years, and hardwood trees have moved in. Several trails fan out of the gap in different directions. The Art Loeb Trail takes off southwest and goes through the Narrows (the spine between Cold Mountain and Shining Rock), leading to Shining Rock Gap.

Make a left on the Cold Mountain Trail [#141], an obvious but unmarked trail. The Cold Mountain Trail is steeper than the Art Loeb Trail: over 1,000 ft. of climbing in 1.5 miles. Here you pass

Frazier's *Cold Mountain*

Inman had pointed out to Swimmer that he had climbed Cold Mountain to its top…Mountains did not get much higher than those, and Inman had seen no upper realm from their summits.

—*from* **Cold Mountain** *by Charles Frazier*

We now know there are at least 30 mountains in western North Carolina higher than Cold Mountain. However, thanks to Charles Frazier's best-selling book, no mountain is more famous. Most content themselves with seeing it from the Blue Ridge Parkway at the Cold Mountain Overlook (milepost 411.8). Hikers reaching the top will enjoy 180-degree views deep into the Shining Rock Wilderness.

blackberry cane and Turk's-cap lilies. Look to your right (due east) for Mt. Pisgah with its identifying tower.

When the trees have not completely leafed out, you can see your goal. This can seem daunting because it's a long way up to the summit. More flowers—cinquefoil, stonecrop, wild strawberries, and purple violets flank the trail. Turk's-cap lilies and lobelia bloom in the second half of August at 5,350 ft. elev.

You'll climb over some downed tree trunks; maintenance is more difficult because trail crews can't use chainsaws in the Shining Rock Wilderness. Notice the orange markers, which are the wilderness boundaries. Enjoy a flat section with southern views on your left. On the right, you'll pass a rock formation with its "finger" pointing up at 4.1 miles (5,600 ft. elev.), as you continue climbing. A spring, also on the right, supplies water for the campsites further up.

The trail makes a right turn, and several good campsites are evident on the left. Make your last climb in this heath bald. Walk through mint in a meadow filling in with heath plants.

At last you'll reach the ridge on the summit with three rocky outcrops, located to the right of the trail, looking south. The first view is just as you get to the top.

Fraser firs look like soldiers marching on the ridge as you view south across Shining Rock Wilderness from atop Cold Mountain.

The Narrows looks wild and seems to go on forever.

Continue on the trail to a second rock outcropping; you'll have the best views from here. If it's not too windy and you haven't already eaten lunch, this is the place for it. With good binoculars and a good imagination, you can see some rock that shines at the end of the Narrows—Shining Rock. The two peaks of Sam Knob are clearly visible; Mt. Pisgah is at the far left. Dark balsam trees, the classic Christmas trees, dot the near landscape like Ents, the walking trees in *Lord of the Rings*. The magnificent panorama makes all the climbing effort worthwhile.

No roads are visible except for the faint cut of the Blue Ridge Parkway. You are in the heart of a green wilderness with its many ridges and spines.

Continue on the trail for the third view and the official summit at 6,030 ft. As you turn into a small, rocky outcropping that is not very obvious from the trail, look for a survey marker embedded in a bare flat rock at ground level. Congratulations! You've climbed another SB6K.

Retrace your steps to the trailhead to finish the hike. As you return, notice another peak close up in front of you. That's the other top of Cold Mountain, located on private land.

Shining Rock

In Cherokee mythology, Shining Rock was the home of the first man and woman, Kanati and Selu. It was their Eden. For hikers, too, Shining Rock is a destination of mythic proportions, and with good reason. This hike starts high and stays high, allowing outstanding views for much of its length. You don't have to go to Switzerland to enjoy alpine scenery and wave upon wave of mountain ridges. Except for the Blue Ridge Parkway which discreetly cuts through the mountains, there are no signs of civilization. However, don't expect to find genuine solitude here.

Though only half of this hike is in the Shining Rock Wilderness, there are no blazes anywhere and few signs even outside the wilderness. Map, compass, and an early start are essential for enjoying the day safely.

Getting to the trailhead: From Blue Ridge Parkway milepost 420.2, turn right onto FS 816 and drive 1.3 miles to the parking lot at the end of the road.

Type of hike: Loop (with several shorter loop possibilities)

Distance: 10.7 miles

Total ascent/descent: 2,200 ft.

Highlights: Views, SB6K, balds, shining rocks, partly in Wilderness Area

USGS map: Shining Rock, Sam Knob

Trail map: Pisgah Ranger District, Pisgah National Forest, National Geographic Trails Illustrated #780

Land managed by: Pisgah National Forest, Pisgah District

The Hike

The parking area is at 5,740 ft. elev., probably the lowest you'll be all day. Walk down the road (FS 816), and at 0.5 mile, turn left on the trail at the Mountains-to-Sea Trail sign. A few steps later, pick up the Art Loeb Trail [#146 – white blazes] on your left as the MST goes right. The trail is good but rocky through bluets and blackberry cane.

Pass a flat area on your right and a second flat area on both sides as the trail rises quickly above treeline. At 0.7 miles, you are already

Black Balsam
FS 816
Graveyard Fields
Blue Ridge Pkwy
Devil's Courthouse
NC 215
★ =Start

enjoying outstanding views; that's the beauty of starting so high. You can see Black Balsam Knob on your right—your first destination.

At the first rocky outcropping on your left (0.8 mile), the world opens up to you. Go out to a second rocky knob straight ahead

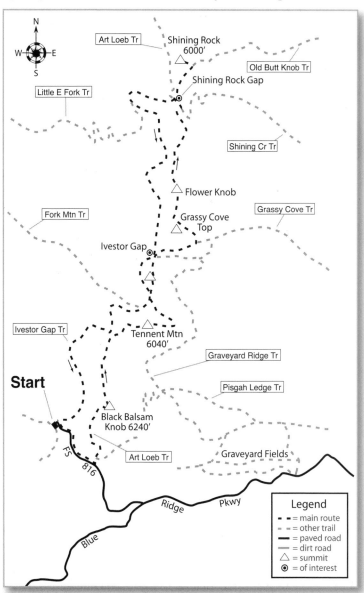

Art Loeb Tr

Shining Rock 6000'

Old Butt Knob Tr

Shining Rock Gap

Little E Fork Tr

Shining Cr Tr

Flower Knob

Fork Mtn Tr

Grassy Cove Top

Grassy Cove Tr

Ivestor Gap

Ivestor Gap Tr

Tennent Mtn 6040'

Graveyard Ridge Tr

Pisgah Ledge Tr

Start

Black Balsam Knob 6240'

Art Loeb Tr

Graveyard Fields

FS 816

Ridge Pkwy

Blue

Legend
= main route
= other trail
= paved road
= dirt road
△ = summit
◉ = of interest

With no blazes in the Wilderness, people come up with all kinds of trail markers.

and a little to the left where you can see Sam Knob with its characteristic two bumps and a dip in the middle, like a sugarloaf. At 1.0 mile, you'll reach a minor summit of Black Balsam Knob as you stare at the higher peak of the same mountain, straight ahead and to the right a little. Stay to the right, (though you might see an Art Loeb sign to the left) and head for the front edge of Black Balsam Knob.

At 1.3 miles and 6,240 ft. elev., you'll reach a rock outcropping on your right. A plaque commemorates the Art Loeb Trail and shows its complete route from the Davidson River, 24 miles to the east, to Camp Daniel Boone, 11 miles to the north. Art

Loeb, for whom the trail was named, was an industrialist, conservationist, and Carolina Mountain Club leader.

With the rock and its plaque on your right, make a sharp left to continue over the summit of Black Balsam Knob. Herd paths go off in several directions, crisscrossing the Art Loeb Trail. Keep looking at the top and continue straight. At 1.7 miles, the trail starts slabbing to the right and down.

Tennent Mountain is now your next goal. If it's windy at the top, you don't have to descend far to get out of it. You're walking in a trench of rhododendron, at their best in mid-June, and blueberries in mid-August. Because there is a 200-ft. drop between Black Balsam and Tennant Mountain, both count on your list of SB6Ks. As long as you see Tennent, you're on the right track. Ignore other herd trails—and there are many. At a gap (2.0 miles, 5,930 ft. elev.), as the trail starts to climb, note the yellow Clinton's lily, which blooms in June at this elevation.

You'll reach the top of Tennent Mountain at 2.3 miles and 6,080 ft. elev. (the sign says 6,040 ft.). The peak was named for Dr. Gaillard Stoney Tennent, a founder of the Carolina Mountain Club who became its first president in 1923.

Here you have an outstanding 360-degree

view. If you stop right here and turn back, you will have seen some wonderful scenery, but there's so much more if you keep going.

The trail goes down from the summit of Tennent as you bob up and down on the rim of a bowl. Once you leave Tennent behind, finding the route becomes easier. At 2.7 miles, the trail turns left and you're getting northbound views. That gently rounded hump ahead of you and to your right is Grassy Cove Top. Trails encircle but do not climb Grassy Cove Top. The rocky trail continues down in a northwest direction through blackberry cane and maples.

As you get down this stretch, there is a wand signed "Art Loeb," but no blazes, even though this is not part of the Wilderness Area. The Art Loeb Trail makes a right to join the Ivestor Gap Trail [#101 – no blazes] for a few hundred feet. At this wide intersection (3.1 miles and 5,730 ft elev.), stay to the right to continue on the Art Loeb Trail. If you look farther to your right, you'll see a road at the base of Grassy Cove, the Graveyard Ridge Trail [#356].

The Art Loeb Trail goes up toward Grassy Cove Top among blueberries, blackberries, and strawberries. At 3.3 miles, you'll reach an area enclosed by pitch pine. At the end of the enclosed pine area the trail splits, but both ends come back to the

The trails are easy to see—it's just a matter of choosing the right one. Always carry a map!

same point. Descend to an open area, go through a split-log fence and reach Ivestor Gap with its signboard and wilderness sign. At 3.5 miles (5,710 ft. elev.), you are now entering the Wilderness Area. (For a shorter loop, you can go back from here on Ivestor Gap Trail to the start of the hike for a total of 5.9 miles).

Go right on a road for 100 ft., and turn left at the Art Loeb wand. There may also be a metal wilderness marker. As you climb up the sides of Grassy Cove Top, pass a huge double fir tree at 4.1 miles.

After coming out of a tree tunnel, the trail continues to offer outstanding views to the east. You'll walk through an enclosed area of balsam and

The Shining Rock itself is a large outcropping of quartz.

come out into the open at 4.7 miles. Look down at an open area, and you'll see your first shining rock straight ahead. As you go down to Flower Gap, you also have head-on views of Mt. Pisgah. At 4.8 miles, reach Flower Gap; the bump ahead is Flower Knob. You'll notice that heath plants are starting to fill in this bald.

Notice also the mica—thin, shining shards of rock—on the ground. Mica was used for electrical insulation until the 1940s; there were several mica mines in Pisgah National Forest.

You're on a flat trail at 5.1 miles. An obscure trail comes in from the right which leads to a spring. A few steps later, also on your right Shining Creek Trail [#363] comes up on log steps. Several spur trails take off on the left to campsites. On summer weekends, this area is filled with tents.

You'll reach Shining Rock Gap at 5.3 miles where several trails take off. The Art Loeb Trail makes a dogleg—first a left, then a right—which leads through the Narrows and eventually to Deep Gap under Cold Mountain. On the right, a spur trail takes off to campsites. The diagonal down to your left is the Ivestor Gap Trail, which you will take on your way back. The trail straight ahead is the Old Butt Knob Trail [#332 – no blazes] to the top of Shining Rock; this is the trail you want now.

You'll walk through a balsam and rhododendron tunnel for a short while, then the trail is lined with high heaths. You're back to a dark tunnel where you start to see quartz rocks, and straight ahead is a rock wall. About 50 ft. before you reach the wall, the trail goes off to the right and up. Log steps have been installed to improve the walking; when you reach them you'll know you're going the right way.

At 5.6 miles (5,960 ft. elev.), the Old Butt Knob Trail makes a right turn. Continue left uphill, and pass an overused campsite with a fire ring. The trail goes back into the bushes with a soft left, soon reaching the overgrown heath summit where the bushes are as high as most of the rocks. One set of rocks still sticks out above the shrubbery at 5.8 miles (6,000 ft. elev.). Scramble up those rocks, and you've summited Shining Rock.

Retrace your steps to Shining Rock Gap at 6.2 miles and make a wide right onto the Ivestor Gap Trail [#101 – no blazes], about 300 degrees west. Several rocky steps lead to the trail into the woods. The Ivestor Gap Trail has a gentle railroad grade, rocky in places. At 6.6 miles, the trail splits. Stay to the left as the Little East Fork Trail [#107] takes off to the right and down to Daniel Boone Camp.

Come out to great views of Grassy Cove Top straight ahead. On the right, Sam Knob will periodically appear for the rest of the hike. At 8.3 miles, you'll reach Ivestor Gap. Follow the wider road bearing softly to the right as it heads about 220 degrees. Outside of the Wilderness Area, the trail widens out into a rocky road. In late summer, the gate is opened to cars for blueberry pickers and much later for hunters, but the road is so poorly maintained that few cars attempt to drive to Ivestor Gap.

At 8.8 miles you'll reach a wide intersection with the Art Loeb Trail. Make a soft right to continue on the Ivestor Gap Trail where it joins the Art Loeb Trail for a few hundred feet. Then the Art Loeb Trail takes off to the left as you continue straight on the road.

The trail goes up gently on a wide road with great views to the right. You may see "rock art"—rocks stacked in various combinations by other hikers—on the side of the trail. At 9.7 miles, cross a huge dip in the road, with seepage. Only a monster truck might be able to get over that hole. At 10.1 miles, look to your right for what might be the best and closest view of Sam Knob. Go around the barrier and back to the parking lot to end your hike.

Sam Knob Loop

This loop can be considered an original rails-to-trails hike, on trails established long before the movement to turn railroad beds into trails became popular in the 1980s. Squeezed in between the Shining Rock and Middle Prong Wilderness Areas, this region was heavily logged and the timber taken out by rail. Hikers now benefit from this logging past by walking on trails created from gentle old railroad grades.

On this hike, you'll climb the two peaks of Sam Knob, walk through sweeping meadows, pass several waterfalls, and enjoy spectacular views at the lookout tower on Devil's Courthouse, all while staying above 5,000 ft. This loop appears to be less traveled than the trails to Shining Rock.

Getting to the trailhead: From Blue Ridge Parkway milepost 420.2, make a right on FS 816 and drive 1.3 miles to the parking lot at the end of the road.

Type of hike: Loop

Distance: 10.6 miles

Total ascent: 1,710 ft

Highlights: Mountain top views, waterfalls, SB6K, Devil's Courthouse lookout

USGS map: Sam Knob

Trail map: Pisgah Ranger District, Pisgah National Forest, National Geographic Trails Illustrated #780

Land managed by: Pisgah National Forest, Pisgah District

The Hike

The trail starts to the right of the toilets where a wand reads "To Sam Knob Summit"—you're on the Sam Knob Summit Trail [#617A – blue blazes]. Veer to the right through blackberry cane, blueberries, ferns, spruce, and maple trees. You're walking on a flat, wide, rocky road, heading northwest. Soon the trail becomes grassy and opens up on the right.

At 0.3 miles, take in the outstanding view of Sam Knob in front of you: two knobs with a slight dip in the middle. The trail veers to the right and descends on a rocky path. The lower, rounded mountain in front of you is Little Sam. The trail crosses the field, heading for Sam Knob, and aims for two wands ahead side by side.

At 0.6 mile (5,680 ft. elev.), you'll reach the wands at the intersection of the Sam Knob

Trail and the Sam Knob Summit Trail. A wand points the way to Flat Laurel Creek here. Make a right to stay on the Sam Knob Summit Trail.

The trail quickly turns left into the woods and climbs through flame azalea and mountain laurel. Note an old piece of metal logging paraphernalia holding up a step on the trail. At 1.0 mile, climb a sturdy ladder with a railing. Looking southeast, you can see Black Balsam Knob on the other side of FS 816. As you go up, Mt. Hardy, the highest knob, is a constant presence on your left.

At the trail split (1.2 miles, 6,030 ft. elev.), go left for the higher of the two tops. The trail has flattened out and you're on a bald which is filling in with wild hydrangeas. You'll pass a

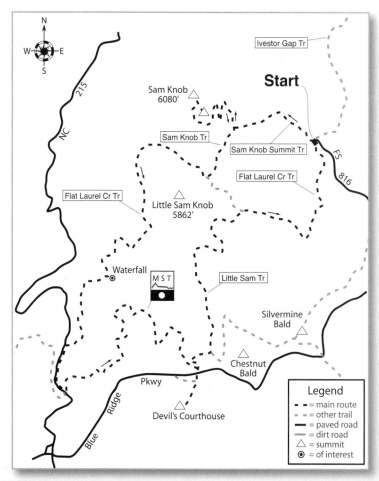

Devil's Courthouse as viewed from Sam Knob.

beautiful hunk of white quartz, which would look good in a landscaped garden. At 1.3 miles (6,080 ft. elev.), you'll reach the top of Sam Knob.

If you look close in on the right, the cut in the forest is the Ivestor Gap Trail. Shining Rock is situated at the end of the Art Loeb Ridge. Pisgah with its identifying tower is east, and beyond that, ridge after ridge as far as the eye can see.

Retrace your steps to go back to the split, and take a left to the other peak of Sam Knob. Looking south, that bump with a rock face is Devil's Courthouse. You can see the devil's profile facing skyward.

Retrace your steps again and return to the two wands. (If you decide to return to the start from here, you will have walked 2.8 miles and climbed less than 600 ft.)

Continuing on the intersection (2.2 miles), take a right on the Sam Knob Trail [#617 – no blazes]. None of the wands say, "Sam Knob Trail," only "To Flat Laurel Creek." The trail goes down and south, on the right-hand side of the field. Several small wooden bridges keep you out of the muck. You're walking toward the base of Little Sam, but you won't climb the mountain. In mid-to-late June, the rhododendron are spectacular.

Cross a shallow creek on rocks at 2.5 miles and pass a flat area, good for camping. You'll pass another "To Flat Rock Creek" wand and intermittent faded blue blazes on rocks. At 2.6 miles (5,440 ft. elev.), you'll cross Flat Laurel Creek on rocks. A few feet later, you'll reach a T junction. Take a right on Flat Laurel Creek Trail [#346 – orange blazes]. (If you went left, the trail would take you back to the parking lot, a shorter loop option of about 4.5 miles.)

You're walking in the gap between Sam Knob on the right and Little Sam on the left on a flat railroad grade trail. Old railroad ties, one with a spike, have been left in the ground from the railroad era. Though you're paralleling the creek on your right, with good camping areas, heath and spruce separate you from the water.

At an open, rocky spot full of mountain laurel at 3.4 miles (5,310 ft.elev.), the road you see twisting down the mountain is NC 215. The sun filters through rhododendron, maples, and birch trees. You'll reach a concrete bridge, left over from railroad days at 4.2 miles (5,130 ft.). On your left, a waterfall on Bubbling Spring Branch hugs the rock as the water comes down in one slow stream on its way to the West Fork of the Pigeon River.

You'll each a graveled parking area and then NC 215 at 5.0 miles (5,070 ft. elev.)—the lowest point on the hike. NC 215 starts outside of Canton, ascends to the Blue Ridge Parkway at Beech Gap, and eventually descends to the South Carolina border.

This road, which separates the Shining Rock and Middle Prong Wilderness Areas in Pisgah National Forest, is different from US 276—NC 215 is its country cousin with few tourist attractions. It has no visitor center, extensive paved parking areas, or educational exhibits. People live on this side of the forest.

North of the Parkway on NC 215 is the Sunburst Campground, the original site of Sunburst logging camp, established in 1906 by Champion Paper when a railroad was built into the area. From 1910 to 1913, the Biltmore Forestry School, headed by Carl Schenck, was based in Sunburst. Farther north is Lake Logan,

Sam Knob is relatively flat on top and wide open.

now the site of an Episcopal Conference Center. Lake Logan was also originally owned by Champion Paper.

Turn left and walk up the road. At 5.3 miles, turn left again on the MST [#440 – white circles] and head back into the woods on rocky steps through mountain laurel, following the white circles through a rhododendron and spruce tunnel. The trail starts to climb gently. At 5.8 miles (a point of possible confusion), do not cross the creek. Instead the trail turns right and keeps the creek to its left. A few hundred yards later, cross the stream on a two-log bridge with a banister and continue on this flat area. The trail has made a U-turn.

At 6.1 miles (5,480 ft. elev.), a huge boulder juts in from the right to meet the trail. When the views open up, you can see NC 215 and Little Sam, and way in the distance to the southwest, Cold Mountain. At 6.3 miles (5,550 ft. elev.), the trail flattens out through heath with maple and yellow birch. You'll enter a dark spruce grove at 6.9 miles and follow the white circles, since the trail is blanketed by pine needles.

When the MST makes a left at 7.3 miles, take a right on a blue-blazed trail to Devil's Courthouse. A paved path comes in from the right; continue straight up on a gravel trail. Here you may meet tourists who have walked 0.2 mile from the Blue Ridge Parkway at milepost 422.4. A large sign explaining the wildlife habitat lets you know that you're now on Blue Ridge Parkway land and you need to stay on the trail.

You'll reach the lookout on Devil's Courthouse at 7.6 miles, where you can see four states— North Carolina, South Carolina, Georgia, and Tennessee—and from the Snowbird Mountains 35 miles west to Caesars Head 20 miles east. Devil's Courthouse is a massive rock outcropping. According to Cherokee mythology, an evil spirit, Judaculla, translated as "slanting eyes," held court and passed judgment in a cave inside the rock.

Retrace your steps back to the MST and make a right at 7.9 miles. As you go down from Devil's Courthouse, when the paved section goes left and down, continue straight. The trail climbs over a boulder and stays rocky as it goes back into the woods.

At 8.1 miles (5,750 ft. elev.), turn left on the Little Sam Trail [#347 – yellow blazes]. The MST continues on the right and goes to FS 816 about 0.6 mile down from the parking lot. You'll reach a wide spot of possible confusion; go straight here, past a campfire ring. Ignore the herd paths on either side.

Huge meadows below Sam Knob are filled with wildflowers.

The Little Sam Trail turns into a grassy field with extended views to the left and periodically goes back into a heath tunnel. At 8.4 miles, step over a metal winch cable lying across the trail, another reminder of logging days. At 9.0 miles, the trail makes a sharp left. Cross a creek and start climbing—here there are some yellow blazes.

At 9.5 miles, (5,560 ft. elev.), the Little Sam Trail ends. Continuing straight ahead (a soft right), take the Flat Laurel Creek Trail. The voices you may hear from your left are probably people on top of Sam Knob.

Walk through mountain ash and spruces. Black Balsam Knob looms ahead, and Sam Knob feels very close on your left as you climb uphill in a rocky trench back to the parking lot to finish the hike.

Great Smoky Mountains National Park

We're the Smoky Mountains hikers
We have nothing else to do
We spend our spare time hiking
Like others seldom do.

—From the 900-Miler Song, sung to the tune of The Yellow
Rose of Texas by members of the 900-Miler Club, a group
of people who have hiked all the maintained trails in
Great Smoky Mountains National Park.

Great Smoky Mountains National Park

Essential Facts

Rules/fees:
No entrance fees. Dogs are not allowed on any hiking trail.

Facilities:
Backcountry campsites and shelters; campgrounds accessible by car. To reserve a campsite at a GSMNP campground, visit www.reservations.nps.gov. Some backcountry campsites and shelters require reservations; to reserve space, call the Park at 865-436-1231 up to a month before your trip. To reserve a space on popular holiday weekends, call as early as possible.

For backcountry campsites not requiring a reservation, self-register for a permit at a ranger station on the day of your trip. All the rules (and backcountry campsites) are clearly laid out on the Great Smoky Mountains Trail Map and Guide available from the visitor center and on the Park website under Camping.

Trail map:
Great Smoky Mountains National Park, National Geographic Trails Illustrated #229

Closest towns:
Bryson City, Cherokee, Maggie Valley, and Waynesville, NC

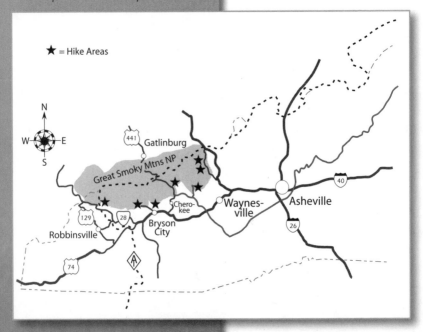

Website:
www.nps.gov/grsm

Related books:
The Wild East: A Biography of the Great Smoky Mountains by Margaret Lynn Brown; *The Great Smokies: From Natural Habitat to National Park* by Daniel S. Pierce

A hiker walks through a sea of white phacelia on the way to Hemphill Bald.

The Great Smoky Mountains National Park straddles Tennessee and North Carolina. Newfound Gap Rd. (US 441), which travels north from Cherokee, NC to Gatlinburg, TN, forms the backbone of the Park and climbs to over 5,000 ft. at Newfound Gap.

If national parks have specialties, the Smokies is a hiker's park. The scenery is diverse: mountain views, old-growth trees, waterfalls, streams, and more shades of green than you'll ever see on a paint chart. Trails are well-maintained and easy to follow. Mile for mile, hiking is much easier here than in the neighboring national forests. Even though there are no blazes on trails in the GSMNP, they are so well-marked at every intersection that you can follow them with confidence.

The Smokies may be the most visited national park in the country, but only the roads and parking lots get congested. With over 800 miles of trails (not the 900 miles in the song), even popular trails are not very busy.

Due to deed restrictions imposed when the Park was established, there are no entrance fees. Counting all the minor entrances, there are 16 entrances into the Smokies, with Gatlinburg being the most popular. It is easy to criticize Gatlinburg, famous for its 20,000 motel rooms, fast food, and t-shirt shops. However, Gatlinburg and Townsend, TN, and Cherokee, NC are the gateway towns that keep the commercialism outside the Park itself. There are no grand lodges in the style of the Ahwahnee Hotel in Yosemite or Old Faithful Inn in Yellowstone. You can't buy a meal or take a shower inside the GSMNP.

If you want to stay in the Park, the developed campgrounds are well equipped with tent pads, picnic tables, cold running water, and group sites, but no showers or hookups. On the North Carolina side, only the Smokemont Campground accepts reservations—all the others operate on first-come, first-served basis.

The comfortable backcountry campsites and the spacious campgrounds make the park an excellent first-time family camping destination. With miles of intersecting trails and over 70 miles of the Appalachian Trail, you can design loop hikes in the GSMNP that will keep you in backpacking options for weeks.

When backpacking, you need to stay in either designated shelters or backcountry campsites. As noted above, all shelters and some campsites require reservations. Both are well laid out with fire rings and the all-important pack suspension devices, placed to help you keep your food away from the bears. Though Smoky the Bear did not come from the Smokies, over 1,800 black bears live in the Park. Bears are shy, so your chances of seeing even the tail end of a bear dashing into the woods are slim.

Yet with all these amenities, the Park is one of the most biologically diverse areas in the world. To date, over 10,000 species have been documented, and scientists expect to find many more. The Great Smoky Mountains are considered a temperate rainforest, defined as an area with an annual rainfall of at least 100 inches. Elevations in the Park range from 876 ft. to 6,643 ft. on top of Clingmans Dome, where you will literally be on top of Old Smoky. This range in elevation is equivalent to traveling from Georgia to Maine, with southern plants in the lower elevations and northern ones, such as spruce, in the higher mountains. The Great Smoky Mountains National Park was declared an International Biosphere Reserve in 1976 and a World Heritage Site in 1983. Even the most industrious hiker focused on covering the miles will slow down to smell the flowers.

The old Cook cabin sits in Little Cataloochee valley.

From the top of Hemphill Bald you look south, east, and west towards the Blue Ridge Parkway.

The GSMNP is not untouched wilderness. For centuries the Cherokees farmed, fished, and hunted here. In the late 1700s and early 1800s, European settlers began arriving in the area and cleared the land to build cabins, schools, and churches. They raised cattle and hogs, planted apple orchards, and built roads to transport their goods in larger towns.

In the 1880s, lumber companies came down to the Southern Appalachians after having logged over the Northeast and upper Midwest. They built sawmills and the railroads needed to bring the trees down to be processed. More workers were attracted to lumbering jobs, many finding it an easier living than farming. The railroads also attracted tourists to Bryson City and Cherokee and took them high up into the mountains.

Logging was devastating the Smokies at the same time as visitors were coming to see its wonders. Regional entrepreneurs realized that tourists coming to fish, hike, and admire the vistas would bring in more money in the long run than logging. Thus the movement to preserve the Smokies was born.

Most of the national parks in the western United States were created from land already owned by the Federal Government. Here the land was bought by the states of Tennessee and North Carolina from individual families and logging companies. The GSMNP was established in 1934 at the height of the Depression. The Civilian Conservation Corps, created to provide jobs to young men, built the trails, fire towers, roads, and bridges which we still enjoy today.

About 5,700 people had to leave their homes when the Park was created. Though some were allowed to live out their lives there, it wasn't easy to stay, since they could no longer hunt, dig roots, or clear fields. In general, Park rangers tried to eliminate evidence of human history, but three churches have been preserved on the North Carolina side: Smokemont Baptist Church, close to the start of the Smokemont loop; Little Cataloochee Church on the Little Cataloochee Trail; and the Palmer Chapel Methodist Church in the Cataloochee Valley.

Over 200 cemeteries remain in the Park. Park employees clean and maintain cemeteries to get them ready for the annual Decoration Day. On Decoration Day—each cemetery has its own day—descendants of the families buried in the cemetery get together to decorate graves, remember their loved ones, picnic on the grounds, and generally reconnect with their home place. In the many cases where descendants no longer live in the area, the Park maintains the cemeteries.

An old wagon wheel possibly used by the Boogerman himself.

Cataloochee

For a quiet, out-of-the way entrance with good hiking and fascinating artifacts, head for Cataloochee in the southeastern section of the Great Smoky Mountains National Park. The word Cataloochee is thought to be a corruption of the Cherokee word Gadalutsi, which has been translated as "fringe standing erect" or "waves upon waves of mountains."

Cataloochee was the largest settlement in the Smokies, supporting about 1,200 people in its heyday. The first families came in 1836, attracted by good farm land and abundant forests. Twenty years later, with the next generation of settlers, the valley became overcrowded. The newcomers migrated over Noland Gap to the next valley, which they named Little Cataloochee.

A hundred years later, the settlements were prospering, with schools, churches, and post offices. The residents were so self-sufficient that they barely felt the Depression in the 1930s and took in relatives who had left the region earlier and were suffering in the outside world. Cataloochee was so isolated that even in the 20th century, women left the valley only once a year to go into town.

Like communities throughout the area, the people of Cataloochee were forced to sell their land to the government and move out when the Park was formed. The National Park Service burned many buildings, concerned that the residents would sneak back to their homes. Thus the Cataloochee valley went from wilderness to settled community and back to "wilderness" in less than a hundred years.

A few artifacts were saved; churches, houses, barns, and a school. They are not laid out neatly in a circle as they are in Cades Cove on the Tennessee side of the Park. In Cataloochee, the buildings were left in their original places, and those who want to see them have to search for them. You can drive into Big Cataloochee, but you must walk or ride a horse to reach Little Cataloochee. To understand Park history at your own pace, consider exploring the Cataloochee valley on foot rather than driving around the often frustratingly crowded Cades Cove loop.

If you are lucky and go very early, at dusk, or in cold weather, you might even see the elk. Elk are native to the area but became extinct before the Civil War, victims of overhunting and habitat loss. As an experiment, the Park Service has reintroduced elk to Cataloochee, and they are doing well. Nothing restricts the elk physically to Cataloochee, so in a few years, they may spread out all over the Park and into neighboring national forests.

Elk are big; a male can weigh over 700 pounds, a female over 500 pounds. These placid grazing machines are wild animals, as warning signs along the road remind you. Since elk reintroduction, the number of tourists in the Cataloochee Valley has doubled, but most come at midday and sit at the edge of the fields with binoculars.

According to Russ Morton, N.C. State Volunteer Chair of the Rocky Mountain Elk Foundation, there are approximately 50 elk in the study, and negotiations are under way to bring more in as soon as possible.

It's an expensive undertaking, all done with money from private donors; none of your tax dollars were used. In fact, the elk might be saving the Park a little money. When settlers moved out of Cataloochee and took their cattle with them, trees began to fill in the fields. The Park Service had to mow the fields to keep part of the land open for views of the mountains and wildlife. Now the elk are doing it for free.

The elk in Cataloochee are closely monitored with radio collars.

Boogerman Trail

This hike, which features old-growth trees, is steeped in the history of the Smokies. Said to be the best maintained trail in Cataloochee, the Boogerman Trail is a good introduction to the Cataloochee Valley. Caldwell Fork was the least populated of three settlements in Cataloochee; the others were Big Cataloochee (the valley bisected by Cataloochee Rd.) and Little Cataloochee over Noland Gap.

Highlights: Streams, old-growth trees, artifacts, and history

USGS map: Dellwood

Trail map: Great Smoky Mountains National Park, National Geographic Trails Illustrated #229

Land managed by: Great Smoky Mountains National Park

The Hike

From the parking area, walk back to the trailhead sign. Cross the log bridge (it's the longest in the National Park) over the creek at its confluence with Caldwell Fork, and start on a well-worn road. Several muddy patches are covered by wooden planks; Caldwell Fork is an obvious horse trail. The trail then plunges into a dark hemlock forest as it parallels Caldwell Fork on your left. Trillium, doghobble, mountain laurel, Christmas fern, speckled wood lily, fleabane, and poison ivy line the trail, which ascends gently as you leave the stream for a short while.

You'll cross a bridge at 0.7 miles (elev. 2,670 ft.) and make a left onto the Boogerman Trail, where horses are not allowed. Start a gentle uphill among old-growth hemlocks, Canada mayflower, galax, and several types of oak trees. You can hear Caldwell Fork down below on the left.

As you climb Den Ridge, you'll have partial views to the north. The trail moderates

Getting to the trailhead:

From I-40, take exit 20/US 276S, and turn right onto Cove Creek Rd., 0.3 mile after the exit. Drive 6 miles to Cove Creek Gap, the entrance to the Great Smoky Mountains National Park and another 1.8 miles into the valley. At the four-way intersection, turn left. Continue 3.4 miles, pass the campground, and park on the left just beyond the Caldwell Fork trailhead.

Type of hike: Lollipop

Distance: 7.5 miles

Total ascent: 1,150 ft.

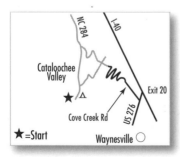

a little as it slabs around the hillside of sassafras and Fraser magnolia. At 3,100 ft., the trail turns dry, and the undergrowth diminishes. Walk through a tunnel of hemlock, rhododendron, and mountain laurel, and look up to the cathedral-like old-growth trees lining the trail.

Once on the ridge, the trail undulates gently. At 2.2 miles (3,280 ft. elev.) among huge trees, twin white pines stand prominently on your right. Soon after, you'll cross Palmer Branch on a log bridge. In spring, brook lettuce and purple Canada violets dot its banks. The area flattens

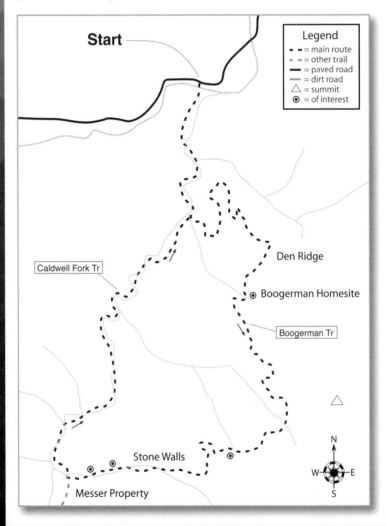

Start

Legend
- - = main route
- - = other trail
━ = paved road
─ = dirt road
△ = summit
◉ = of interest

Den Ridge

Caldwell Fork Tr

◉ Boogerman Homesite

Boogerman Tr

△

Stone Walls

◉

Messer Property

N
W ✦ E
S

out; this was Boogerman's homesite. The trail climbs gently but steadily. Trees line both sides of the trail, like an entranceway to a grand palace.

At 2.5 miles, a lugged metal wheel leans against a tree on the right. It probably belonged to Robert Palmer, the "Boogerman" who built a road to his property by hand. The trail continues its gentle climb in this dark forest where oak and hemlock dominate.

You'll rock hop across a tributary at 3.2 miles. After another short, steep climb, the trail turns right and climbs up to 3,720 ft. elev. at Sag Gap, the high point, and immediately goes down. At 3.7 miles, after another couple of short, steep climbs, the trail switchbacks down sharply. Though it is heavily wooded, this section does not have the huge trees you saw at the beginning of the Boogerman Trail.

At 3.9 miles (3,500 ft. elev.), you'll cross a creek coming in from the left and soon pass the first of three long stone walls on your right. On the right, a tulip tree has a hollow trunk so large you can stand inside it. At 4.2 miles, Snake Branch comes in from the left with a small cascade, and crosses the trail on its way to Caldwell Fork.

You'll cross Snake Branch a second time; it's now on your left and getting wider. You'll pass the second dry

> ## The Boogerman
>
> *Robert Palmer was the Boogerman, a name he acquired in school. According to legend, Robert was a very shy child. When the teacher asked him what he wanted to be when he grew up, he answered the first thing that came into his head: "The boogerman!" The name stuck. As an adult his full beard and gruff demeanor frightened children—he really did become the boogerman. Cataloochee was a settled area, but Boogerman did not sell out to the logging companies or even allow his neighbors to cut trees on his property. He is remembered as a stubborn loner. Today, the old-growth trees live on long after the landowner is gone.*

wall, about 2 ft. wide on the right where the land is almost flat. The third stone wall, shaped like an L, bisects several spur trails to homesites. Cross the main creek a third time on rocks.

At 4.7 miles, look to your left for two big pieces of timber in a depression in the ground, which may have originally been part of a root cellar, or led to a spring. You are now on the Messer property; Messer is another prominent Cataloochee family name.

At 4.8 miles, you'll reach the second intersection with

Caldwell Fork Trail; make a right turn here. The trail is lush and wet, filled with galax, ferns, rhododendron, and doghobble. In this section, you'll follow Caldwell Fork on a wide and rocky trail and keep crossing it (you'll cross no fewer than eight times) on wide split-log bridges supported by rock pilings. Look for a turn to each footbridge; in several instances, if you miss the turn, the trail straight ahead will lead you to a horse crossing. If you end up at one, you've missed the bridge by just a few feet. Most of the area looks logged over, though a few trees, hemlocks in particular, escaped the axe. Suddenly the trail goes uphill on good log waterbars. Caldwell Fork is far below you on the left. At 6.6 miles, reach the second intersection with the Boogerman Trail. You've now closed the loop.

On the way back to the trailhead from here you'll cross two more bridges, including the last one back to the road, to finish the hike.

Bridges come in all shapes and sizes. This one is crossing Caldwell Fork.

Little Cataloochee

The hike starts from the gate on NC 284. Some say that if you want to know what most mountain roads were like 80 years ago, this is the one to drive. Though the road is not paved, it is maintained. You can hike into the Little Cataloochee Valley from the gate, go as far as you want on the Little Cataloochee Trail, and return the same way. You will pass cemeteries, cabins, and the Little Cataloochee Chapel. However, if two cars are available, a shuttle hike will give you a good feel for the difficulty of traveling between the two valleys in the days when they were inhabited. On a shuttle hike, you climb up to Davidson Gap and come down to meet the Pretty Hollow Gap Trail, which takes you into Big Cataloochee.

the Cataloochee Valley. At the 4-way intersection, continue straight on NC 284, following the sign for Big Creek and Cosby. Drive the dirt road for 6 miles, passing a gauging site to a gate on the left and signs to Little Cataloochee Trail. Park at a wide spot on the road just before the gate.

Shuttle hike directions:
Place a second car at Pretty Hollow Gap trailhead on Cataloochee Rd first. From the four-way intersection, make a left into the Cataloochee Valley and drive 4.9 miles. The Pretty Hollow Gap trailhead is on your right, close to the Beech Grove School.

Type of hike:
Out and back or shuttle

Distance: *As a shuttle:* 6.6 miles – 1,490 ft. ascent and 1,460 ft. descent
To the Little Cataloochee Chapel and back: 5 miles – 1,050 ft. ascent
To Cook Cabin and back: 6.3 miles – 1,270 ft. ascent

Highlights: History, artifacts, church, cabins, cemetery

USGS map: Cove Creek Gap

Trail map: Great Smoky Mountains National Park, National Geographic Trails Illustrated #229

Land managed by: Great Smoky Mountains National Park

Getting to the trailhead:
Take I-40 to exit 20/US 276. Once on US 276, make the first right onto Cove Creek Rd. and drive 6 miles to Cove Creek Gap at the Great Smoky Mountains National Park entrance. Continue down into

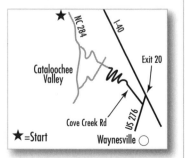

The Hike

At the gate on NC 284, take the Little Cataloochee Trail into the Little Cataloochee Valley. You'll parallel the Little Cataloochee Creek, with poison ivy, rhododendrons, galax, maples, and ferns along the sides. Cross a wide bridge at 0.4 mile.

At 1.1 miles, turn right on the Long Bunk Trail for a short side trip (0.2 mile and 100 ft. ascent) to the Hannah Cemetery. The Long Bunk Trail is lined with mountain laurel as it goes up to the cemetery, which is surrounded by a fence with yucca plants. In the cemetery

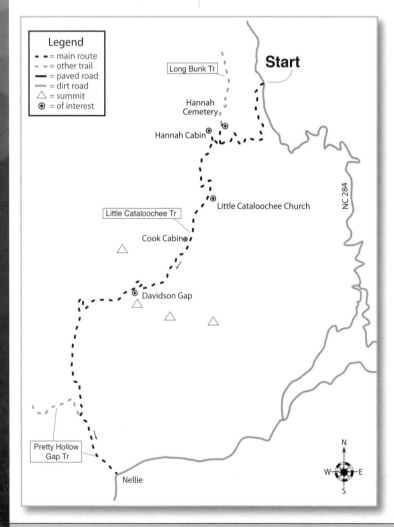

Legend
- – = main route
- – = other trail
— = paved road
= dirt road
△ = summit
◉ = of interest

Start

Long Bunk Tr

Hannah Cemetery

Hannah Cabin

Little Cataloochee Church

Little Cataloochee Tr

Cook Cabin

Davidson Gap

Pretty Hollow Gap Tr

Nellie

NC 284

N
W   E
S

Life in Cataloochee

The Little Cataloochee Valley was established by the children of the original Cataloochee residents. In 1854, the first settlers went over Nolan Mountain from Big Cataloochee because they found it too crowded. Little Cataloochee is called an island community because one can trace the community from its birth to its death in the 1930s when the area became part of the Great Smoky Mountains National Park.

To explore Little Cataloochee, you must walk or ride a horse. Though there is a road into the community, it is opened only once a year for cemetery decorations, adding a new meaning to the term "gated community." Each year, former inhabitants and their descendants gather around the church to eat, pray, and clean up the cemeteries.

In the old days, when people walked over the mountain from Big to Little Cataloochee, they would stay a while rather than returning the same day. One woman raised in Big Cataloochee remembers the trek through the gap to visit her grandmother for a couple of days, and the hike back home. "It was a tough walk," she recalled.

and of course, Hannahs. At burial, bodies are oriented with their feet pointing east. In this way, they could rise up and face east at the time of the Second Coming.

Return to the Little Cataloochee Trail. At 1.75 miles, turn right for a side trip to the Hannah Cabin. Raised on rock piles, the cabin was built in 1864 and restored in 1976 by Park personnel using period tools. Note the puncheon floor with boards over 2 ft. wide.

Cross the creek on a bridge at 2.1 miles, and take a look at the mossy stone work on the far side of the creek. Soon after, you'll find a rock-covered spring on the right. The trail climbs and reaches the Little Cataloochee Baptist Church at 2.7 miles.

Built in 1889, the chapel sits on a ridge top. It has a small square belfry atop a gable roof. Like the outside, the inside is plain and painted white, without even a cross or a picture on the wall. There is a potbellied stove in the middle of the room which would block the view of anyone preaching from the small pulpit.

The cemetery to the right of the knoll is well-maintained. At their yearly cemetery decoration day, attendees bring extra plastic flowers so that every grave is remembered with a flower. After a remembrance ceremony in the chapel, food is laid out for everyone to share on the high picnic tables in the back.

itself, a few graves have large, imposing stones; some have numbers; and others are marked by unreadable stone stumps. The cemetery has many Woodys, Valentines,

Continue on the trail following the creek, passing level homesites on both sides. At 3.3 miles (3,320 ft. elev.), you'll reach the Cook Cabin, a restored structure with a stone chimney and a porch on three sides. A split-log fence surrounds the lawn. The stone enclosure on the left is the remains of an apple house; apples were a cash crop in this valley.

Past the Cook Cabin, the trail starts its climb to Davidson Gap. You'll pass a long stone wall on the left at 3.5 miles. This was the site of Will Messer's first farm complex before he moved his family farther into the valley.

It's a steady climb up the sides of Nolan Mountain to Davidson Gap, separating Big and Little Cataloochee Valleys. Here the trail is filled with nettles, but you can see it was a road. Trail maintainers have installed log steps in an effort to mitigate some of the mud created by horses.

You'll reach Davidson Gap at 4.1 miles. It's a nice flat area with several logs—good for a break. Now the trail goes downhill steeply in a muddy trench created by horse traffic. In one place a side trail was built to avoid the worst of the mud. It's a quiet forest walk through Solomon's seal, Solomon's plume, spiderwort, and whorled loosestrife.

A long stone wall parallels the trail at 4.2 miles on the right. Beyond the wall on your right, look for a house foundation with notched logs stacked together and a faint trail leading up to the foundation.

At this point the trail is no longer as steep. Two creeks come in from the right to cross the trail. You'll cross Davidson Creek at 4.9 miles and make a second crossing at 5.1 miles.

At 5.8 miles, turn left on Pretty Hollow Gap Trail, here a wide road which parallels Palmer Creek on the right. It's a pleasant downhill. You'll pass a horse camp and picnic area at 6.3 miles, which explains the mud that you walked in on Little Cataloochee Trail. The hike ends in Nellie.

Little Cataloochee Baptist Church.

Mount Sterling

This out-and-back hike goes from the historic Little Cataloochee Valley to the Long Bunk Trail, past the Hannah Cemetery and then to the Mt. Sterling Trail, which takes you to the top of Mt. Sterling. The altitude on this hike ranges from 2,960 ft. at the trailhead to 5,820 ft. at the summit. Once on top, you can get even higher by climbing the fire tower for outstanding 360-degree views.

Getting to the trailhead:
Take I-40 to exit 20 at US 276. Once on US 276, make the first right onto Cove Creek Rd. and drive 6 miles to Cove Creek Gap at the Park entrance. From there, drive down into the Cataloochee Valley. At the four-way intersection, continue straight on Old NC 284, following the sign for Big Creek and Cosby. Drive the dirt road for 6 miles, passing a gauging site, to a gate on the left and signs to Little Cataloochee Trail. Park at a wide spot on the road just before the gate.

Type of hike: Out and back

Distance: 13.3 miles

Total ascent: 3,260 ft.

Highlights: Cemetery, history, views on Mt. Sterling

USGS map: Cove Creek Gap

Trail map: Great Smoky Mountains National Park, National Geographic Trails Illustrated #229

Land managed by: Great Smoky Mountains National Park

The Hike
The Little Cataloochee Trail starts at the gate and is still maintained as a rough road for the annual family reunion and cemetery decoration day. At 1.0 mile, turn right on the Long Bunk Trail. This trail, which starts out as a road, climbs slowly on the lower slopes of Long Bunk and crosses several streams. Look for level home sites on the right. At 1.1 miles, pass Hannah Cemetery on the right. Hannah is an important name in the Cataloochee Valley. The Hannah cabin is a short way past the Little Cataloochee Church. After the area was incorporated into the park, Mark Hannah, a former resident, was hired as the first ranger in Cataloochee.

The trail becomes narrower as it follows a creek upstream, and it can get a little mucky in the spring. Cross a minor creek at 2.7 miles. On the right, the trail parallels the main stream with several small cascades—sometimes, the trail is *in* the stream—and goes up a little more steeply.

Cross the main creek at 3.3 miles and enter an area with abundant spring wildflowers—bloodroot, purple violets, cut-leaf toothworts, Dutchman's britches, spring beauties, halberd-leaved violets, and trout lilies. After the third crossing of the major creek at 4.1 miles, the trail becomes drier with fewer flowers.

At 4.5 miles, you'll reach the junction with Mt. Sterling Trail; turn left here. The Mt. Sterling Trail starts at Mt. Sterling Gap, a historical and legendary gap, about 0.5 mile downhill from here.

Long ago, buffalo used the gap to get from one grazing range to another. Cherokee hunters followed the buffalo, and later European settlers improved the road which then became the Cataloochee Turnpike. In 1810, Francis Asbury, the first elected Methodist bishop in the United States, rode over Mt. Sterling Gap to deliver a sermon at a home located on the Pigeon River in present-day Clyde. Asbury was a circuit-riding preacher who traveled from New England to the South every year for

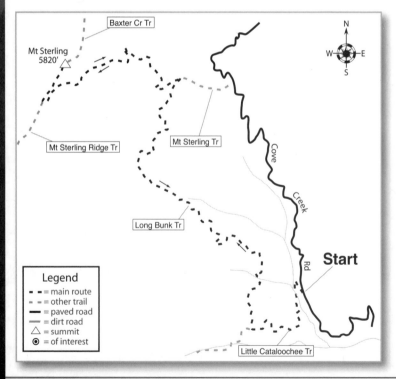

45 years to seek converts and organize churches in isolated areas. Though he only passed through Mt. Sterling Gap once, his route has been commemorated as the Asbury Trail, a 27-mile walk partly on road and partly on trail. The local Boy Scout troop maintains the trail, which lies outside the Park boundaries.

The Cataloochee Turnpike, finished in 1860, was one of the first substantial roads connecting the Tennessee and North Carolina sides of the Smokies. The road made it more convenient for Cataloochee residents to get their goods to market, but it also enabled Union soldiers and Confederate Home Guard to raid the area. The Home Guard, a paramilitary organization consisting of men too old to be conscripted into the regular army, were charged with finding army deserters and forcing them back to their regiments.

Some Home Guard members, like Albert Teague, a real-life villain who shows up in the novel *Cold Mountain*, killed deserters, tortured their relatives, and looted family homes. In the spring of 1865, Teague captured three deserters and marched them over Sterling Gap. Anderson Grooms, one of the prisoners, had taken his fiddle with him. When the party stopped in the woods, Grooms was asked to play a tune and he chose *Bonaparte's Retreat*, a sad, meditative melody. Though the fiddle playing impressed Teague, he ordered his men to shoot the three captives and left them on the road.

The trail switchbacks and goes up steeply; there is no way to sugarcoat it. Because it is an old, well-graded jeep road, the climbing is easier than it may sound. The Mt. Sterling Trail is still maintained as a road to service the fire tower and transmission tower. The trail becomes rocky and goes through a tunnel of rhododendrons as it slabs the mountain. Look for views of the sides of Mt. Sterling.

As you near 5,000 ft. in elevation, you begin to see the Fraser fir and red spruce trees that do well only above that altitude. Look to the left in the distance at Hemphill Bald, an inverted brown bowl. The Cataloochee ski area is to its left.

After 6.2 miles, turn right at the intersection of the Mt. Sterling Trail with the Mt. Sterling Ridge Trail in a grassy area. Continue on the Mt. Sterling Trail as it descends slightly and then continues up to the top of the mountain. This section is flatter, covered with pine needles, and softer underfoot. Farther on, the trail is lined with blackberry cane.

Then comes the reward for all this effort: the trail ends at a backcountry campsite (#38); at 5,840 ft., it's one of the highest in the Park. This area was actually more open in the early 19th century, since it was used as high summer pasture by mountaineer farmers who herded their cattle there to graze.

Climb the fire tower for 360-degree views: Balsam Mountain and Luftee Knob to the west, Mt. Guyot to the northwest, and the Cataloochee Valley to the south. This is the Smokies at its best, with wave upon wave of blue mountain ridges.

After you've soaked in the views, retrace your steps to return to the trailhead and end the hike.

A winter view from the Mt. Sterling lookout tower.

Hemphill Bald

If you missed the spring flowers and wish to prolong the season, come on up to 5,000 ft. where spring starts later. The flowers, coupled with outstanding views from Hemphill Bald, make this out-and-back hike a spring and summer favorite. The Hemphill Bald Trail follows the spine of the Cataloochee Divide on the southeastern rim of the Cataloochee Valley. At the beginning of the hike, left-handed views of the Cataloochee Valley and the ridges dominate. At Hemphill Bald, the views southeast into Maggie Valley and farther out into Pisgah National Forest are breathtaking. The trail is at the edge of the Great Smoky Mountains National Park which is marked by a split-log fence, but on the other side, property owned by Cataloochee Ranch looks much the same.

Getting to the trailhead:
The trailhead is at Polls Gap, off Heintooga Spur Rd., in the southeastern corner of the Great Smoky Mountains National Park (GSMNP). From the Blue Ridge Parkway at milepost 458, go south (toward GSMNP) for 0.2 mile,

★ =Start

then right on Heintooga Rd. toward Balsam Mountain Campground. Drive on for 6.2 miles to Polls Gap and park on the right.

Type of hike: Out and back

Distance: 9.6 miles

Total ascent: 1,910 ft.

Highlights: Views, flowers, Hemphill Bald

USGS map: Bunches Bald, Dellwood

Trail map: Great Smoky Mountains National Park, National Geographic Trails Illustrated #229.

Land managed by: Great Smoky Mountains National Park

Related movie: *Songcatcher* (2001) with Janet McTeer and Aiden Quinn

The Hike
The Hemphill Bald Trail, at 5,180 ft. elev., begins on the right-hand side of the parking area. Almost immediately, spring flowers explode on the banks—wake robin and sweet white trillium, violets, chickweed, Solomon's seal, wood anemone, and trout lily. The trail is flat on a good railroad grade around the curve. Fringed phacelia spill over the sides like white paint spattered on the trail.

In early summer, purple-fringed orchids, considered an "occasional" flower (one step up from rare), appear along with mayapples. As the trail goes gently uphill, look for churned-up soil on the right, as if a rototiller passed through. This damage was done by feral boars.

On your left, views into the Cataloochee Valley and the mountains above it will be with you most of the way. The highest mountain on the horizon is Mt. Sterling. At 1.0 miles, you'll cross a muddy, stagnant creek lined with squirrel corn and jewelweed. The trail climbs gently at 1.6 miles and reaches its first knob at 1.9 miles. As you come down the other side, the trail is enclosed in rhododendron and hemlock. On the right at 2.3 miles, a large rock with an overhang creates an open cave. Split-rail fencing, put up partly to keep cattle out of the Park, lets you know that you are at the edge of the Park boundary.

You're likely to pass a patch of ramps here, with their lily-like leaves and white flowers in summer. A distinctive onion-garlic flavor makes ramps a favorite traditional Southern Appalachian green used in early spring cooking. Digging ramps—or anything else in the Park—is forbidden, but in late spring you can find ramps harvested outside the Park at local produce markets.

At 2.8 miles, the trail turns east as it starts switchbacking to the flanks of Little Bald Knob. At 3.0 miles, the trail reaches its high point on Little Bald Knob with good views. At Pine Tree Gap, the grassy

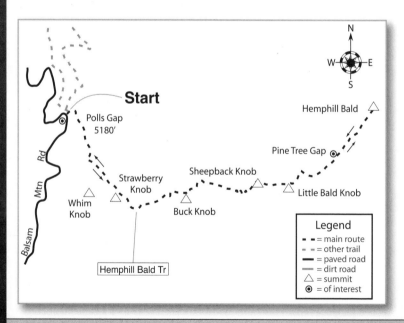

A memorial plaque is embedded in a stone table atop Hemphill Bald.

low point before Hemphill Bald, the trail parallels a trail-road in Cataloochee Ranch. You may see cows grazing behind a second fence.

At about 4.2 miles, you'll start the climb to Hemphill Bald as the trail offers first northern views and then southeastern ones. On the right, you have open views of pasture and serviceberry trees. You'll reach the top of Hemphill Bald at 4.8 miles; turn into the picnic area.

Cataloochee Ranch was founded in 1933 by Tom and Judy Alexander; the green plaque you see here, embedded in a stone tabletop, is a memorial to them. The original ranch was located in the Cataloochee Valley, but

when the Park was formed they moved it to its present location, which was then a potato and rutabaga farm. The grassy bald is kept open by summertime grazing. The current owners of Cataloochee Ranch put 220 acres into a conservation easement which protects Hemphill Bald from development. A stone picnic table and several picnic logs have been placed, inviting hikers to enjoy their lunch here.

On a clear day it will be hard to leave the outstanding 180-degree views behind. The mountain straight ahead is Cold Mountain, and to its right is Shining Rock. To the left is Mt. Pisgah with its tower. All those are in Pisgah National Forest.

The buildings you see close-in on your left belong to The Swag. This upscale resort, also just outside the boundary of the Park, is about 2.2 miles trail miles away. The wood frame buildings on the right, also close-in, are part of Ghost Town theme park. Straight down and a little to the left of Cataloochee Ranch are the ski slopes in the Cataloochee Ski Area.

When you're ready, return to the trailhead the way you came, to end the hike.

Smokemont Loop

This is a low-altitude loop hike, suitable year-round. It starts on the Bradley Fork Trail, an old road paralleling the Bradley Fork of the Oconaluftee River. Then it crosses the creek and meets the Smokemont Loop Trail which goes steadily up and then down the other side of Richland Mountain. You'll visit the Bradley Cemetery before returning to the campground.

Since the hike starts in Smokemont Campground, one of the three most popular campgrounds in the park, you might think this loop gets heavy use by tourists. However, once you're on the Smokemont Trail, you won't have many others climbing with you.

Getting to the trailhead:
From the Oconaluftee Visitor Center, take US 441 north for 3.3 miles to the entrance to the Smokemont Campground. Drive through the campground; the trailhead is at the far end of the D loop.

Type of hike: Loop

Distance: 6.2 miles

Total ascent: 1,400 ft.

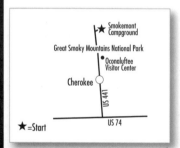

Highlights: History, stream, cemetery, church

USGS map: Smokemont

Trail map: Great Smoky Mountains National Park, National Geographic Trails Illustrated #229

Land managed by: Great Smoky Mountains National Park

Facilities: Smokemont Campground comprises 140 campsites and is open year-round. There are restrooms with cold water but no showers. Advance reservations for campsites are highly recommended.

The Hike
The trail starts to the left of the parking area at the far end of the D loop of the campground on a wide road which ascends gently. Bradley Fork is on the left and a high bank of rosebay rhododendron, doghobble, nettle, and Christmas fern on your right. At 0.2 mile, a horse trail comes in from the right. Stay left and pass a maintenance building. A maintenance road takes off to the right.

Several creeks ripple through from the right to join Bradley Fork, lined with hemlock, maidenhead fern, doghobble, bee balm, mountain laurel, wild geranium, and poison ivy. You'll pass a large moss-covered rock on the left at 1.1

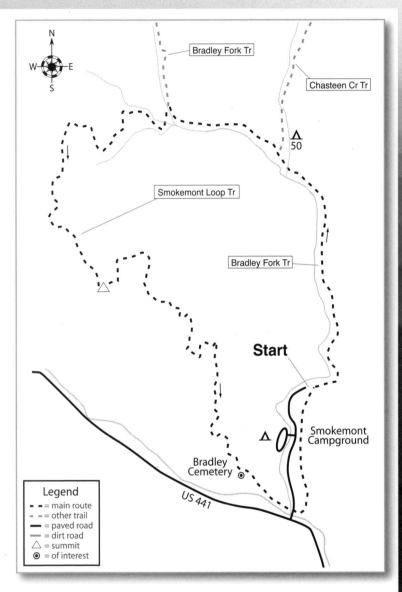

Start

Smokemont
Campground

Bradley
Cemetery

US 441

Legend
- – = main route
- – = other trail
- ▬ = paved road
- ▬ = dirt road
- △ = summit
- ◉ = of interest

Bradley Fork Tr

Chasteen Cr Tr

△
50

Smokemont Loop Tr

Bradley Fork Tr

N
W — E
S

miles, then cross Chasteen Creek which joins Bradley Fork. At 1.2 miles, Chasteen Creek Trail comes in from the right. Bradley Fork has narrowed, and so has the trail. As you climb above Bradley Fork, now wide again, there is a moss-covered bench at 1.4 miles. Pass a rhododendron grove on your left as the trail flattens; the creek is far below you.

At 1.8 miles (2,490 ft. elev.), you'll reach the intersection of Smokemont Loop Trail, with a good wooden bench on the left. A sign says "3.9 miles to the campground." Go down stone steps to cross Bradley Fork on a long, narrow split-log bridge with a steel cable hand rail. You'll notice the bridge has been creosoted to prevent moss from growing and making it slippery underfoot.

Immediately cross a smaller bridge, then turn west away from Bradley Fork and start climbing toward a ridge of Richland Mountain. It's a long, steady uphill as the trail switchbacks through rhododendron, Clinton's lily, Solomon's plume, and violets. At 2.7 miles (3,100 ft. elev.) the trail turns south and flattens out, but not for long. The trail has changed direction, and the winter views are to the right. Periodically you can hear the traffic on Newfound Gap Rd. roaring below you. You'll reach the top at 3.5 miles (3,550 ft. elev.), a flat spot with several logs to sit on where you can stop for a drink. You've done all the climbing for the day.

At 3.8 miles, pass a well-defined grassy saddle under a grove of trees to your left. The trail continues pleasantly downhill. At 5.2 miles, you might be able to see the first of the graves in the Bradley cemetery on your right. Several eroded side trails have been created to reach the cemetery. Rather than adding to the erosion problem, walk down a few hundred yards

Smokemont

The Smokemont community was first known as Bradleytown, named for settlers who came to the area in the early 1800s. According to **Churches of the Smokies** *by Charles Maynard, the earliest known church congregation there was organized around 1829, though families had been living in the valley since the 1790s. By the early 1900s, Champion Fibre Company established the headquarters for its massive logging and sawmill operation in Smokemont. The company town had a school, store, and boarding houses. Other than the Bradley cemetery and a few clearings which are filling in with vegetation, little evidence of human habitation is left now on the trail.*

Daniel S. Pierce, in his **The Great Smokies: From Natural Habitat to National Park***, writes that the cleanup of the Champion Fibre Company's Smokemont mill proved difficult. It involved removing a locomotive, railroad cars, large buildings and homes, and several miles of railroad tracks—all paid for by the National Park Service. However, the Smokemont Baptist Church, also known as the Lufty Church, was saved, and regular services were held here until 1935. The church is not on the trail but sits off on a densely wooded hillside.*

where the trail reaches a T junction and continues left.

To visit the Bradley cemetery, turn right on a wide side trail. When the side trail splits, stay to the right. Most of the graves in the gently sloping cemetery are stone stumps with no identification. The Bradley patriarch and matriarch have large readable stones:

> Mother R. Palistine Bradley
> May 10, 1859 – Sept 11, 1922
> Father Jasper Bradley
> Mar 31, 1851 – Sept. 22, 1924

Once a year, descendants of those buried in cemeteries within the Great Smoky Mountains National Park gather to decorate the graves with silk or plastic flowers. These events are known as Decoration Days, which usually include a prayer service and a communal buffet lunch. All the cemeteries in the Smokies are maintained by the Park Service, so they need drivable access; hence the wide service road. On Decoration Day, the gate is open to allow people to drive in. If the graves are bare when you visit the cemetery, it probably means that Park Service workers have cleaned up the old flowers in preparation for the next Decoration Day.

Retrace your steps to return to the Smokemont Loop Trail, now a wide road. At 5.6 miles, cross on a big stone bridge, go through the gate, and make a right on a paved road. Take a left where the wooden sign points to "campground." You are at the beginning of the campground loop. Follow the road back to the D loop to end the hike.

Extra—Luftee Church:
After your hike, consider visiting the Smokemont Baptist or Luftee church. The church is hidden by trees and foliage on a steep slope and is hard to see from the road. When you turn off Newfound Gap Rd. at the Smokemont campground, you'll cross the Oconaluftee River and drive across the paved road up to a gravel road. (Do not turn left toward the Smokemont campground.) There is a parking area on the right.

Look up the hill and a little to the left where you should be able to see the church. A gravel path will take you to the front of the church, passing a piped spring. The inside is very plain with dark paneled walls, several rows of benches on three sides, and a pulpit in front—no decoration or cross. In the summer, church services are held before the annual homecoming for descendants of those who lived in the Smokemont area.

Deep Creek Loop

This low-altitude hike can be done any time of the year. The hike, which follows creeks much of the way, goes past old homesites and several campsites good for an introduction to backpacking.

Campsite #57, the last campsite on this hike, is also the site of Horace Kephart's last camp. Kephart is well-known in the Southern Appalachians for writing **Our Southern Highlanders***, a first-person account of his years with mountain people. A librarian, husband, and father of six children, Kephart ditched his old life to move to the North Carolina Mountains in 1904. He stayed in several places in the Smokies, finally basing himself in Bryson City. He was an active proponent of the Smokies and the Appalachian Trail. Mt. Kephart on the Tennessee side of the Park and the Kephart Prong Trail are named after him. He died in 1931 in a car accident on his way to a bootlegger; he is buried in Bryson City.*

Getting to the trailhead: From the center of Bryson City, make a left on Everett Street. After 0.3 mile, make a right on Water St., signposted Deep Creek Campground, which becomes Toot Hollow Road. After 1.8 miles, at the stop sign, make a left on W. Deep Creek Rd. Drive 1.2 miles and park at the Deep Creek trailhead.

Type of hike: Loop

Distance: 13.4 miles

Total ascent: 1,880 ft.

Highlights: Creeks, waterfalls, history

USGS map: Bryson City, Clingmans Dome

Trail map: Great Smoky Mountains National Park, National Geographic Trails Illustrated #229

Land managed by: Great Smoky Mountains National Park

The Hike

From the Deep Creek Trailhead, at 1,810 feet, follow a wide road paralleling Deep Creek. Almost immediately, pass a left turn for the Juney Whank Falls Loop Trail, about 0.7 mile round trip. On the Deep Creek Trail, mountain laurel borders the creek as the road goes up gently.

At 0.3 mile, don't miss Tom Branch Falls, a waterfall on the other side of the creek which tumbles 60 ft. The bottom

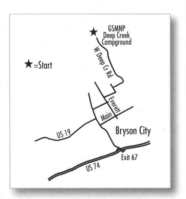

looks like a cascade but it starts from high up. Cross a bridge at 0.4 mile where you may see people tubing. The trail climbs above the creek but always comes back to it. Doghobble, poison ivy, and nettle dot the trail.

At 0.6 mile, stay left on the Deep Creek Trail when it

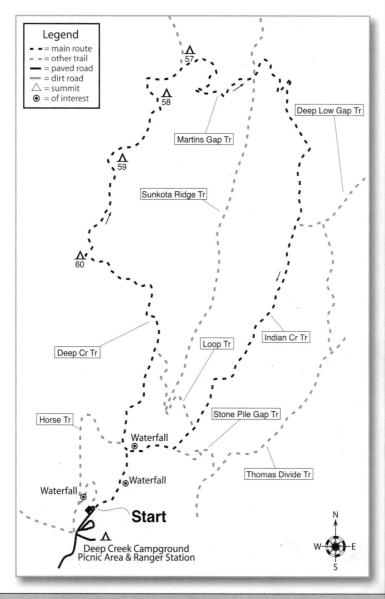

Legend

- **= = main route**
- **- - = other trail**
- **▬ = paved road**
- **= dirt road**
- **△ = summit**
- **◉ = of interest**

△ 57

△ 58

Deep Low Gap Tr

Martins Gap Tr

△ 59

Sunkota Ridge Tr

△ 60

Deep Cr Tr

Loop Tr

Indian Cr Tr

Horse Tr

Stone Pile Gap Tr

Waterfall ◉

Waterfall ◉

Thomas Divide Tr

Waterfall ◉

Start

△ Deep Creek Campground
Picnic Area & Ranger Station

N
W ◉ E
S

This old millstone marks one of Horace Kephart's favorite camping sites on Deep Creek.

At 2.1 miles, where you see logs and several faint trails on the left, turn right to follow Deep Creek Trail. Bicycles are allowed up to this point. The trail climbs; it is no longer a road. There are partial ridge views to the left as the trail levels out above the creek. At 2.3 miles, a rushing watercourse comes in from the right to join Deep Creek. Cross a large creek on a bridge at 2.5 miles. The horse traffic has hollowed out a trench in spots.

Pass Campsite #60 at 2.5 miles. Then climb away from the creek and come back down several times among toothwort, Solomon's plume, Solomon's seal, trillium, and wild geranium. The trail is muddy red clay. In some places, wooden planks have been laid down to alleviate the mushy conditions.

At 4.5 miles, a tall hemlock has been saved in the center of the trail, creating a two-lane trail. Pass Campsite #59 at 4.9 miles, and after a minor climb, Campsite #58 at 5.4 miles.

At 5.9 miles, as the trail rises, look to your left for a flat area where a millstone memorializing Horace Kephart is located (this is not an official campsite). Go down and turn left. The millstone, surrounded by rocks and moss, was erected by the Horace Kephart Boy Scout Troop from Bryson City on May 30, 1931. Given that Kephart died on April 2, 1931, that was quick work. If the inscription looks modern,

intersects the Indian Creek Trail. The second bridge is the end of the tubing area. On a hot day, especially if you're staying in the campground, there's no better way to end the day than by renting a tube (just outside the Park) and floating down the creek.

Cross the third bridge; to the left you'll see a horse trail. Stay on the gravel trail which starts climbing. The trail continues through mountain laurel, hemlock, tulip tree, and yellow buckeye. Cross the fourth bridge, and the trail narrows.

The upper part of the loop is at 1.6 miles. For a short day (4.4 miles), turn right and follow the loop trail to Sunkota Ridge Trail and down Indian Creek Trail.

Beyond this point, you have left most of the tourists.

that's because the millstone was recently refurbished.

At 6.0 miles, reach Campsite #57, a horse camp with two high picnic tables. Turn right on the Martins Gap Trail, which is also part of the Mountains-to-Sea Trail (MST) and Benton MacKaye Trail. The Deep Creek Trail continues around the campsite and up to Newfound Gap Rd. (US 441).

The Martins Gap Trail starts out steeply but switchbacks in a gentle manner characteristic of Smokies trails. The mud has disappeared, though horses are permitted here also. As you climb Martins Gap Trail away from Deep Creek through speckled wood lily,

crested dwarf iris, galax, and tall, imposing hemlock, a minor creek on your right follows you. Cross a bridge at 6.4 miles and continue up. Reach Martins Gap at 7.5 miles (3,410 ft. elev.) at a four-way intersection. Cross the Sunkota Trail; both the MST and Benton MacKaye Trail go left and up. Continue straight on the Martins Gap Trail. The rest of the hike is downhill from here.

Martins Gap Trail switchbacks downhill and soon parallels Indian Creek on the right. You'll follow the creek the whole trip back. Cross Indian Creek on a split log bridge at 8.4 miles. Take care not to have too many people on the bridge

Just before joining Deep Creek, Indian Creek makes a final plunge.

at the same time. At 8.8 miles, cross the creek twice more on split-log bridges.

You'll reach a wide spot at 8.9 miles with a Martins Gap Trail sign and a split-log bench. This is the beginning of Indian Creek Trail, though there are no signs to that effect. Martins Gap Trail seems to flow into Indian Creek Trail, an old road.

Soon you cross Indian Creek on a substantial bridge; you have left the mossy, rickety bridges behind you. The trail is smooth and wide and you feel you're going into an inhabited area with flat homesites. At 9.6 miles, the trail intersects Deeplow Gap Trail which goes off to the left. After several more crossings of Indian Creek, the trail meets the Loop Trail at 11.8 miles on the right. A log bench at the intersection is very welcome because the flat sides of the trail make it difficult to find a comfortable place to sit.

At 12.1 miles, the Stone Pile Gap Trail goes off to the left. The creek gets wider. At 12.5 miles, take a short side trail on the right to Indian Creek Falls, a sliding cascade coming down in three streams. Take a left on the Deep Creek Trail. When the weather is good, on this last stretch, you will see people tubing or walking with tubes as you return to the trailhead to end the hike.

Shorter option: A Deep Creek/Indian Creek Loop of 4.4 miles can also be done which takes in two waterfalls.

Hot summer days bring out the tubers on Deep Creek.

Road to Nowhere

This hike is two loops with a connector. The smaller loop starts by going through the tunnel on Lakeshore Trail and returns on the Tunnel Bypass Trail. The larger circle is the loop formed by Whiteoak Branch Trail, Forney Creek Trail, and the return trip on Lakeshore Trail.

The tunnel itself is at the end of the "Road to Nowhere," a remnant of Lakeview Drive, originally intended to replace NC 288, which was flooded when TVA built Fontana Dam during World War II. In the early 1960s, 6.2 miles of the replacement road were built from the entrance to the Park, but the project was halted for environmental reasons. For a more complete story, see the discussion preceding the Shuckstack–Lakeshore Loop hike.

Type of hike: Figure eight with a long middle section

Distance: 9.4 miles

Total ascent: 1,370 ft.

Highlights: Tunnel, history, current controversy, Forney Creek

USGS map: Noland Creek

Trail map: Great Smoky Mountains National Park, National Geographic Trails Illustrated #229

Land managed by: Great Smoky Mountains National Park

Getting to the trailhead:

From downtown Bryson City, travel 9.0 miles on Fontana Road, which becomes Lakeview Drive. Park in the last parking area before the barrier and tunnel.

★ =Start

The Hike

Park at the barrier and walk through the 365-ft. tunnel, wide enough for two lanes of traffic. In the middle it is very dark; take a flashlight or you'll have to depend, literally, on the light at the end of the tunnel. On the other side, the Lakeshore Trail stays paved for a couple of hundred feet and then becomes a trail into the woods. The whole Lakeshore Trail is 33.5 miles long and approximates the route of the proposed North Shore Rd. Its western end can be hiked as part of the Shuckstack–Lakeshore Loop from Fontana Lake.

The Lakeshore Trail (in this section also part of the Benton MacKaye Trail), contours and slabs around the hill with good winter views southwest. At the first

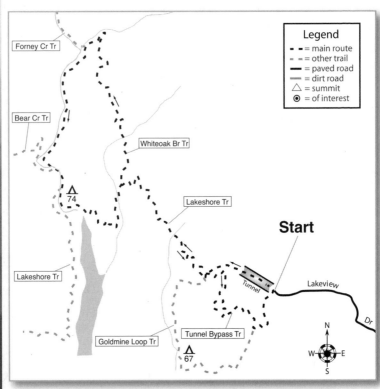

Start

Legend
- ■ ▪ = main route
- ▪ ▪ = other trail
- ▬ = paved road
- ▬ = dirt road
- △ = summit
- ◉ = of interest

Forney Cr Tr

Bear Cr Tr

Whiteoak Br Tr

Lakeshore Tr

△ 74

Lakeshore Tr

Goldmine Loop Tr

Tunnel Bypass Tr

△ 67

Tunnel

Lakeview

Dr

N
W — E
S

intersection, stay to the right and bypass both intersections with the Goldmine Loop Trail. On the way back, you'll take the first intersection of the Goldmine Loop Trail.

The trail goes slowly and steadily down. At 1.1 miles, cross a little stream coming in from the right. There are good winter views of mountain ridges to the left (southwest). The trail meanders up and down through rhododendron, mountain laurel, and in the spring many blooming wildflowers. At 1.6 miles, you'll cross a boggy area and a low stream crossing.

The trail goes steadily down, paralleling a creek on your left.

At 2.0 miles, turn right on Whiteoak Branch Trail, where the hike starts its large circle. The Whiteoak Branch Trail goes up through a muddy, still creek to a gap and descends as it slabs the hill. At 2.4 miles, Gray Wolf Creek parallels the trail upstream. Rock hop across a tributary of Gray Wolf Creek. On the left, at 2.8 miles, a jumble of chimney rocks is all that remains of a home long gone.

The trail makes a sharp left turn and goes down toward the creek. Cross

Whiteoak Branch to reach the junction with the Forney Creek Trail at 3.7 miles. The junction of both creeks is a delightful spot to sit and listen to the rippling water. Turn left on the Forney Creek Trail. The trail rises above Forney Creek and continues a gentle climb. This area was heavily logged and suffered several fires before all logging ceased in the 1930s.

Forney Creek, which starts below Clingmans Dome, is now a wide river, paralleling the trail on the right. This is a beautiful, flat section of trail, with rivulets coming out of moss-covered rocks. On the left, nearly horizontal tree trunks hang on to huge boulders. Pass the junction with the Bear Creek Trail, and continue left on Forney Creek Trail toward the Lakeshore Trail. At the intersection with the Lakeshore Trail at 5.1 miles, continue on Forney Creek Trail for 0.1 mile to Campsite #74. Though the campsite is well-used in season, the picnic table is a comfortable place for lunch.

Retrace your steps and make a right on the Lakeshore Trail. As you ascend, look right to see Forney Creek going into Fontana Lake. The Lakeshore Trail climbs up about 200 ft. and flattens as it zigzags around the mountain. You can hear water below on your right. Several well-maintained, unsigned roads leave the Lakeshore Trail. Stay on the trail and cross the bridge.

Soon the trail makes a sharp left and heads uphill. At 6.8 miles and the junction with the Whiteoak Branch Trail, make a right to stay on the Lakeshore Trail. At 7.6 miles, take a right at the second intersection with the Goldmine Loop Trail, which will take you to the Tunnel Bypass Trail. Despite the name, there was no gold on Goldmine Loop Trail. Don't confuse this trail with the Gold Mine Trail at the extreme western side of the Park in Tennessee.

Goldmine Loop Trail goes down into a hollow and climbs back up with good open views to the right. At 8.8 miles, make a left on the Tunnel Bypass Trail. This trail, built originally for tunnel-shy horses, appears very narrow for horses. It's a gentle descent to the parking lot and the end of the hike.

Forney Creek runs fast and cold.

Shuckstack–Lakeshore Loop

This hike is a loop which takes you on the Appalachian Trail up to Shuckstack Tower, where on a good day, you can see the world: 360 degrees of wilderness within the largest unbroken tract of mountain forest in the eastern United States. It then heads downward on Lost Cove Trail on a railroad grade. You'll return to the trailhead on the Lakeshore Trail, where you'll see artifacts left by the residents before they moved out in 1943. The trailhead serves as the start of two trails: the Apalachian Trail on the left, which is your starting trail, and the Lakeshore Trail on which you'll return.

Type of hike: Loop

Distance: 11.7 miles

Total ascent: 3,010 ft.

Highlights: Current events, Fontana Lake, history, old cars, and artifacts

USGS map: Fontana Dam

Trail map: Great Smoky Mountains National Park, National Geographic Trails Illustrated #229

Land managed by: Great Smoky Mountains National Park

Special challenge: The Lost Cove Trail has about 13 stream crossings, some of which may be challenging in high water.

Related movie: Nell (1994) with Jodie Foster.

Getting to the trailhead:
From the center of Robbinsville, take 143 east for 9.1 miles. At the NC 28 intersection, turn left (north) and drive 10.3 miles. Turn right at the Fontana Village sign. Stay on the road, cross the dam, bear right, and follow the road until the barrier. The Appalachian Trail (A.T.) starts on the left. It's 2.4 miles from the turn at the Fontana sign to the trailhead.

The Hike
Head north on the A.T., which climbs Shuckstack Mountain through a dry section filled with yellow star grass, toothwort, blackberry and blueberry bushes, and poison ivy. At 0.2 mile, there are winter views of Fontana Lake on the right. Don't dismiss these, since there are not many opportunities to see the lake. A second view of the lake comes in on the right at 0.7 miles.

At 1.6 miles, a log seat on the left makes for a welcome break. The poison ivy diminishes above 3,000 ft. Farther up, mountain laurel, ferns, galax, and speckled wood lily line the

★ Fontana Dam

NC 28

Robbinsville NC143 ○ Tsali

US 129

US 19/76 ★ =Start

trail along with a solitary group of lady slippers. At 2.7 miles, the trail heads west and slabs with views to the left.

You'll reach a rocky area with great views to the left at 2.9 miles (3,610 ft. elev.). Soon, the trail climbs steeply among an abundance of Solomon's seal and Solomon's plume. As the trail zigzags east again, note a big sliced rock on the left.

At 3.3 miles (3,890 ft.), the A.T. goes left and down.

Take the side trail to the right for 0.1 mile up to Shuckstack Tower at 4,000 ft. elev. On the way, spiderwort and Dutchman's pipe dot the trail. From Shuckstack Tower, you can see Fontana Lake, the ridges of the Smokies, and peaks in the Joyce Kilmer Wilderness. The site also has the remains of a fire warden's cabin. Coming down from the tower, to continue on the A.T., make a right. The trail goes down and passes a large rock with rock tripe on the right.

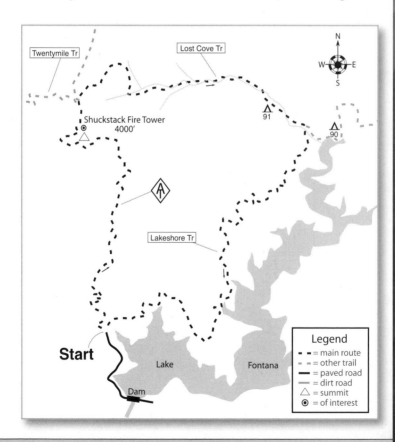

Origins of The Road to Nowhere

The area north of Fontana Lake was not part of the original Great Smoky Mountains National Park, formed in the 1930s. Until the 1940s, several communities lived in and north of the area now covered by the lake. Their only access was NC 288, a narrow, twisting road from Bryson City to Deal's Gap southwest of the Smokies. At the time, hundreds of families—mostly farmers, after loggers had moved out of the area—depended on the road. When World War II was declared, the Tennessee Valley Authority came into the region almost immediately and built Fontana Dam on the Little Tennessee River to create electricity for the war effort. The dam flooded the road and several communities; the residents had to move out. The land north of the lake was then amalgamated into the Park.

The Federal Government promised to build a road on the North Shore after World War II. The National Park Service constructed a less than one-mile segment of the road west of Fontana Dam, which ends at the trailhead for this hike. It also built 6.2 miles from the eastern boundary of the Park. In 1971, construction stopped when road builders hit acid-bearing rock that would cause serious water contamination. That road, known as "The Road to Nowhere," now ends in a tunnel. (See the **Road to Nowhere** hike, p. 247).

Construction of a North Shore road, which would follow the northern shore of Fontana Lake for 35 miles from outside Bryson City to Fontana Dam, is still advocated by descendants of the settlers who moved out. For those who wish to visit cemeteries where their ancestors are buried, the Park Service provides free boat transportation across the lake and a shuttle as close as vehicles can get to the cemeteries.

At 3.9 miles, reach a four-way intersection. The A.T. continues straight on. Twentymile Trail comes in from the left, a railroad grade trail which was the access to the fire tower. Note the wide spot on the trail where vehicles may have parked.

Make a right on Lost Cove Trail. The trail goes downhill steeply among trillium, speckled wood lily, geraniums, violets, and an occasional yellow lady's slipper. Cross Lost Cove Creek at 4.7 miles. There will be twelve more creek crossings as you descend and the creek gets wider.

As you continue down, the trail moderates to a comfortable walking grade. This was the route of a spur line of a logging railroad. As you can see, giant hemlocks were left standing.

You'll reach Campsite #91 at 5.8 miles, a good campsite by the creek for hikers and horses. After this point, you need to pay attention and cross creeks very carefully; the creek gets deeper and swifter. Don't worry about getting your boots wet, and don't cross barefoot or in "water shoes." Your feet need the protection of boots on the submerged rocks.

Look for a chimney on the left as you start to see homesites. The last creek crossing is just before Lost Cove Trail intersects Lakeshore Trail.

At 6.5 miles, turn right on Lakeshore Trail. (On the left, Lakeshore Trail continues to Eagle Creek and eventually to the Road to Nowhere tunnel outside of Bryson City.) The trail switchbacks up steeply for 0.1 mile and reaches a level area above the creek. Dappled sunlight sparkles on the trail as you catch glimpses of Fontana Lake, but there are no open views of the lake on this section of trail. The trail meanders up and down with wide spots at several local ridges.

Cross a creek at 7.9 miles and continue going uphill. At 9.2 miles, you'll pass a hiker sign. Look down to your left—that is old NC 288 veering toward the lake. You are now walking on the remains of NC 288, a flat, wide road. Here you have what is possibly the best view of the lake through the trees so far.

At 9.9 miles, look for an old car body down on its side and a second one with a tree growing through it. The third car may be the best remaining specimen, though little is left of it. Car buffs have suggested that the first two old cars were Ford models made between 1933 and 1936. The third car with the starter button on the floor is not easily identified, but is the same era as the others—maybe a Chrysler product, perhaps a Plymouth, which was the low-end car in those days. These cars might not have been running very well 10 years later. With gas and tire rationing, men off to war, and many women not able to drive, families left their cars behind when they moved out. There is a fourth remnant of a car at 10.0 miles.

At 10.3 miles, this end of the road goes into the lake. A sign points to the right for hikers to follow Lakeshore Trail, which is now trail-sized. An old boar trap is filled with weeds. A newer boar trap stands ready as you walk back to your car to end the hike.

Nantahala National Forest

The rhododendrons, plots of wild strawberries, flame azaleas, Solomon's seal, sweet shrub, mountain laurel, ginseng, Fraser magnolia...create a seemingly infinite green tapestry that surrounds the trail.

—William Bartram, botanist and explorer (1739–1823)

Nantahala National Forest

Essential Facts

Facilities:
Facilities in the Nantahala National Forest range from primitive to modern. Check the individual hike description for each destination.

Website:
www.cs.unca.edu/nfsnc

Nantahala, in the Cherokee language, means *land of the noonday sun*, which refers to the Nantahala Gorge, where the sun reaches the valley floor only in the middle of the day. The Nantahala National Forest, established in 1920, is now a diverse collection of noncontiguous protected land in western North Carolina, the largest of the four national forests in the state. The forest is divided into four districts (Wayah, Tusquitee, Cheoah, and Highlands) with several sections within districts. It is spread out from west of Pisgah National Forest to the borders of Tennessee and Georgia.

The area is packed with hiking, rafting, camping,

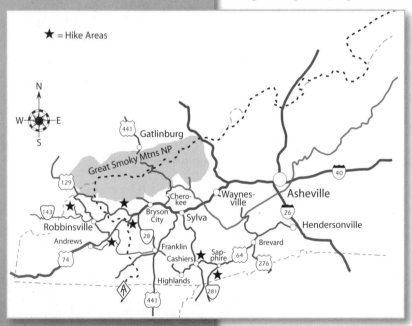

The Horsepasture River is home to many a waterfall. This hiker is enjoying a break below Stairway Falls.

and fishing opportunities. Three long-distance trails—the Appalachian Trail, the Mountains-to-Sea Trail, and the Bartram Traill—go through the Nantahala National Forest. Yet, perhaps because it is not close to large population centers and not well publicized, most of this forest is quieter than the adjoining lands in Pisgah National Forest and the Great Smoky Mountains National Park.

The Wayah District is dominated by the Nantahala River Gorge, internationally known for whitewater rafting and kayaking. The Gorge runs about 10 miles from Nantahala Lake northeast to Fontana Lake.

South of the Gorge in Macon County, the trails around Appletree Group campground offer good hiking of moderate difficulty. They are not used much and consequently are a great place to go if you're looking for solitude. The Bartram Trail passes through the Appletree Campground, part of a multistate project to approximate the route William Bartram took when he explored the Southeast.

William Bartram was the son of John Bartram, the English royal botanist for the North American Colonies. William traveled with his father and later by himself, collecting seeds and plants through the Southeast. After his final trip, he recounted his journeys in his 1791 *The Travels of William Bartram*, a dense book cataloguing all that he saw. The 100 miles of the Bartram Trail in North Carolina are located mostly in the Nantahala Forest, entering the state from Georgia near the town of Highlands and progressing northwest to the summit of Cheoah Bald, close to the Tennessee border.

The Cheoah District offers excellent hiking in the Joyce Kilmer-Slickrock Wilderness Area, from the easy two-mile loop in Joyce Kilmer Memorial Forest to challenging trails climbing to high mountain balds. You can also hike in the Tsali Recreation Area, known for its mountain biking trails. Tsali is advertised as a mecca for mountain bikers and horseback riders, but

Mountain bikers are frequent visitors to the Panthertown area.

why should they have all the fun? For hikers, the area provides gentle, impeccably maintained trails with loops of varying lengths. There are no blowdowns to scramble over or under, since these trails are maintained for horses and bikers. Even the muddy spots are better cared for here than on most hiking trails.

Hikers can get good views of several branches of Fontana Lake. The trail system consists of four loops. Hikers are allowed on any trail at any time, but bikers and horses alternate trails according to the day of the week. Walking with bikers on the trail is not a problem if you start out early and stay alert. There will be fewer horses than bikes on the trail on their respective days. Check with the Cheoah Ranger District for the schedule.

Tsali's low elevation (around 1,700 to 2,000 ft.) makes it a good place to hike in the winter months.

In the Highlands District, the eastern section of Nantahala Forest, the trails in Panthertown and along the Horsepasture River are peppered with spectacular waterfalls created by an abundance of water in a rugged landscape.

Panthertown Valley is found just northeast of Cashiers, at an altitude of between 3,600 and 4,000 ft. Despite its outstanding waterfalls and great

The view across Lake Fontana to the Great Smoky Mountains National Park at the Tsali Recreation Area is well worth the hike to get there.

views, this area has yet to really be discovered by mainstream hikers and mountain bikers. With all its rare and endangered plants, it's important for users to stay on the trail.

The land has suffered from fire and erosion. Like a good number of recovering areas, Panthertown has rough spots such as wide dirt roads, logged areas, cut and downed trees, and a maze of trails of varying quality; however, there are such gems—waterfalls, solitude, and views—that it's worth putting up with the rough spots.

In the end, it's what's missing that keeps crowds away: there are no trail signs. If not for Burt Kornegay's map, it would be even more difficult to negotiate your way in and out of the hodgepodge of trails. Kornegay is a wilderness guide who runs Slickrock Expeditions, which takes people hiking and camping all over the country. He literally hand-drew the trails over a modified topographic map. Hiking Panthertown has the same feeling as hiking Dupont State Forest, without the trail signs and other amenities. At this point, there are no plans to put up signs. Though hiking in tire grooves over dirt roads may not seem exciting, the area contains such outstanding highlights that it is worth the walk.

Horsepasture River

What is it about waterfalls that attracts people–the rush and force of water, the roar overwhelming all other sounds, the mesmerizing effect of the water tumbling down? As a hiker, you might be willing to walk several miles to reach one lovely waterfall. On the Horsepasture River Trail, you'll see five waterfalls and take side trips to other cascades, rapids, and watercourses.

Drift Falls, Turtleback Falls, and Rainbow Falls are popular and easy to get to. The last two, Stairway Falls and Windy Falls, are off the main trail and more challenging to find. The following hike describes the route to all of them, leaving Stairway Falls for last on the way back. The information board states that it takes 105 minutes to hike from the first waterfall to the last, but that's not counting all the diversions: foot-dipping, photo-taking, and oohing and aahing.

Getting to the trailhead:
From Brevard, take US 64W for 18.7 miles to its intersection with NC 281S.

Turn left and drive 1.1 miles to the entrance to Gorges State Park on the left.

Type of hike: Out and back

Distance: 8.9 miles

Total ascent: 2,110 ft.

Highlights: Waterfalls, waterfalls, waterfalls

USGS map: Reid

Trail map: The North Carolina Sierra Club Guide to the Jocassee Gorges; Horsepasture, Bearwallow, & Toxaway Region by Bill Thomas (N.C. Chapter of the Sierra Club, 1998), available at local bookstores

Land managed by: Nantahala National Forest, Highlands District. A small section is in Gorges State Park.

Facilities: Portable toilets in the Gorges State Park parking area

Closest town: Cashiers, NC

Related book: One Foot in Eden by Ron Rash

The Hike
From the parking lot at Gorges State Park, go back out to NC 281 and make a left on the trail which parallels the road (don't walk on the road) and follow it into the woods. If you miss that trail, go around the gate on an emergency vehicle road and walk down.

You'll pass an information board at 0.8 mile which will have the latest trail and waterfall conditions. You've now left the State Park and are in the Nantahala National Forest, where there's a wand for the Horsepasture River Trail. Soon you'll start hearing the river. At 1.0 mile, turn right on a side trail heading for the base of Drift Falls, and then walk over a board to cross a minor creek coming in from the right. At 1.2 miles, you'll have a good view of Drift Falls. The actual waterfall is on private property, as you can see by the many private property signs posted. The water cascades over a gigantic rock slide and into a deep pool. Don't even think of going past the private

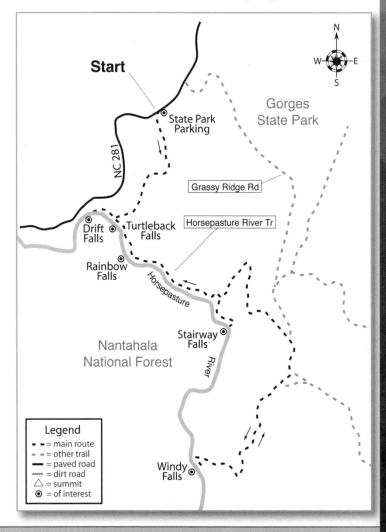

property signs, to photograph the falls from a better angle or for any other reason.

Go back to the main trail and make a right. The trail here is rocky and quite slippery, even when dry. You approach Turtleback Falls, a wide and sloping slide, from the rear at 1.4 miles. On summer afternoons people congregate here to jump off the rocks, swim, take pictures, or just hang out. However, the water is swift, and if you get swept away by the current, a very dangerous waterfall waits downstream.

The trail continues to the left of Turtleback Falls under the shadow of a boulder on good wooden steps and then over a bridge. The trail then turns to face Turtleback Falls,

Just above Windy Falls is a nice place to soak your feet.

and this is the best place from which to photograph it.

Continue downhill on a slippery rock before the trail moderates to approach Rainbow Falls, which conservationist Bill Thomas refers to as the "scenic climax" at 1.6 miles (2,760 ft). The water over Rainbow Falls, a nearly vertical cascade 125 ft. high, crashes down with a thunderous roar. A steep side trail on the right leads to a lower viewing area. A wooden railing has been built at the upper and lower observation points to protect the slope from erosion. The rainbow is visible at the pool level, and the view is best on sunny mornings—good reason to get an early start.

After Rainbow Falls, the trail is steeper, and you've left most of the casual walkers behind. The power and sound of the water drowns out bird song and conversations as you follow the trail through a rhododendron and hemlock tunnel.

Any side trail will show you the calmer side of the river and might be a good place for a snack break. The water flows rapidly through rocks, smoothing boulders and sweeping away trees that fall in its path. The main trail has some roots but fewer rocks. Sounds of the river are constant as you go in and out of the rhododendron tunnel.

At 2.1 miles (2,560 ft. elev.) you'll reach a wide spot on your left which would make a good campsite, and then the trail crosses a small creek and goes up gently. This is the farthest you've been from the river. At 2.3 miles, stay to the right on the main trail when it splits, but remember this fork because you'll need it to identify a side trail to Stairway Falls on your way back.

Walking on a pleasantly flat trail, you can't hear the river anymore, and the bird sounds have come back. At 3.1 miles you'll reach Grassy Ridge Rd., a graveled maintenance road. Turn right here and go down a couple of hundred feet to a wide cleared area on the right. In about 0.1 mile, turn right onto a side trail. When you see a boulder blocking the trail, you'll know you're in the right place.

At this point, you must decide if you want to go down almost a mile and 800 ft. in elevation to Windy Falls. The trail, an old woods road with many blowdowns, is not well maintained. At the bottom, it delivers you to the top of the waterfall; there is no safe way to see the water actually drop, but the rocks at the top of the waterfall make a good destination for lunch. Because of its remoteness, you won't have much company.

As you go down the side trail to Windy Falls, you leave the Nantahala National Forest

Falls and Friends of the Horsepasture River

All the spectacular beauty and water power of the Horsepasture River might have been fodder for a hydroelectric plant if not for the action of one man named Bill Thomas. He organized the Friends of the Horsepasture River and managed to get 4.2 miles of the river designated a National Wild and Scenic River in 1985. The Horsepasture River empties into Lake Jocassee along with three other rivers— Toxaway, Thompson, and Whitewater—each of which has its own outstanding waterfalls.

Now that the Horsepasture River and the waterfalls are protected, people have to be protected from the waterfalls. The water current is strong and the rocks are smooth and slippery. If you fall in, serious injury or death is likely.

and enter the North Carolina Wildlife Gamelands. Descending into the forest, you may feel like you're heading into a canyon. Ignore several old roads going off the main trail. At this point you may be wondering how you are going to get back up and if it is really worth it. The trail gets steeper and rockier as you get further down, and you can hear the torrential waterfall.

Brave swimmers enjoy the plunge over Turtleback Falls.

The path bottoms out at a campsite (4.2 miles, 2,080 ft. elev.). Continue to the left to the rocks at the top of Windy Falls, where there may be several safe places to dip your feet. From your idyllic seat at the top of the waterfall, look upstream where the river crashes over and around boulders to make several U-turns.

On the climb back up from Windy Falls, the trail moderates as it goes up. About halfway up, a large wooden arrow guides you to stay left. You'll reach Grassy Ridge Rd. again at 5.3 miles. Turn left on the road and 0.1 miles later, turn left again. You are now back on the main trail.

To find Stairway Falls, the last waterfall on this hike, look for the split in the road you noted at 2.3 miles on the way out. Past that split and just before the trail makes a sharp curve going down to the right at 6.3 miles, take a left on a side trail to Stairway Falls—it's a good narrow trail through rhododendrons.

The side trail is short, though steep; you can hear the river get louder. Come down to a flat area, a good campsite at 6.4 miles (2,510 ft. elev.). The small cascade you see in front of the campsite is not Stairway Falls.

Turn left at the campsite and go into the woods. The trail, though obscure, is obviously maintained because blowdowns have been cut. It heads downhill in a narrow, dark heath tunnel and veers right toward the river. When you get to the bottom in 0.1 mile and look right, there is no question: you've reached Stairway Falls. The water tumbles down a set of stairs and continues into a maze of rocks.

From here return the way you came, first back to the campsite by the river and then up to the main trail. If the side trail to Stairway Falls which seemed so clear on the way down is now confusing, stay close to the river until you see a good path which takes you up and away from the river.

At 6.8 miles, make a left on the main trail to retrace your route back to the parking lot and end the hike. When you get to Rainbow Falls, take the upper trail on the right, which will take you to the finish a little faster. On the other hand, you might want to take the lower trail and admire the views all over again.

Hiking alternatives:

The mileage and altitude gain on this hike varies depending on how many waterfalls you visit and how many other side trips you make. You can take the main route, the Horsepasture River Trail, as far as you want and return when you hike back. The beauty of this hike is that you can spend all day enjoying just one waterfall or hike in and out of every side trail. The trail as described here descends from 3,170 ft. elev. at the parking lot to about 2,000 ft. elev. at the bottom of Windy Falls.

Panthertown Loop

This hike makes an oval-shaped loop on major trails—old roads, really—from west to east and back again with diversions to four memorable waterfalls and two outstanding viewpoints. Granny Burrell Falls and Schoolhouse Falls, each a short walk from the western and eastern parking lots, respectively, are popular hang-outs on sunny summer weekend afternoons. Greenland Creek Falls and Warden's Falls are more difficult to find. Climbing down to those will make you feel you've discovered waterfalls even the natives don't know about.

Getting to the trailhead:

From Cashiers, take US 64 east for 2.0 miles to Cedar Creek Rd. (SR 1120) on the left. Take Cedar Creek Rd. 2.3 miles to Breedlove Rd. on the right. Follow Breedlove Rd. 3.5 miles to the Forest Service gate. The road is unpaved the last 0.2 mile. Park at the Salt Rock Gap Trailhead, the western entrance to Panthertown.

Type of hike: Lollipop with several tails

Distance: 11.2 miles

Total ascent: 1,700 ft.

Highlights: Views of plutons, waterfalls

USGS map: Big Ridge

Trail map: A Guide to Panthertown Valley (rev. ed., 2003) by Burt Kornegay, available in area map stores or at Kornegay's website, www.slickexpeditions.com. A trail map and compass are necessary for any hike in Panthertown.

Land managed by: Nantahala National Forest, Highland District

Closest town: Cashiers, NC

Special note: At times, even when following Kornegay's map with a compass and the hiking instructions below, you may have an unsettled feeling that comes from a lack of trail blazes and trail names. To help you keep them straight, on this hike each one is referred to with a capital letter. You might want to pencil in the letters as you walk. Though it is tempting to name the trails, that honor should be left to Burt Kornegay, since he created the first map.

The Hike

Walk down Main Trail through hemlock, rhododendron, white pine, and pitch pine. This trail from Salt Rock Gap Trailhead, if followed with all its twists and turns, will take you to the eastern entrance. Look for interpretive signs low on posts describing various plants. At 0.3 mile, stop at an open view on Salt Rock where you can see across the Panthertown Valley east to Little Green Mountain and Big Green Mountain.

As you go down the trail, it feels as if you're entering a bowl. Ignore the first right turn at 0.6 mile. Continue on the trail as the road narrows. At 0.9 mile, you'll reach a four-way intersection. If you went straight ahead on the Main Trail, you would reach the eastern side of Panthertown. The left turn is where you'll come out at the end of the hike.

Turn right onto Trail A for Granny Burrell Falls, your first destination. Walk through a white pine forest with a flat camping area and a block of bricks on the left. After crossing a small bridge, walk about 100 ft. and turn right onto a small trail. (You will come back to this point after visiting Granny Burrell Falls). Walk along a very still creek. After 0.1 mile on this side trail, you'll reach Granny Burrell Falls at 1.3 miles. This broad waterfall is great for sliding, swimming, and just hanging out.

Backtrack 0.1 mile to Trail A and turn right, away from the bridge. You are heading southeast toward Little Green

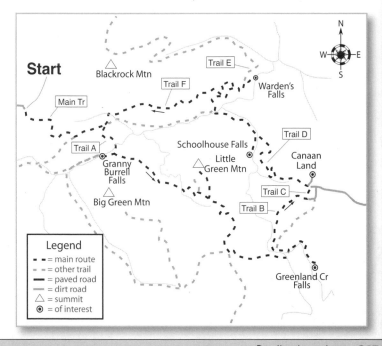

Start

Blackrock Mtn

Trail E

Trail F

Warden's Falls

Main Tr

Trail A

Granny Burrell Falls

Schoolhouse Falls

Little Green Mtn

Trail D

Canaan Land

Trail C

Big Green Mtn

Trail B

Greenland Cr Falls

Legend
- ▪ ▪ = main route
- ▪ ▪ = other trail
- ▬ = paved road
- ▬ = dirt road
- △ = summit
- ◉ = of interest

Be sure and take the side trail to view Warden's Falls. It serves as a marker for the beginning of the Tuckasegee River.

Mountain. On this woodlands walk, there are several wide, flat expanses on both sides of the trail, good for camping. At the end of one such flat area, cross the stream.

At 2.3 miles, Trail A reaches a Y; take the right fork which goes up. Continue on Trail A for another 0.2 mile and look for a trail on the left. Make that left turn to go up to Little Green Mountain. Soon, you are walking on beautiful stepwork. The stairs disappear as you continue climbing north through rhododendron. It is particularly important to stay on the trail here and not trample rare plants. The trail leads to a large flat expanse of rock.

At 2.8 miles, from the flat rocky expanses on Little Green Mountain, you can see Salt Rock west across Panthertown Valley. Several private houses dot the mountainside. If you're here in mid-July, don't miss the abundant blueberries edging the rocks.

Follow the arrow on the rock back and retrace your steps down to meet Trail A again, and turn left to continue on Trail A. After Mac's Gap, the trail goes up steeply. Look for mica in the rock, and enjoy the good winter views to the right across the valley as the trail flattens out. A creek comes in from the right; the trail continues up and to the left. Ignore the side trails; some are faint trails and others are just drainage ditches.

At the T make a left, which keeps you on Trail A

going downhill through a thick forest. You'll cross a minor creek—the rocks before the creek are always wet and slippery. Rock hop the next crossing, then cross Greenland Creek, the widest creek so far, which is a wet-boot crossing.

After crossing the creek, turn right to face a clearing and note two footpaths. Take the wider of the two, the one on your left (the right footpath only goes a few hundred feet back to the creek).

This footpath will take you to Greenland Creek Falls in 0.3 mile. It twists around through rhododendron and vines and crosses a couple of muddy places; with its roots and rocks, it is rougher than the trails you've been on so far on this hike. On this trail, you may feel that you are going through the jungles of western North Carolina. This is what Panthertown looked like before the loggers got to it—a temperate rainforest. At 4.7 miles, you'll reach Greenland Creek Falls.

Greenland Creek Falls has two parts, a steep top section and a lower and wider section. You can find a rock for your lunch spot without having to wade out into the river.

Retrace your steps to the wide spot and continue on Trail A, with the creek on your left. In about 0.1 mile, look for a narrow trail coming in on your left at 5.2 miles, and take it. This is Trail B,

which will eventually lead to Schoolhouse Falls. The trail starts out very green through rhododendron, goes down to the creek, and climbs up away from the river, heading north through a dry forest. At the top, you'll be standing under a Duke Power transmission tower. Veer right and down to a gate and an access road.

Immediately after the gate, look for a trail—this is Trail C—to your left, and take it. If you pass a line of rocks on the right side of the road, you've gone too far. A survey marker on the ground at the start of Trail C tells you that you're on the right path.

This trail goes downhill through the woods to another unpaved road, Trail D. Turn left here; if you look to your right, you'll see a sign indicating the entrance to the Canaan Land Christian Retreat, a private facility. The road (Trail D) veers to the left and downhill in a series of long switchbacks. Cross a new bridge and take the first left trail, lined with gravel, to Schoolhouse Falls. Near the halfway point, the trail has a wooden boardwalk.

At 7.2 miles you'll reach Schoolhouse Falls, the most popular waterfall in Panthertown because it is the easiest one to walk to from the eastern gate. Now, with the growth of private communities around Panthertown, finding parking at the eastern gate can be tricky. Schoolhouse

Falls has a small sandy beach in front. In the logging days, a schoolhouse was built near the falls, which gave it its name.

Backtrack to Trail D and make a left.Follow the creek on your right. Cross a bridge, reach a T junction, and make a right on Trail E at 7.9 miles, which will take you to Warden's Falls. Trail E is a wide trail through pine forest with flat camping areas on the both sides. Ignore the first left and look for a second left turn on a dirt road, Trail F, but do not take it now—you'll come back to this point after visiting Warden's Falls.

Continue up; about 100 yd. after the intersection with Trail F, make a right on the first side trail, which may look like a drainage ditch at the beginning. The side trail then immediately makes a left. You're descending 150 ft. in elevation on a narrow, rough trail similar to the one that took you to Greenland Creek Falls. This trail to Warden's Falls is easy to follow.

Go past a few large hemlocks and follow the sound of water. About half-way down, the trail makes a sharp left. At 8.6 miles, you'll reach the bottom of Warden's Falls where the trail is muddy and opens up on slippery rocks; be careful here. Warden's Falls is a long and wide waterfall over rippling rocks. You are standing at the headwaters of the Tuckasegee River, formed by the confluence of Panthertown and Greenland Creeks. From this small start, the Tuckasegee flows northwest, where it enters the Little Tennessee in Swain County.

Climb back up, regaining your lost elevation, and turn left on Trail E. Very shortly after, turn right on the wide trail you noted before, Trail F. This wide trail heads southwest through scrawny white pines. In the winter, the Forest Service spreads hay on the side of the trail to encourage wildlife. As you walk, you can see obstructed views of the plutons (see box p. 187) on your left. Trail F makes a sharp left as it crosses a bridge and goes up.

You'll reach the intersection with the Main Trail at 10.3 miles. If you look straight across, you'll see the road to Granny Burrell Falls. Turn right and in 0.9 mile, the Main Trail will take you straight to the trailhead to end the hike.

Tsali Loop

The Right Loop is not the longest of Tsali's four loop trails, but it provides the most flexibility. You can shorten your hike by taking one of several side trails that cut through the loop. This hike has good views of the inlets, and from one vantage point a magnificent view of Fontana Lake and the Great Smokies beyond. For more than eight miles the trail bobs up and down as it meanders close to the shoreline and then heads inland. After an optional climb to an overlook, you'll walk back on County Line Rd., a wide trail with ridge views which descends quickly and easily back to the trailhead.

Getting to the trailhead:
From Bryson City, take US 19/74 west for 9 miles. Turn right on NC 28 north. Drive for 3.6 miles, turn right into the Tsali Recreation Area, and follow the road 1.5 miles to the large parking lot. The left and right loops start beyond the restrooms and fee pay area.

Type of hike: Loop

Distance: 12.3 miles

Total ascent: 1,140 ft.

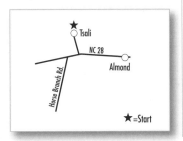

Highlights: Views of mountain ridges and Fontana Lake; gentle, well-maintained trails

USGS map: Noland Creek

Trail map:
Available at the trailhead

Land managed by:
Nantahala National Forest, Cheoah Ranger District

Rules/fees: $2 per person; no fee for hikers. Dogs must be kept on a leash.

Facilities: Restroom, picnic tables, campground

Closest town: Bryson City, NC

Website: www. cs.unca.edu/nfsnc

The Hike
It begins with a flat path banked by maples, white pine, ferns, and plenty of poison ivy. Then the trail starts to go down toward Lake Fontana, and on your right at 0.9 mile you get your first glimpses of Lemmons Branch, a side arm of the lake.

At 1.3 miles, the trail proceeds through mountain laurel, Fraser magnolias, and blueberry bushes, with good lake views, depending on the water level. You can hear and see an occasional boat below. At 2.2 miles, a side trail comes in from the left, the first of several opportunities to make a shorter loop. Continue to the right.

The trail is now wider as it descends. There are mileage markers every 0.5 mile through most of this right loop. You'll meet another side trail on the left at 2.7 miles, but stay right. If you're lucky you might see a pileated woodpecker; these birds like open areas.

If you're hiking in spring as you round into the fingers of Battles Branch, you'll notice some flame azaleas.

At 3.6 miles, there's another bail-out option on the left for a shorter hike. Continue right for good views of Battles Branch. At 4.1 miles, the land

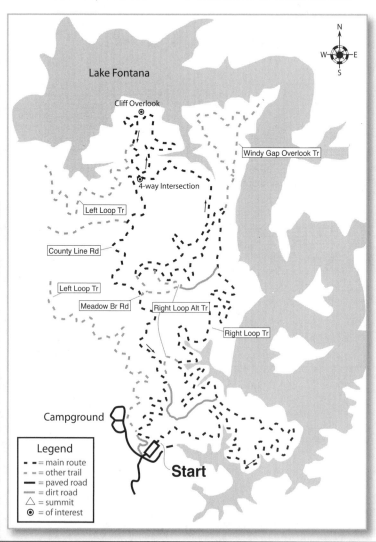

Wooden posts mark every 0.5 mile on the Tsali trails.

Continuing on, the trail goes down and changes direction sharply, now going southwest. At 6.2 miles, you'll cross a wildlife opening, a cut created by the Forest Service for birds and animals that like living on the edge.

At 6.4 miles ignore a trail coming in on the left, signed Right Loop Second Alternate. Continue straight on as you enter an area thick with mountain laurel. At 6.7 miles, turn right to stay on the Right Loop as a road comes in from the left.

Cross on a bridge over a small creek at 7.2 miles. Any hiker can rockhop across

is dry and more open, and you're above the inlet in holly and white pine scrub. Soon, the trail leaves the edges of the lake going northeast. You'll climb your first sustained but gentle uphill as you follow a tiny creek on your right with good ridge views at 4.5 miles.

The trail turns away from the lake, higher and dryer, and switchbacks northeast and northwest. The hillside you are climbing stays with you, first on the right, then on the left as the trail goes north and inland. At 5.5 miles, you'll have views of the lake on your left, and soon the trail makes a left turn at 5.6 miles. If you want some extra mileage and another view, make a right turn for Windy Gap Overlook, then retrace your steps back to this point.

What's in a Name?

The recreation area was named for Tsali, a Cherokee hero who fought against the removal of his people to Oklahoma in 1838. Not all Cherokees left their homes in the Trail of Tears. Tsali and hundreds of others hid out from Federal troops in the Nantahala Mountains. According to legend, when Federal troops attempted to capture them, Tsali and his sons killed two soldiers. After combing the mountains for weeks, the soldiers enlisted the aid of other Cherokees to find Tsali, who agreed to be executed so that his people still left in the mountains would be allowed to stay on their land.

Milkweed in full bloom just off Tsali's Right Loop trail.

that water, but cyclists use a bridge to keep from degrading the stream bank.

At 8.3 miles, you'll reach a four-way intersection. Going straight would take you to the Left Loop. To get back to the trailhead from here, make a left—but it would be a pity for you to miss the best view of the lake. Take a right and head for the Cliff Overlook. At 8.7 miles, the trail turns left and starts climbing to the overlook. You'll reach the top at 9.0 miles and 2,030 ft. elev., the high point of the loop. You are looking north at Fontana Lake and into the Great Smoky Mountains National Park.

Coming down from the overlook, the trail goes gently downhill, with limited lake views to the right. At 9.6 miles at the three-way intersection, the trail turns left and climbs to go toward County Line Rd. Complete the Overlook Loop at 9.8 miles and make a right onto County Line Rd., which separates Graham and Swain counties.

This road is wide and dry with good western views to the right. At 10.2 miles, continue left at a clearing and avoid the trail on the right which goes to the Left Loop. The walking is easy; you can stay to the right and allow horses and cyclists to pass on your left without having to stop.

At 10.9 miles, Meadows Branch Rd. enters from the left. At 11.6 miles, a minor road (blazed orange) enters from the left. Soon after, also on the left, another road takes off uphill. You'll pass a gate at 12.1 miles. Turn left beyond the gate to head back to the trailhead and finish the hike.

Fontana Lake Levels

The lake views depend on when you hike this trail. The Tennessee Valley Authority, which operates Fontana Dam for hydropower generation, flood control, and downstream navigation, controls the water level in the lake. TVA starts its drawdown of the lake after Labor Day. The lake is at its lowest in the winter.

Joyce Kilmer Memorial

The Joyce Kilmer Memorial Forest is a fine example of old-growth cove hardwood forest. The Memorial Forest was never logged because of the Great Depression and falling timber prices. The Forest Service bought this 13,055-acre tract in 1936; in 1975 it became part of the Joyce Kilmer-Slickrock Wilderness. Here you'll find lots of moisture, rich soils, and a variety of ferns, wildflowers, and moss—this is an enchanted forest, especially after a soft rain. However, people come here primarily to see the large trees, some over 100 ft. tall and 20 ft. around.

Getting to the trailhead:
From Robbinsville, take NC 143W. After about 12 miles, turn right on Joyce Kilmer Rd. (SR1134). Drive 3.0 miles and turn left to the Memorial Forest Parking area.

Type of hike: Figure-eight loop

Distance: 2 miles

Total ascent: 400 ft.

Highlights: Old-growth forest, variety of plants, spring wildflowers

USGS map: Santeetlah Creek

Trail map: Map at the trailhead

Land managed by:
Nantahala National Forest, Cheoah Ranger District

Rules/fees: Maximum group size is 10 people

Related movies: *The Fugitive* (1993) with Harrison Ford; *Nell* (1994) with Jodie Foster

The Hike
The loop starts past the signboard and picnic area. Cross Little Santeetlah Creek. As the trail climbs, the trees get bigger and more impressive. At the intersection of the lower and upper loops, there is a plaque on a rock memorializing Joyce Kilmer, the poet whose best-known poem, "Trees," begins with the famous lines,

> *I think that I shall never see*
> *A poem lovely as a tree*

Continue on the left to the upper portion of the loop, known as Poplar Cove. As the trees get bigger, families like to link hands and see how many people it takes to encircle a large tree.

Kilmer, a soldier from New Jersey who was killed in World War I, probably never set foot in the mountains of North Carolina. The Veterans of Foreign Wars asked the U.S. Government to name a suitable forest as a living memorial for Kilmer.

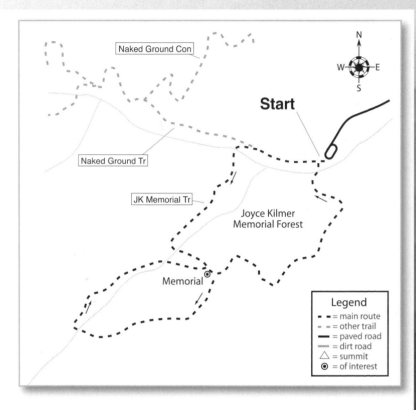

Although the Joyce Kilmer Wilderness Area has miles of other trails, for most visitors, this loop is almost synonymous with the whole forest. It is possible that more people know who Joyce Kilmer was from having walked the Memorial Loop than from walking through the Kilmer Campus of Rutgers University, also named for him.

Naked Ground Loop

If after walking the two-mile Joyce Kilmer Memorial Loop you want to see more of this amazing old-growth forest, try this hike. Though it requires a commitment of more time and energy, the Naked Ground Trail will take you through an outstanding poplar, oak, and hemlock forest. Named for the grassy, high-elevation meadow at its summit, Naked Ground is the only trail—other than the popular Memorial Loop—in the old-growth forest.

This hike is in a wilderness area without trail blazes, but at this writing there are good wooden signs at every trail junction. This trail is particularly beautiful after a rain when everything looks even greener than usual.

Type of hike: Loop

Distance: 10.5 miles

Total ascent: 3,500 ft.

Highlights: Cascading stream, ridge views, spring flowers

USGS map: Santeetlah Creek and Tapoco

Trail map: Fontana & Hiwassee Lakes, National Geographic Map #784

Land managed by: Nantahala National Forest, Cheoah Ranger District

Rules/fees: Maximum group size is 10 people

Related movies: *The Fugitive* (1993) with Harrison Ford; *Nell* (1994) with Jodie Foster

Getting to the trailhead:
From Robbinsville, take NC 143 west. After about 12 miles, turn right on Joyce Kilmer Rd. (SR1134). Go 3 miles and turn left at the four-way stop, toward the Joyce Kilmer Memorial Forest. The trail starts to the right of the parking lot, past the restrooms.

The Hike
The Naked Ground Trail [#55] starts on the right fork of the Joyce Kilmer Memorial Loop, right of the Little Santeetlah Creek. The first 0.25 mile is the same for both trails. Then the Naked Ground Trail turns right and for a while pulls away from the creek.

You'll climb up the hillside with ferns and robin's plantain. At 0.5 mile, the Jenkins Meadow Connector comes in from the right. This is where you will return to close the loop. (The connector trail is not on the 2002 National Geographic Map.)

The Naked Ground Alternate [#55A] comes in

from the right and crosses Little Santleetlah Creek. Stay on the main trail where Solomon's plume, trillium, dwarf crested iris, and bluets bloom in spring. Small creeks cross the trail, their waters heading for Little Santleetlah Creek. Here the trail rises quickly, allowing limited ridge views on the left.

At 1.5 miles, look to your left and get off the trail for a moment to enjoy a series of cascades. You'll then pass a campsite and soon cross the creek on a split-log bridge. Notice a larger waterfall at 1.8 miles. At 1.9 miles, you'll pass a huge hollow poplar on your right. You could probably step inside its trunk and keep dry during a rain shower.

At 2.6 miles, a short side trail leads to an outstanding set of cascades on the creek. You'll cross Little Santeetlah Creek and pass several flat camping areas, after which the trail starts climbing more seriously. Round a local top at 3.5 miles at 4,230 ft. As the trail switchbacks right, look ahead and to the left for a double waterfall cascading down.

At 4.3 miles, the trail ends at Naked Ground Gap, a major, multiple-trail intersection at 4,900 ft. elev. This flat area separates Little Santleetlah Creek from the Slickrock Creek watersheds. Because hikers can reach this spot in several ways, it is a popular camping area.

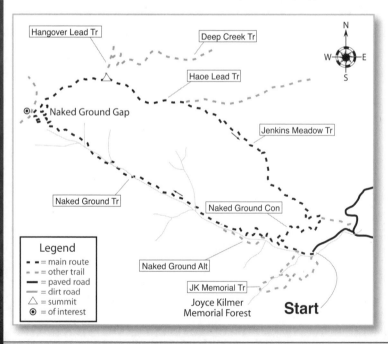

Hangover Lead Tr

Deep Creek Tr

Haoe Lead Tr

N
W—E
S

Naked Ground Gap

Jenkins Meadow Tr

Naked Ground Tr

Naked Ground Con

Legend
- - = main route
- - = other trail
— = paved road
= dirt road
△ = summit
◉ = of interest

Naked Ground Alt

JK Memorial Tr

Joyce Kilmer Memorial Forest

Start

Make a sharp right onto Haoe (pronounced *hey-o*) Lead Trail [#53]. Legend has it that Bob Stratton, who owned the land, liked to walk around his property yelling out "Hey-o." Try shouting "Hey-o." It feels good, especially when it's foggy on top and you can't see your own feet. Fog has its own beauty and is particularly entrancing on Haoe Lead as gnarled trees peek out of the mist.

A *lead* is a long ridge or ridge spur that leads to higher ground; the Haoe Lead Trail traverses generally west to east. Here there are no old-growth trees. Judging from the leaning trees, this ridge

Cherohala Skyway

On your way to the Naked Ground trailhead you'll pass the entrance to the Cherohala Skyway. This scenic stretch of NC 143 winds for 36 miles and to nearly 5,400 ft. elev. as it stretches between Robbinsville, NC and Tellico Plains, TN. Completed in 1996, it has the distinction of being North Carolina's most expensive highway at a cost of $100 million. The road passes through the Cherokee and Nantahala National Forests, from which it takes its name "Chero-hala."

must be windy most of the time. At 5.3 miles, the trail goes through a rocky patch and seems to head in two different directions, but the left and right forks rejoin quickly.

At 5.3 miles (and 5,250 ft. elev.—the highest point of the hike), the trail meets the end of the Hangover Lead Trail [#56], which comes in from the left. A flat rock face marks the junction. Make a sharp right to stay on Haoe Lead Trail as it goes down steeply. (This junction is not clearly connected on the 2002 National Geographic map.)

At 6.4 miles, the trail cuts over. You are no longer looking at the northern views to the left, but at southern views to the right.

In the Joyce Kilmer Wilderness, you spend a lot of time looking up at the massive trees.

At 6.5 miles and 4,570 ft. elev., the Haoe Lead Trail takes off to the left. Take the Jenkins Meadow Trail [#53A] which comes in from the right. Here on the dry side of the mountain, the trail feels rougher, though it is very easy to follow. The trail descends steeply with outstanding views of the mountains on your right. The meadow has disappeared now that cattle are no longer brought up here to graze.

Crossing the creek, note the first hemlocks on this trail. Look southwest (right) just below the ridge for a road—the Cherohala Skyway.

At 7.5 miles, the trail makes a sharp right. Straight ahead, a flat area is outlined with two logs and a fire ring in the middle. The path beyond the fire ring does not go far. Continue on the Jenkins Meadow Trail as it descends into a tunnel of rhododendron, hemlock, and mountain laurel.

At 8.9 miles, turn right onto the Naked Ground Connector. If you went straight, you'd stay on the Jenkins Meadow Trail and end up with a 0.5-mile walk on the road. The connector meanders down (with some uphill stretches) through the woods. You'll cross a creek at 9.4 miles. Turn left onto the Naked Ground Trail at 9.8 miles and retrace your steps to the Joyce Kilmer Memorial Forest parking lot to end the hike.

Little Santeetlah Creek rushes boldly through the forest to keep you company during your hike.

Haoe Lead

If you're looking for solitude, this is the hike for you. The first half of this lollipop hike is literally off the beaten track—you are truly in the middle of the forest. Few people seem to walk the Deep Creek Trail, finding the route too challenging. Though several helpful signs have been placed at confusing junctions, there are no blazes. Trail maintenance has been kept to wilderness standards, and blowdowns stay down.

Beyond solitude, this hike offers a contrast of moist green paths crossing creeks and minor rivulets to dry terrain with an almost Mediterranean feel. The elevation ranges from 3,360 ft. at the trailhead to about 5,260 ft. at the height of the land. Because of the low level of maintenance and foot traffic, this hike is more challenging than its distance and elevation gain alone would indicate.

Getting to the trailhead:
From Robbinsville, take NC 143 west. After about 12 miles, turn right on Joyce Kilmer Rd. (SR1134), and go 3 miles. At

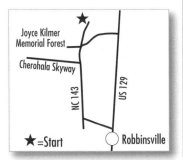

★ =Start

the four-way intersection, go straight toward the Maple Spring Observation Point. At 4.4 miles, park at the Forest Service signboard on the right. The Haoe Lead Trail starts across the road and beyond the guard rail.

Type of hike: Lollipop

Distance: 10.2 miles

Total ascent: 2,640 ft.

Highlights: Cascading stream, ridge views, solitude

USGS map: Tapoco

Trail map: Fontana & Hiwassee Lakes, National Geographic Map #784

Land managed by: Nantahala National Forest, Cheoah District

Rules/fees: Maximum group size is 10 people

Related movies: *The Fugitive (1993)* with Harrison Ford; *Nell (1994)* with Jodie Foster

The Hike
The Haoe (pronounced *hey-o*) Lead Trail [#53]starts over the guardrail and takes off to the right, rising quickly. Ignore what looks like a switchback to the left. Going west among ferns, mountain laurel, and galax, you get good ridge views to the left. A sign on a rock to your right explains that the trail was built by the U.S. Young Adult

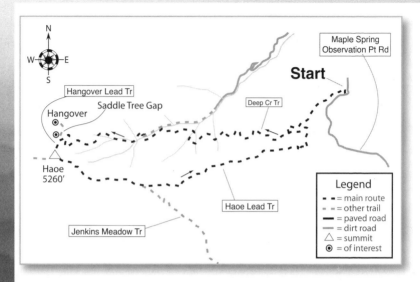

Conservation Corps in 1979. At 0.5 mile, it becomes a gentle, uphill ridge walk. Here you might frighten a grouse protecting her chicks. With her screeching and injured bird act, she might frighten you. You'll reach a large boulder at 1.0 mile on the right.

At 1.1 miles (3,830 ft. elev.), make a right onto the Deep Creek Trail [#46] on the slopes of Rock Creek Knob. Haoe Lead Trail, which goes off to the left, is the way you'll come back down. The Deep Creek Trail is a rocky trail with wet moss in many spots, making it slippery. You'll pass several massive boulders in this lush section lined with Canada violets, speckled wood lily, foam flower, and blackberry cane.

The trail goes generally west and down, alternating between slick rocky sections and gentle downhills on firm soil. At 1.8 miles, an imposing boulder on your left comes right down to the trail. Soon the trail turns left into a rhododendron tunnel and you hear the roar of Deep Creek below to your right. Cross a muddy spot at 2.2 miles with mossy, slippery rocks and several minor rivulets.

At 2.5 miles, you'll have to negotiate around a huge blowdown. Cross one cascade and soon another, coming in from the left. At 2.7 miles among tall nettles, a sign with an arrow leads you to the left, and later, a second sign with an arrow leads you up.

The trail ascends steeply away from the river, and at 3.0 miles reaches an overgrown road. Make a right on the road, which has filled in with nettles and other low foliage. You can hear the stream below to your right. At 3.1 miles, (3,530 ft. elev.), you'll cross Deep Creek on a bridge and continue in the same general direction. On the right, a sign shows the Deep Creek Trail going both ways, with Saddle Tree Gap to the right. Saddle Tree Gap is your goal, so continue right.

Cross above the creek on slippery rocks—the creek is now on your left. You're walking uphill on another road which has filled in with ferns and low bushes, except for a worn thin line which is the trail. At 3.2 miles, look for a beautiful set of cascades to your left. A little farther up, a flat area invites a well-deserved break.

At 3.5 miles, at a three-way muddy area (a point of possible confusion), the trail continues left and up. If you went straight, you'd hit a dead end.

With a hillside of hemlocks to your right, you're walking on an overgrown road going uphill. At 3.7 miles, you start to get views of the ridge on your left—your destination which, from here, looks far away. You're in a giant green bowl and you can now see all of it, with the hollow below and a semicircular ridge above on the left.

At 3.9 miles, (4,060 ft. elev.), the trail goes steeply up and to the right on a narrow side road—do not go straight. With rhododendrons on your right, you can hear Hudson Deaden Branch on your left. Make one more branch crossing and continue up.

At 4.6 miles, you've left the creek for good and are walking in a forest of maple and silverbell. When you get to an intersection with a cairn, go left. At 4.9 miles (5,120 ft. elev.), reach the ridge. A sign shows Hangover Lead Trail [#56] in both directions.

This is the end of the Deep Creek Trail. Turn left and you're on the Hangover Lead Trail going toward the Haoe Lead Trail. When the Hangover Lead Trail swings to the right and down, continue left on a short, unnamed path.

At 5.1 miles (5,260 ft. elev.), at the Hangover Lead/

Trees such as this are prime spots to see a pileated woodpecker

Haoe Lead intersection, your solitude will be broken as hikers move across the western end of Haoe Lead Trail to its intersection with Naked Ground Trail. (See the *Naked Ground Loop* hike, p. 277). Make a left to go down on the Haoe Lead Trail, veering southeast toward Jenkins Meadow. Violets, bluets, rue anemone with its mitten-shaped leaves, and blackberries abound. On the right, you start to get views of the Cherohala Skyway.

At 6.3 miles (4,580 ft. elev.), you'll reach the junction with the Jenkins Meadow Trail and make a left to stay on Haoe Lead. On the left, two large rock faces stick up like cathedrals.

The trail continues as a dry path through blackberry, wood betony, bluets, yellow star grass, and trillium. With many blowdowns to climb over and nettles and blackberry cane sticking into the trail and onto your clothes, the walking is slower going than you would expect, given the gentle, downhill trail. Once past the intersection with Jenkins Meadow Trail, your solitude returns, as few people climb up the Haoe Lead from the road.

Cross a boulder field at 6.9 miles. The trail continues down and to the right. Reach a flat area on the right among large, second-growth trees with an obstructed view on the far side. At 7.8

miles, the boulder-lined trail heads uphill. At the top of the rise, you can see layers upon layers of mountains.

Soon you get glimpses of Santeetlah Lake on your right. Cross a minor creek at 8.7 miles and reach a rocky promontory on the right. At 9.0 miles, you'll pass a massive, mossy rock wall on the left and reach the junction with the Deep Creek Trail at 9.1 miles—you have closed the circle. Make a right to stay on Haoe Lead. You have 1.1 miles to go back to the trailhead to end the hike.

Extra – Maple Springs Observation Point:

Once back to your car, drive up to the Maple Springs Observation Point. This road (SR 1127) was destined to be a state highway that would go into the Slickrock watershed. When the area was designated a Wilderness Area, construction was stopped, leaving another "road to nowhere." A short, paved loop trail takes you to outstanding 180-degree views of mountain ranges.

Wesser Bald

Over the years the Appalachian Trail has been rerouted numerous times. On this hike, you'll walk on what was once the A.T. before it was rerouted along the top of the ridge running from Wesser Fire Tower down to the Nantahala Outdoor Center. The firetower burned years ago, but was not a complete loss. You can still climb the steps to a more modern platform; the view from the top is extraordinary. You'll enjoy the "new" A.T. as you complete your hike.

Type of hike: One-way, requiring a short shuttle

Distance: 10.8 miles

Total ascent/descent: 2,760 ft./3,250 ft.

Highlights: 360-degree views, cascades, flowers

USGS map: Noland Creek

Trail map: Fontana & Hiwassee Lakes, National Geographic Map #784

Land managed by: Nantahala National Forest, Wayah Ranger District

Getting to the trailhead:

The hike begins at the Wesser Creek Trail trailhead and ends at the Nantahala Outdoor Center (NOC). Place a car at NOC first; to get there, drive west on US 74 from Bryson City approximately 13 miles. Next drive the second car to the start. From NOC in Wesser, drive 0.9 mile east and turn right onto Wesser Creek Rd. Drive about 1.9 miles to the end of the road.

The Hike

The Wesser Creek Trail (blue blazes) starts at the right corner of the parking lot at the end of Wesser Creek Rd. Because it was once part of the old A.T., the trail is still largely well-maintained. It generally parallels Wesser Creek. In spring, foam flowers, chickweed, purple violets, trillium, and banks of crested dwarf iris line the trail.

You'll soon reach an area with large rocks and wooden debris, the remains of a washout after a flood. The trail is passable, but pay attention to your footing while negotiating the rocks. Cut diagonally across to the right through the mess, then cross the creek on a little plank bridge. Take a sharp left and you're back on the trail with the creek to your left. You'll pass an old picnic table on your right. Watch for the

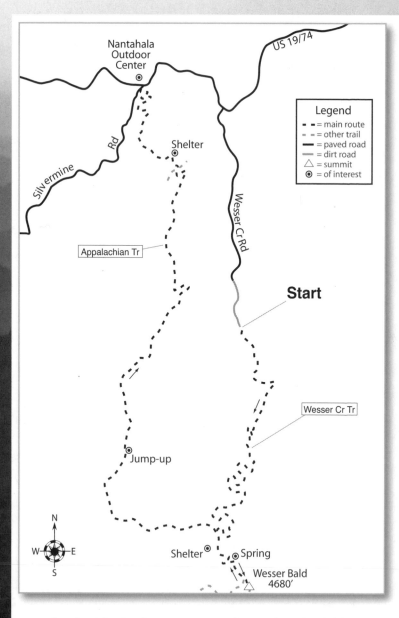

occasional patch of poison
ivy as the trail switchbacks
away from the creek.
At 0.6 mile, cross a small

creek on a three-log bridge
and continue on up. The trail
switchbacks up the mountain
and may leave the creek

temporarily, but you can always hear the rushing water.

The trail climbs slowly out of the gorge as it passes big boulders on the right at 0.75 mile. You'll pass a stone retaining wall and a level house site behind it. As you climb, the trail rejoins the creek with good views of the water tumbling over rocks. You'll see evidence of cut-throughs created by other hikers, but stay on the trail and walk the full switchback.

At 1.1 miles, look down and see two creeks, one with two small cascades. Farther along on the side you'll notice rock jumbles left by a flood, but the trail is not affected here.

At 1.5 miles, a flat rock on the left is a good place for a rest—time to contemplate the two creeks flowing down. You'll pass a thin, high waterfall enclosed by rhododendrons in about 2.0 miles. The trail makes a sharp left and doubles back for a closer view of the falls. Climb up above and past the falls to reach an upper falls, a tiered cascade with thin streams of water. Enjoy the view across the gorge.

Crisscross several more creeks as you climb toward the ridge. If you look up you can see the ridge you're aiming for, though it may look daunting.

The trail skirts around the hillside and becomes rockier. On the left, a small bridal veil falls drips softly as you walk on wet rocks around the hollow.

As you switchback up toward the ridge and move out of the Wesser Creek drainage, you can now see mountains on all sides.

At 3.5 miles and 4,140 ft. elev. you'll reach the A.T, but the climbing isn't over yet. Turn left and walk south on the A.T. Pass the sign for the Wesser Bald Shelter built by the Nantahala Hiking Club in 1994. Walking the A.T. south, you won't see the shelter from the trail.

This was the first Nantahala-style shelter— the familiar three-sided construction, but with an extended front roofline for a sheltered cooking and eating area with a picnic table. The design was developed by the Nantahala Hiking Club, and later used for shelters built by the Potomac Appalachian Trail Club and the Georgia Appalachian Trail Club.

Continuing on, the trail climbs steadily. A few hundred feet from the junction at the shelter, the trail makes a sharp right and goes up several steps. A sign points to the water source for the shelter. At the end of April, the serviceberry (shadbush) is in bloom on the ridge. It's a steep climb on a well-groomed trail up to the tower, where views can be characteristically "smoky."

Turn left on a short side trail to the tower. At 4.3 miles and 4,680 ft. elev., climb to the observation tower, which offers a 360-degree view with few visible signs of civilization. From the large platform, admire the panoramic views of the Smokies: Fontana Lake to the north and the Nantahala Mountains to the south. The trees have reestablished themselves on Wesser Bald, and without the tower, there would be no views.

Retrace your steps and head north on the A.T. At 5.1 miles, you're back at the junction with the Wesser Creek Trail. Continue downhill on the A.T. It's a good up-and-down ridge walk. At 6.3 miles, a steep, short climb takes you to good views on both sides of the trail. You'll descend sharply on a good set of steep steps. Soon, a rocky outcropping, the Jump-Up, opens to the world with outstanding views of the Smokies across the valley and an arm of Fontana Lake below. Descend steeply to the right after the Jump-Up.

At 8.0 miles, views to the east become limited as the trees obscure them. On the right, an old broken-down cabin can be seen in the flat area below.

At 9.1 miles, the trail crosses the ridge, and now you can see the western ridge as the trail continues down. At 9.6 miles, you'll cross an old road. At 10.1 miles, you'll pass a camping area and the A. Rufus Morgan Shelter on the right. Rev. Morgan founded the Nantahala Hiking Club and helped establish and maintain the North Carolina section of the A.T. On your left, the Nantahala River roars on steadily. The trail comes down to Silvermine Road in back of the NOC Information Office to end the hike.

The A.T. crosses the road at the Nantahala Outdoor Center.

Appletree Loop

The area around the Appletree Group Campground, named after the apple trees that used to cover the vicinity, is located between Andrews and Wesser. A small network of trails allows several loops of moderate difficulty. The terrain varies from lush, wet areas full of flowers to a hilly ridge walk with great views of the surrounding mountains and Nantahala Lake. If you're looking for solitude in the Nantahala Gorge, this is the hike for you.

Getting to the trailhead:
From Wesser, drive south on US 19 for 8 miles. Turn left on Wayah Rd. (SR 1310) and drive 4.1 miles along the Upper Nantahala River. This road has a couple of pulloff views of the cascades. Turn right on Old River Rd. for 3.3 miles and turn right again on Junaluska Rd. (SR 1401). Cross the bridge over the Nantahala River and continue for 3.7 miles to Junaluska Gap and the trailhead. Park on a wide spot by the county line sign that

reads, "Leaving Macon County, entering Cherokee County."

Type of hike: Loop

Distance: 12.2 miles

Total ascent: 2,170 ft.

Highlights: Woodlands walk, solitude, views of mountain ridges and Nantahala Lake

USGS map: Topton

Trail map: Fontana & Hiwassee Lakes, National Geographic Map #784

Land managed by: Nantahala National Forest, Wayah Ranger District

The Hike
At Junaluska Gap (3,560 ft. elev.), start on the London Bald Trail [#19C – blue blazes]. After a couple of hundred feet, make a right on the Junaluska Trail [#19 – blue blazes]. The Junaluska Trail goes generally northeast to the Appletree Group Campground. Walk downhill on a pleasant soft trail lined with rhododendron and hemlock.

The trail goes sharply left. You'll cross a creek and start following it upstream, then pass through a short burned stretch where painted trilliums have come up through the ashes. The trail, cut into a hillside through the forest, parallels Junaluska Rd. Bluets and purple and white violets line the creeks and muddy patches. This trail through the heart of Nantahala National Forest is delightful and quiet.

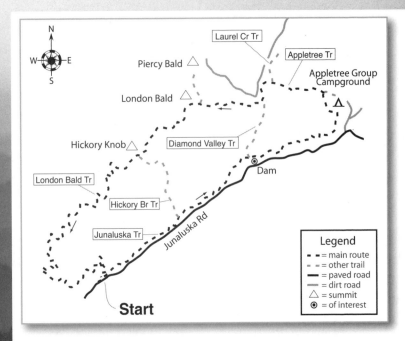

Except for the trail itself and intermittent blazes, there is little evidence of civilization, though occasionally the silence in this section is interrupted by noise from the road below.

At 0.7 mile, you'll cross Matherson Branch and bear left where you'll see the blue blazes. The trail parallels the road and crosses Hickory Branch at 1.3 miles. The Hickory Branch Trail [#19A] comes in from the left at 1.4 miles; the trail sign may be missing. Make a sharp left at 1.5 miles.

At 2.5 miles, the Diamond Valley Trail [#19D] comes in from the left. Continue right on Junaluska Trail. For a short diversion, follow the creek downstream on the approach to the Diamond Valley Trail to see a small waterfall, several cascades, and a little concrete dam. Retrace your steps and cross the creek on rocks to follow the blue blazes of the Junaluska Trail.

The trail is now above the road and in the heart of the forest where it crosses minor creeks and skirts up the hill. You'll reach an open area with dogwood, gnarly mountain laurel, and robin's plantain at 3.5 miles. At 4.0 miles, work your way around several boulders from which you can see water pipes and open fields on the right across the road. In spring, foam flowers, violets, and white trillium proliferate.

At 4.5 miles, the Junaluska Trail ends. Make a left on the

Appletree Trail [#19B – yellow blazes], following a creek upstream. The trail to the right leads to the campgrounds in 0.4 mile and the Bartram Trail in another 0.2 mile.

The Appletree Trail climbs steadily through Clinton's lily, violets, and poison ivy, following Appletree Branch. At 5.0 miles, the creek disappears as you continue on an old road. The Laurel Creek Trail [#19F] comes in from the right at 5.3 miles. You'll cross an old road and soon after, at 5.5 miles, the Diamond Valley Trail comes in from the left. Continue right, with views ahead of you and to the south as you climb the flanks of London Bald; there is no trail to the top of the Bald. At 5.8 miles and 3,890 ft. elev., you'll reach a flat area with good ridge views.

At 6.3 miles, make a left onto the London Bald Trail. There is no sign at this T intersection. The trail starts on a gentle downhill. You'll cross a rock bridge over the headwaters of Youngs Camp Branch; this trail feels like an old road bed whose sides are slipping down the hollow.

At 7.2 miles in the distance, to your left (southeast), you can see Nantahala Lake. The lake was created at the beginning of World War II to supply power for the war effort and is now regulated and maintained by Duke Power Company. You'll have views of the lake along most of this trail. At 7.4 miles, look east to see the bump which is London Bald.

At 7.7 miles, the Hickory Branch Trail comes in from left; it's the upper end of the trail you crossed at the beginning of the hike. You'll pass a burned area, part of the same burned section that you saw at the bottom of the Hickory Branch Trail. The burned area comes and goes for the remainder of the London Bald Trail as new growth revitalizes the hillside. Without a thick green cover of vegetation, fiddlehead ferns and wildflowers are taking over.

You'll cross four creeks within the next 1.5 miles. After the fourth crossing, the trail gently contours the hills and starts downhill through a cove of hemlocks and rhododendrons, holding tightly to the hillside. Cross one last creek before arriving at the junction with the Junaluska Trail, to end the hike.

Fern fiddleheads emerge from the dark rich Appalachian soil.

Appalachian Trail

Hiking takes more than heel.

—Emma "Grandma" Gatewood, the first woman
to thru-hike the Appalachian Trail.

Appalachian Trail

Essential Facts

Facilities:
The Appalachian Trail, though part of the National Park Service system, does not have official entrances or visitor centers. You can get on and off the trail in hundreds of places. Shelters are located along the trail but you should always carry a tent. In most places, you can sleep in a shelter on a first-come, first-served basis. In some parks, you need reservations.

Website:
www.appalachiantrail.org

Related books:
As Far As the Eye Can See by David Brill; *A Walk in the Woods* by Bill Bryson; *There are Mountains Tto Climb* by Jean Deeds.

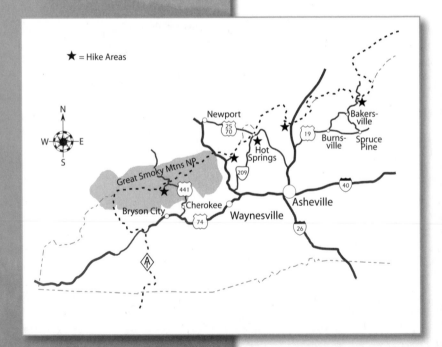

In the Southern Appalachian Mountains, the Appalachian Trail moves back and forth between North Carolina and Tennessee for about 380 miles. It climbs to Clingmans Dome in the Smokies, the highest point on the trail, and dips down into gaps and coves only to ascend again. When hikers talk about "the Trail," they are referring to the Appalachian Trail(A.T.), part of the National Park System and now entirely on public land. The A.T., blazed with white rectangles, may be the most documented trail in the world. The Appalachian Trail Conservancy, a private nonprofit organization charged with caring for the 2,175-mile greenway from Georgia to Maine, is also the umbrella organization for the 30 volunteer clubs who built and now maintain the trail.

Several names will always be associated with the Appalachian Trail, including Benton MacKaye, Myron Avery, Earl Shaffer, and Emma Gatewood. MacKaye was the thinker and advocate for wilderness who in 1921 first proposed a footpath through the wilderness connecting the mountains from the highest point in New England to the highest point in the South. Myron Avery was the doer who organized hiking clubs, developed volunteer groups who would construct much of the trail, and took charge

In Hot Springs the AT emblem is marked right on the sidewalk.

of the Appalachian Trail Conservancy (then known as the Appalachian Trail Conference) for many years. He became the first 2,000-miler by walking the whole A.T. in sections in 1936. Earl Shaffer was the first thru-hiker, walking the whole A.T. in four months in 1948.

In 1955, Emma "Grandma" Gatewood was the first woman to complete the trail. After raising 11 children in Southern Ohio, she first hiked the A.T. at age 67 and went on to hike it twice more, becoming the first person to walk the trail three times, the last time at age 76. This was before the days of lightweight, ergonomically designed backpacks and sleeping bags. She wore tennis shoes and carried her gear—an army

The open balds in the Max Patch region are popular destinations for AT hikers.

blanket, a raincoat, and a shower curtain—in a duffle bag swung over her shoulder. One of her famous lines was "Most people are pantywaists. Exercise is good for you."

Hiking the whole trail is not for those who like to commune with nature. Spring flowers, mountaintops, and dramatic sunsets are the rewards, but they don't happen every day. An A.T. hiker must be a linear thinker: go north (or south), follow the white blazes, make your miles, stop for the night before you drop.

Both thru-hikers and section hikers need to follow this routine to finish. Thru-hikers are trying to walk the trail in one continuous hike during the six to seven months between the end of March and the beginning of October. If they start earlier, they can be walking in snow or caught in a blizzard in the Georgia and North Carolina mountains. If they reach Baxter State Park in Maine too late in the fall, they will arrive to find the park closed. Section hikers walk the trail over many years, usually on their vacations. They start at one point and need to reach their endpoint by a set date. Neither group can follow their own muses; they need to follow the white markers.

The Appalachian Trail Conservancy does not distinguish between those who thru-hiked and those who section-hiked the trail, calling them all 2,000-milers. In 2005, 510 people completed the trail, 99 of them section hikers. Though thru-hiking is the most popular perception of the A.T., many more casual day hikers and weekend backpackers than thru-hikers walk the trail.

Backpackers can stay overnight in shelters or in their own tents. Shelters, planned about a day's walk apart, are three-sided structures with a tin roof and the fourth side open to the elements. Shelters are a good place to get out of the rain and meet other hikers. They are typically located off the trail near water on short, blue-blazed side trails.

As a day hiker, you may want to stop at a shelter for lunch or just to read the trail register or log book, which can be thought of as a diary for the shelter. Originally notebooks were put in shelters for safety so that hikers could enter their intended route. Now, log books are used mostly for musings, exaltations, and complaints about the trail, nature, and food. Food is very important on the A.T. Entries like this are sometimes accompanied by elaborate drawings:

Walked 15 miles today, saw a snake heading into the grass. Looking forward to some chow. Curry noodles tonight.

When you hike the A.T., you might meet trail maintainers wielding loppers, clippers, a chainsaw, or a weed-whacker. To keep trails in hiking conditions, volunteer trail maintainers regularly clip, clean, and mow down weeds. Otherwise, in a couple of years, you would not be able to find the trail.

When A.T. directions say North or South, they are referring to "trail north," heading toward Maine, or "trail south," heading toward Georgia. Sometimes that's the complete opposite from the compass direction you'll have on the trail as it winds and wiggles through the mountains. Many side trails diverge from the A.T., allowing for loop hikes. The hikes which follow start from various sections of North Carolina where it borders Tennessee and are grouped together because they are all on the Appalachian Trail.

Grassy Ridge

The diversity of the Roan Mountains stems, in large part, from the diversity in altitude. Bakersville, NC is at 2,470 ft. elev. and Grassy Ridge is at 6,190 ft. Altitude determines the environment: flowers, trees, animals, temperature, humidity, and the seasons. Climbing 4,000 ft. is the climatic equivalent of traveling 1,000 miles north, which would put the top of the Roan Mountains in the same zone as Canada. Luckily you don't have to climb almost 4,000 ft. in elevation to explore the Roans. At Carvers Gap on the North Carolina/Tennessee border where the Appalachian Trail crosses, you are already at 5,512 ft. elev.

Getting to the trailhead:
From Bakersville, NC, take NC 261 north for 13 miles to Carvers Gap. The hike starts at Carvers Gap on the North Carolina/Tennessee line.

Type of hike: Out and back

Distance: 5.0 miles

Total ascent: 1,130 ft.

Highlights: Views,

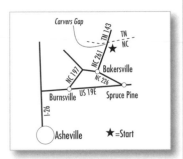

outstanding heath balds, rare plants, SB6K

USGS map:
Carvers Gap, Bakersville

Trail map: Appalachian Trail Guide to Tennessee-North Carolina

Land managed by:
Pisgah National Forest, Appalachian District

The Hike

The hike starts on the Appalachian Trail heading north through the opening in the fence. The beginning of the path from Carvers Gap has been hardened with geotextile, a porous plastic fabric which feels like canvas and gravel has been laid over it. This material, coupled with mesh, prevents the gravel from washing away. Without it, the large number of people who start on this trail would be walking in a muddy trench.

The A.T. here is lined with rhododendrons and blackberry plants and soon enters a dark spruce tunnel with a barbed-wire fence on the left. At 0.6 mile (5,830 ft. elev.) as you come out into the open, you'll pass a cluster of spruces planted to see if they would grow on this grassy bald. Reach Round Bald at 0.7 miles (5,830 ft. elev.); there is a sign on the left side. From here, you can see the Blue Ridge and the Unaka Mountains.

To keep the balds clear, the Forest Service brought in

goats and sheep for a few years, but now they just mow and weed-whip the grasses. If left to nature, the balds would fill in with trees, rhododendron, and azalea bushes, and the views would disappear.

The thin plant that predominates here is hair grass, which looks like wheat waving in the breeze. The other ground-cover, Pennsylvania sedge, looks more like grass on a lawn that needs cutting. The spongy moss underneath, together with the sedge and grasses, prepares the ground for the growth of other plants. Schweinitz's ragwort, a rare plant, grows among the grasses and sedges.

The trail descends to Engine Gap at 1.0 mile. During the logging days, timber was pulled up the mountain and taken away by rail. The gravel path ends at Engine Gap, and most walkers turn around here.

Continue up on wet, steep rocks where water always seems to be flowing. The trail is enclosed in green alder among the wild strawberry, filmy angelica, and bluets. You'll pass a rock formation that allows outstanding views of your journey so far. At 1.5 miles the trail goes across Jane Bald, named after a woman who died after passing this spot in 1870.

There is always a strong breeze up here, even on the warmest day. If it's foggy, as it often is, don't let that deter you from continuing on; fog adds to the mysterious feeling, and it's part of the adventure.

At 1.9 miles (5,910 ft. elev.), the A.T. goes left and descends. Continue straight up to Grassy Ridge on a good trail. The open balds, famous for Catawba rhododendron and flame azalea, explode with color in

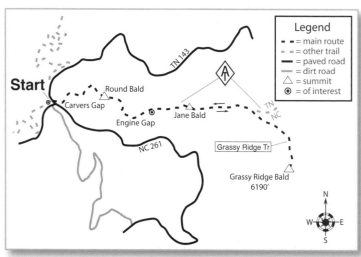

Roan Mountain

"It is the most beautiful mountain east of the Rockies," said Asa Gray, the leading authority of his time on plant life in the United States, as he explored the Roan Highlands in 1841. That's where he discovered a new lily, which was named after him: Gray's lily, Lilium grayi, a rare flower found in only a few places in western North Carolina. Gray's lily is not as colorful or imposing as the daylily or Turk's cap lily. Gray's lily has small, funnel-shaped blooms that dangle downward. Deep crimson outside and orange-red inside with reddish-purple spots, these small flowers with narrow petals are about two inches long, carried on slender stems with whorled leaves. Some wildflower books omit this lily out of concern that people would pick it after they've identified it.

Gray's lily is only one of many attractions on your way to Grassy Ridge in the Roan Mountains. In the fall, you can pick wild blueberries with little effort. The bald's open grasslands, Catawba rhododendron, azalea, and the views—especially the views—attract countless visitors.

mid-to-late June. However, the views from the Roans are outstanding at any time.

As you walk up toward Grassy Ridge looking east, you can see Grandfather Mountain and the infamous ski condominium on Sugar Top Mountain. From this distance, Grandfather Mountain and the condo look like they are next to each other, though in reality they are separated by a wide valley. The condo sticks out of the mountain skyline like the proverbial sore thumb. Public protest against this building led to the Mountain Ridge Protection Law of 1983, which now limits the height of buildings on ridges over 3,000 ft. elev. You can also pick out Table Mountain and Hawksbill in Linville Gorge. To the southwest you can see Mt. Mitchell on a clear day.

You'll come out of a rhododendron tunnel into a grassy alpine meadow. In the fog, people disappear and reappear straight ahead of you. If it happens to be clear, you'll be able to see forever.

At 2.4 miles, the trail splits. Take the right fork and aim for the boulder on Grassy Ridge. On this boulder, the Forest Service has placed a plaque to honor the memory of Cornelius Rex Peake (1887-1964), a local man born in the valley below who operated the highest cultivated farm east of the Rockies and helped protect the Roans. You are now on top of the world and have left nearly all the people below you.

For hikers headed north on the A.T., Grassy Ridge is the last 6,000-ft. mountain they encounter until they reach Mt. Washington in New Hampshire. As you retrace your steps heading back to the trailhead to end the hike, look to your left and across the gap to see the round top of Roan High Knob.

Gray's lilies bloom at Engine Gap.

Rugged terrain makes for outstanding scenery—and photos.

Roan High Knob

At Carvers Gap on the Appalachian Trail, you're 1,803.1 miles south of Mt. Katahdin in Maine and 371.8 miles north of Springer Mountain, Georgia. On this short hike, you'll get to the highest shelter on the A.T., reach the site of the Cloudland Hotel and, optionally, walk through the spectacular natural Rhododendron Gardens to Roan High Bluff. Locals know that in winter this area provides the best cross-country skiing in the South.

Getting to the trailhead: The hike starts at Carvers Gap on the North Carolina/Tennessee line. From Bakersville, NC, take NC 261 north for 13 miles to Carvers Gap. Park in the parking lot at Carvers Gap.

Type of hike: Out and back

Distance: 4.6 miles

Total ascent: 1,110 ft.

Highlights: Views, A.T. shelter, hotel site, Rhododendron Gardens, two SB6K

USGS map: Carvers Gap

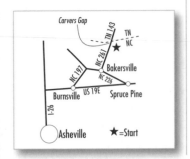

Trail map: Appalachian Trail Guide to Tennessee-North Carolina

Land managed by: Pisgah National Forest, Appalachian District

The Hike

The Appalachian Trail, heading trail south, starts on the Tennessee side of TN 143N. Walk on the road to the end of the parking lot on your left until you see the white rectangle A.T. blazes going down into the woods.

The graveled trail, bordered by logs, descends a little. You'll cross several creeks on plank bridges, partly covered with chicken wire. The trail then starts to climb through a dark spruce grove. In 0.25 mile, the gravel and the logs end, and the trail passes a cluster of stones on the left, remnants of an old chimney toppled over. Because trees cut out the sunlight, the bottom branches of the spruces are dead.

At 1.3 miles, a point of possible confusion, the trail switchbacks right and up. You're walking on a wide, rocky railroad grade trail in a fir and spruce forest with occasional rhododendron; runoffs coming in from the left keep the trail constantly wet here. At 1.5 miles, make a left on the blue-blazed trail, which will take you to the top of Roan High Knob and the shelter. Roan High

Knob Shelter, the highest on the A.T., was built in 1933 by the Civilian Conservation Corps to house the fire warden staffing the nearby fire tower. By 1940, the tower had been dismantled. The shelter is an enclosed cabin with a covered porch and an outside cooking table. It was renovated by volunteers from the Tennessee Eastman Hiking and Canoeing Club, which maintains over 130 miles of the A.T., including the section through Roan Mountain. Like most A.T. shelters, this one has a log book where backpackers record their plans and experiences on the trail.

Continue past four stone pilings, the base of the old fire tower, to a cluster of rocks about 100 yd. from the shelter. This is the top of Roan High Knob at 6,285 ft. elev.

Go back down to the A.T. and take a left; the trail bobs up and down. At 2.1 miles, you can see a road to the Rhododendron Gardens on your left. Pass a well-maintained chimney on the left as you switchback and continue up on log steps. At 2.2 miles, leave the A.T. and go left on rocks into a field to the site of the Cloudland Hotel. The A.T. continues on the right.

The Cloudland Hotel was built in 1884 as a three-story resort hotel which attracted an upper crust clientele. To get there, guests traveled by narrow-gauge railroad to Roan Mt. Station in Tennessee and then by wagon for 12 dusty miles on the newly constructed Carvers Gap Rd.

A plaque at the site, the only existing evidence of the hotel, states that the lodging rate was two dollars a day and included three meals. The hotel area offered no hunting or fishing, just scenery and relief

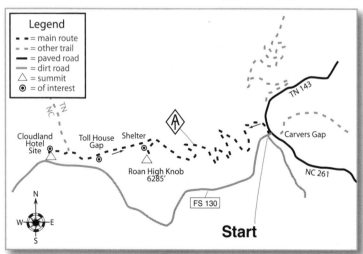

Legend
- – = main route
- – – = other trail
- ▬ = paved road
- ▬ = dirt road
- △ = summit
- ◉ = of interest

Cloudland Hotel Site

Toll House Gap

Shelter

Roan High Knob 6285'

TN 143

Carvers Gap

NC 261

FS 130

Start

N
W — E
S

The trail to Roan High Knob is well marked.

from hay fever. John Muir, one of the founders of the Sierra Club and an environmentalist most often associated with the American West, stayed at the Cloudland when he visited the Roan Mountains in 1898. The hotel was open for just three months of the year and operated for 20 years.

From here, this hike has several possible endings. You can simply retrace your steps and return on the A.T to where you started. Your second option is to continue to the four-way trail intersection. Going straight at the intersection, you'll reach a gravel path leading to a picnic table on your left and, soon after, a parking lot with restrooms on your right. Walk to the parking lot entrance. From here, you'll turn left and walk down the blacktop road for 1.7 miles back to Carvers Gap to return to your car.

Your third option is to walk to the Rhododendron Gardens in 0.2 mile and continue an additional mile to Roan High Bluff. Take the Cloudland Trail, blazed yellow, which starts to the right of the entrance to the parking lot; there is a sign to the right of the trailhead and a water fountain on the left. The gravel trail goes past the Gardens, crosses several roads, and ends at an octagonal observation tower on Roan High Bluff. Returning from Roan High Bluff to the Cloudland Hotel, you'll then retrace your steps to the trailhead to end the hike.

Extra – The Rhododendron Gardens: The U.S. Forest Service bought the top and sides of the Roan Mountains in 1941 to protect the rhododendrons from being carried off. The Rhododendron Gardens are entirely naturally occurring; no one planted them here. The rhododendron have survived and spread, pruned only by wind and severe winter weather.

If you elect to make the Rhododendron Gardens your destination on this hike, on your way back, you can explore hundreds of acres of Catawba rhododendrons on several short trails. Most tourists drive directly to the Gardens from Carvers Gap, and many are unprepared at the cool and misty conditions, even at the height of the summer.

Of course, the easiest way back to Carvers Gap is to have someone pick you up at the Gardens. There is an entrance fee to drive in the Rhododendron Gardens.

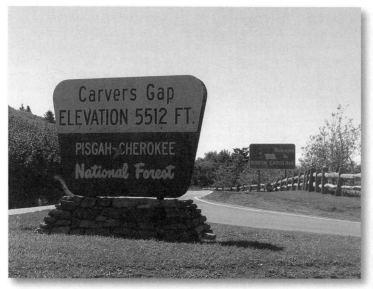

Carvers Gap straddles the North Carolina/Tennessee border.

Sams Gap

You'll begin this hike under I-26, a new stretch of the interstate which has been discovered by trucks and tourists, but the trail quickly goes into the woods where it quiets down. The trail is in the trees most of the time, and you might see a hawk, a turtle, or a snake slithering across the path or even a great horned owl. You will find solitude here, too, since this part of the A.T. is used only by backpackers and local hikers.

Getting to the trailhead:

The hike starts at Sams Gap and ends at Devils Fork Gap. Place a car at Devils Fork Gap first. To get there leave I-26 at exit 5 (Flag Pond Rd.) in Tennessee, and make a right at the exit ramp, a left at the Flag Pond sign, and a right at the stop sign. Drive for 2.2 miles on Flag Pond Rd. (also TN 81) and turn left on TN 352W. Drive 4.3 miles to Devils Fork Gap on the Tennessee/North Carolina border. The parking area is on the left.

Next drive the second car to the start. To do that, drive back to Flag Pond Rd. (TN 81),

turn right, and continue for 8 miles on TN 81. Go under I-26 and park on the right at the Sams Gap trailhead. Do not get back on I-26.

Type of hike: Shuttle

Distance: 8.2 miles

Total ascent/descent: 1,700 ft./2,460 ft.

Highlights: Typical A.T. section, shelter, waterfall, solitude

USGS map: Sams Gap, Flag Pond

Trail map: The Appalachian Trail Guide to Tennessee-North Carolina

Land managed by: Pisgah National Forest, Appalachian District

The Hike

From the parking area at Sams Gap (3,760 ft. elev.), walk on US 23N and cross under I-26. Stay to the left and turn on a steep, paved driveway. The paved path quickly turns left into the woods. You'll pass a small environmental monitoring station on the right.

The trail goes up on good log steps and leads into a maple forest. In mid-May to early June, the trail explodes with a full catalog of wildflowers including Solomon's plume and Solomon's seal, bloodroot, trillium, squaw root, violet, and Jack-in-the-pulpit.

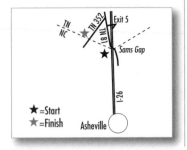

Pass the first of many barbed-wire fences as the trail ascends gently into the woods. This land is a former cow pasture. You can hear and see I-26 from the first high point, but the noise soon dissipates and the trill of juncos takes over. White pine, tulip tree, oak, and wild hydrangea line the route. The trail goes north from the start of the

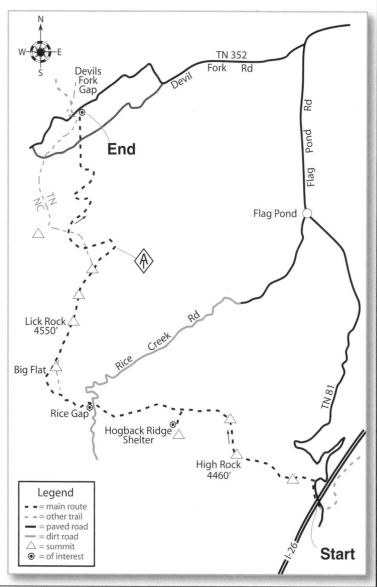

hike, though it zigzags east and then west. It continues to cross and run parallel to fence lines from formerly grazed lands as sunlight filters through the trees. At 1.7 miles, reach High Rocks (4,460 ft. elev.) with good winter views. The trail then turns right and descends on log steps. Soon you'll reach an obviously cleared view on your right.

At 2.2 miles, turn left on a blue-blazed trail to go to Hogback Ridge Shelter, 0.1 mile off the A.T. This shelter, built by the Carolina Mountain Club in 1984, has a typical design for its era—one level, with an overhang and a picnic table in front.

Stiles make crossing fences a good deal easier.

Spend a few minutes reading the entries in the log book for a taste of the A.T. experience.

In for the night, hot meal and a good night sleep (cold – or hot or wet or tired).

Log books give hikers something to do and to read in the shelter. Sometimes you get art work or poetry.

Oh if I were a shelter, where do you think I'd be?
Up ahead? Round the bend? Past the little tree?

The privy on a side trail about 300 ft. east of the shelter has a throne with a view. The water source is in the opposite direction, about 450 ft. west of the shelter. Return to the A.T. and turn left to continue the hike. The trail first descends steeply, then gently, through fire pinks and squaw root. At 3.3 miles (3,800 ft. elev.), you'll reach Rice Gap. [A trail to the right would take you down to Rice Creek Rd., about 5 miles from the center of Flag Pond.]

The A.T. crosses Rice Gap and climbs out of the Gap straight ahead. Here the trail is an old, wide road. On this section, several minor roads of various widths intersect the A.T.; most have been barred with logs. Ignore them and continue on the A.T., which is well-marked. In less than a half-mile, the A.T. veers off the road and continues as a narrow, conventional trail. The trail climbs west, gently and then more steeply, to reach a flat area with fire rings.

At about 4.7 miles, you'll pass a huge boulder on the left—there is much more rock behind the part of the boulder you can see from the trail— and soon you'll reach the top of Frozen Knob (also referred to as Lick Rock) at 4,550 ft. elev. Descending through an apple orchard, you may find some tiny green apples (in summer) before you begin climbing to a second summit.

Come down to a good eastern view of I-26 and the mountains. Trees were cut by the Appalachian Trail Conservancy to prevent the entire A.T. from becoming a green tunnel. The trail hugs the wire fence on your left as you come down. You'll reach a second section of downed trees on your right; you can decide for yourself whether cutting trees to create views is desirable.

You'll reach a good sitting rock on your right with a boulder in the back and a creek in front, which makes a relaxing lunch spot. Then the trail reaches Sugarloaf Gap, a flat open field, as it crosses back into Tennessee at 4,000 ft. elev. and descends in tight switchbacks down log steps. Cross a stream coming in from the left with a small cascade above. Then at 6.8 miles,

Best of the A.T.

The Appalachian Trail through the Southern Appalachians boasts many "bests and biggests" on the A.T.—best view, best waterfall, highest point. The section from Sams Gap to Devils Fork Gap might get the prize for offering the best feel for the whole A.T. experience. If you've completed part of the A.T. and are contemplating thru-hiking the whole trail, this segment will give you a glimpse into a typical day on the A.T., at least the southern half. Throughout this archetypal A.T. day hike, you'll walk mostly in a new forest and have occasional views, crossing minor creeks and visiting a trail shelter.

However, each A.T. section is distinctive and has its own quirks. Here, though you are walking the A.T. south, the trail goes mostly compass north as it zigzags along the North Carolina/ Tennessee border. In certain sections, Tennessee is east of North Carolina. Though a compass and map are recommended as essential equipment for all hikes, here your compass can also serve as a source of entertainment.

you'll cross the creek again at the base of a waterfall.

Here the trail displays more evidence of life (and lives past) as it gets closer to Devils

Fork Gap. Passing a dismantled log cabin on the left, go down log steps and pass the remains of a second cabin on the right. Cross the creek coming in from the left, and go up more log steps before the trail turns left and continues downhill. The small cemetery on the right has only two graves, marked

Dorothy Hensley
May 2 1865 to April 30, 1965
Joe Riddel
May 16, 1877 to July 9, 1967

The A.T. continues down through the first rhododendron tunnel of the hike. When you cross an old forest road to your left, you can see a gate and houses.

The trail, now level, leads through a field. You'll cross Laurel Branch on a two-log bridge and then Rector Laurel Rd., a paved road. The trail starts up again on the other side, passing a huge hemlock on the left as it approaches the top of this section. At the top, go through an angled fence designed to keep cattle out. Climb over the stile and head down through pasture. You'll end the hike by climbing another stile and coming out onto the road at Devils Fork Gap.

Hogback Ridge shelter has welcomed hikers on the A.T. since 1984.

Lover's Leap

This half-day loop from Hot Springs makes a perfect short hike any time of the year, but shines in winter when the trees are bare and the views are spectacular. The first half is on the Appalachian Trail; the trail climbs up to a ridge with mountains on both sides. Then you return on the Pump Gap Loop Trail, following Silvermine Creek.

Getting to the trailhead: Hot Springs, on US 25, is in Madison County, NC, close to the Tennessee border. Park in the public lot next to the railroad tracks.

Type of hike: Lollipop

Distance: 5.4 miles

Total ascent: 1,050 ft.

Highlights: Views of mountain ridges, French Broad River

USGS map: Hot Springs

Trail map: Appalachian Trail Guide to Tennessee-North Carolina; also a map from the Hot Springs Visitor Center

Land managed by: Pisgah National Forest, Appalachian District

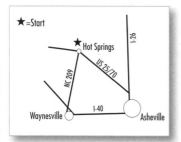

★ =Start
Hot Springs
I-26
NC 209
US 25/70
Waynesville
I-40
Asheville

Closest town: Hot Springs, NC. Hot Springs is too small for fast food restaurants. A couple of restaurants are open year-round, but most close in the winter. Soaking in the mineral waters at the Hot Springs Resort and Spa is a great way to end a hiking day.

Website: www. hotspringsnc.org

Related books and movies: *The German Invasion of Western North Carolina* by Jacqueline Burgin Painter; *The French Broad* by Wilma Dykeman

All the Real Girls (2003) with Paul Schneider

The Hike

After parking, turn left and cross Bridge St. (US 25). Cross the railroad tracks and pass the Hot Springs spa. Walk across the bridge, following the white A.T. rectangle blazes. At the eastern end of the bridge, climb over the barrier down to the street below by the French Broad River. Turn left and pass the Nantahala Outdoor Center rafting take-out point. NOC, considered the Harvard of outdoor recreation, brought recreational rafting to western North Carolina in the early 1970s.

A street comes in from the left where you'll come back to close the circle. Bear right to continue on the A.T. The A.T. (going trail north) parallels the river, passing a massive rock on the left and an old gauging station on the river side.

The French Broad begins its life in the mountains of Transylvania County with a North, a South, an East, a West, and a Middle Fork. These five forks converge in the small town of Rosman to create the main stream of the French Broad. Once in Rosman, the French Broad does something very unusual for an American river; it flows north, first to Asheville and then on to Hot Springs. The French Broad picks up several tributaries as it travels and eventually joins the Pigeon River to become the Tennessee River. The river was called "French" because it flowed into French-held territory before the French relinquished all its holdings east of the Mississippi river in the 1763 Treaty of Paris. "Broad" is another name for a wide river, so calling it the "French Broad River" is redundant.

Since the A.T. was designed to follow mountain ridges, such a pleasant river walk on this trail cannot last too long; you'll start climbing on manicured switchbacks at 0.8 mile. Every bend allows better views of Hot Springs and the river below.

Ignore the first blue-blazed trail and stay on the A.T. to Lover's Leap Ridge, which has several lookouts. The rock outcropping, where the sharp edge of the ridge crest drops 500 ft. to the river, gave this spot its name. A Cherokee Indian legend recounts the tale of a maiden who threw herself from the cliffs after learning her lover had been killed by a jealous suitor. Beyond Lover's Leap at 1.3 miles, signs for the Silvermine

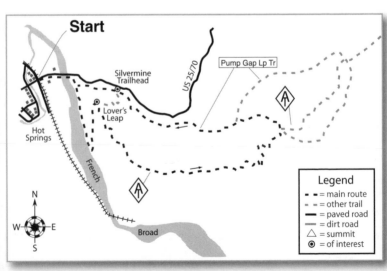

The warming springs of Hot Springs are still in operation, so be sure to plan time for a soak after your hike.

Trail and Lover's Leap Trail point left as alternatives to the A.T. (For a shorter loop, turn left on the Lover's Leap Trail; it's only 1.6 miles to the Silvermine Trailhead.)

Continuing on the A.T., at 1.5 miles take a right at the blue blazes for a short while for another outstanding lookout on a rock outcropping. So far the river has been in sight continuously, but now the trail is above the river and heads inland. Soon you'll reach a flat area on the right with an illegal campfire ring and limited views at 1.9 miles (2,190 ft. elev.).

The trail is a classic ridge walk with steep banks on both sides through maple, sassafras, oak, and white pine. It bobs up and down with chickadees flitting about and winter mountain vistas in view at all times.

Keep your eyes peeled on the right for two islands at a wide spot on the river at about 2.1 miles. The trail contours down the hillside toward Pump Gap, and the river disappears from sight. You can hear an occasional freight train passing through Hot Springs.

At 3.2 miles (2,130 ft. elev.), the Pump Gap Loop Trail intersects the A.T. (The A.T. continues up and will cross the Pump Gap Loop Trail again farther north.) There are several good sitting logs for a snack break.

Bear left on the wide and steep Pump Gap Loop Trail which will take you all the way down to Hot Springs. On each side, piles of branches lie in a jumble. This area was badly hit by a hurricane and not cleared for a long time. If you can walk this trail, thank a trail maintainer. You'll cross Silvermine Creek— you'll crisscross it several times on your way down—and reach the other section of the Pump Gap Loop Trail at 3.6 miles.

If you made a sharp right here and went up, you would eventually reach the A.T. north of where you left it. Instead, go down to the left and straight into the hollow—that's the stick part of the lollipop of Pump Gap Loop. This trail is not very busy because most people who go to Lover's Leap return the same way or do the short Lover's Leap Loop. As the trail flattens out, a small concrete building on the left has a sign "Explosives Dangerous" painted on it. Railroad ties, a diesel fuel tank, concrete support beams, and a second building were left here after US 25 was modernized. You'll reach a barrier at the Silvermine Trailhead, the end of Pump Gap Loop Trail. The area has a restroom (closed in winter), picnic area, and group campground with a sign that reads, "Pets must be leashed."

From here, walk on a short street with trailers, old cars, and small houses to complete the circle at 5.1 miles, and return to US 25 to end the hike.

Lover's Leap outcrop.

Max Patch

On this hike, you walk to Max Patch first and then get on the Appalachian Trail, heading north to Lemon Gap and back. Since most people make Max Patch their destination, you won't encounter many day hikers after you leave the top of the bald. In the spring, fields of trillium, wild geranium, and other flowers take over. Put a small wildflower book in your pack to help you identify all the species you'll find.

Getting to the trailhead:
Take I-40 to exit 7 (Harmon Den). Turn right at the exit and follow Cold Spring Creek Rd. for 6.7 miles. Stay left and on the main gravel road. Turn left on SR 1182 and drive for less than 2 miles to the Max Patch parking area.

Type of hike: Out and back

Distance: 10.5 miles

Total ascent: 2,640 ft.

Highlights: 360-degree views, spring flowers, creek, new shelter

USGS map: Lemon Gap

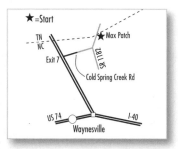

Trail map: Appalachian Trail Guide to Tennessee-North Carolina

Land managed by: Pisgah National Forest, Appalachian District

The Hike
An access trail leads from the parking area to the A.T. At 0.5 mile, take the A.T. south to the top of Max Patch. Enjoy the top-of-the-world feeling but hold on to your hat, because Max Patch is always windy.

Retrace your steps and head A.T. north. In mid-spring, purple and yellow violets, spring beauty, and trout lily line the trail as you leave the meadow. Take the right fork and follow the A.T.'s rectangular white blazes. This well-maintained section of trail descends gently but steadily.

Go around a fenced-in area as the trail makes a left and then right. East of the enclosure, the trail climbs. At 1.5 miles, make a left turn toward Lemon Gap and go through a short rhododendron tunnel to come out on a windy bald. On your right is the Buckeye Ridge trail for horses. Stay left on the A.T.

Go through an opening in the barbed wire fence at 1.8 miles, cross an old road and then follow the trail on the left through a gate. At about 2.0 miles, you'll reach trillium land—fields and fields of wakerobin (purple), sweet, and white trilliums, which bloom in May. After crossing the creek, pass a patch of trout lilies as you enter a rhododendron tunnel.

At 2.9 miles, turn right at the Roaring Fork Shelter. The shelter, dedicated in 2005, replaces the old Roaring Fork Shelter, which had been located too close to a road at Lemon Gap and abused by nonhikers. The new one, built by volunteers from the Carolina Mountain Club, is dubbed the "McDonald Hilton," after its designer, Howard McDonald, a retired engineer and leader for the shelter construction crew. McDonald is currently the head of the A.T. trail maintainers for the CMC. The shelter, which sleeps eight on its main deck, has the latest

in shelter conveniences, from a cooking shelf outside the shelter to a moldering privy. (A moldering privy uses the active biological soil layer, the first six inches, to break down waste.) As McDonald explains, "Spread a little duff as a starter, like sourdough starter. Then throw a handful of leaves after each use to keep the material loose. That's very important to the process." The shelter meets the requirements of the Americans with Disabilities Act, as does the access trail and the trail to the privy.

Cross the stream and make a sharp right to go uphill. At 3.1 miles, look to your right for a double waterfall. At the switchback at 3.3 miles, the rushing stream forms a small cascade. Cross a side creek on a two-log bridge. At about 4.0 miles, the trail is open, with trillium fields and large boulders covered with rock tripe.

You'll pass a sign reading "Lemon Gap 0.4" and a side trail on the right to the site of the old shelter, which has been removed. On the left, a short path leads to logs and a flat area, good for a picnic. The turn-around point is the road at Lemon Gap with parking – you've walked 5.5 miles to this point.

On the return, the trail always looks different. The sun is at a different angle for pictures, and it's like a different hike altogether. As you come up around the fenced-in area to end the hike, look up for a great view of Max Patch.

Extra: If you still have some energy and time, continue past the access trail and back to Max Patch for a really spectacular finish.

About Max Patch

At 4,630 ft. elev., Max Patch is an open, grassy summit with glorious views. Tourists come to exercise their dogs, fly kites, picnic, and just hang out. One writer suggested it is the perfect place to propose. Appalachian Trail hikers consider Max Patch one of the highlights of their journey and a spot they will remember long after they've forgotten the details of most of their trek.

Max Patch was a grazing area from the 1800s. The bald was also once used as a landing strip for small planes. Until 1982, Max Patch was privately owned and in danger of becoming a ski development. The U.S. Forest Service bought the 392 acres comprising Max Patch, and the Appalachian Trail was relocated to go over the top in 1984. If the area was left alone, trees would fill the field and cut out the views. The Forest Service currently manages the bald by mowing and controlled burning.

Clingmans Dome

This ridge hike starts by walking up to the Clingmans Dome tower and then follows the A.T. north to Newfound Gap on US 441. The trail straddles the Tennessee/North Carolina border. Both ends of the hike attract many tourists, but you will meet few people on the trail itself. Hiking at 5,000 ft. to over 6,600 ft. means walking in the clouds (i.e., in wet and cool weather) much of the time, even when the sun is shining below. The terrain feels more mysterious and even greener than if it were sunny. In April, you will meet A.T. thru-hikers.

Getting to the trailhead:
This hike starts at Clingmans Dome and ends at Newfound Gap. Place a car at Newfound Gap first. To get there, take US 441 through the Great Smoky Mountains National Park (GSMNP), to Newfound Gap on the state line. Drive the second car to the start at Clingmans Dome. To do that, drive 7 miles to the end of Clingmans Dome Rd. If you have just one vehicle, park at the end of Clingmans Dome

Rd. and walk to the Fork Ridge trail and back for a 7.6-mile hike. Clingmans Dome Rd. is closed from December 1 to April 1 and whenever weather conditions dictate.

Type of hike: Shuttle

Distance: 8.2 miles

Total ascent/descent: 1,070 ft./2,450 ft.

Highlights: Views from Clingmans Dome tower, ridge walk, highest point in Tennessee, two SB6K mountains

USGS map: Clingmans Dome

Trail map: Great Smoky Mountains National Park, National Geographic Trails Illustrated #229

Land managed by: Great Smoky Mountains National Park

The Hike
The hike starts on pavement and first climbs to the top of the corkscrew-shaped Clingmans Dome tower. In the morning you'll find few tourists here. At the top, enjoy the panoramic views in all directions. Notice the dead Fraser fir trees, victims of the balsam wooly adelgid, a non-native invasive insect that infests and kills stands of Fraser fir in the spruce-fir zone. Descend fom the tower and from its base, make a right on a short side trail and another right on the A.T. going north.

You'll descend steeply on rocky steps where, in April, spring beauties blanket the trail. As you go farther down, Fraser firs dominate the trail in the 5,000- to 6,000-ft. zone.

At 0.5 mile, there is a limited view through the trees on the left. Tree roots hug boulders as the trail stays above 6,000 ft. The trail is rocky with intermittent steps; blackberry cane and trout lilies grow alongside. At 1.1 miles, it makes a sharp right and continues downhill. There is another sharp right at 1.5 miles on stone steps. The trail parallels the road for a short while but then goes below the road.

At this point the trail is more open, with banks of spring beauties and blackberry cane. In 2.0 miles, the trail has descended almost 1,000 ft. in elevation. You'll reach a saddle and start the ascent to Mt. Collins. Passing a big hunk of marble on the right as you climb up, note the huge uprooted trees. You are back under the cover of the spruce and fir forest.

The trail summits Mt. Love, a local top of Mt. Collins, at 2.4 miles and continues to a view in a flat area to the right.

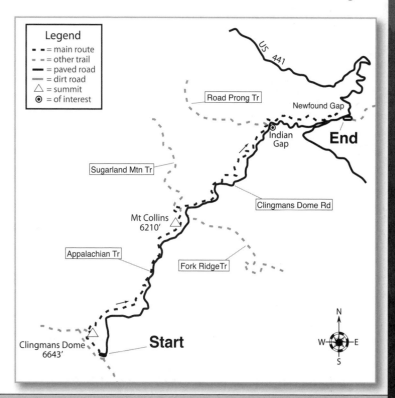

About Clingmans Dome

At 6,643 ft., Clingmans Dome has the distinction of being the highest point in Tennessee. It is also the starting point of the Mountains-to-Sea Trail as it winds its way for over 900 miles through North Carolina. Clingmans Dome honors Thomas Lanier Clingman, a Civil War politician and officer in the Confederate Army who extolled the virtues of the North Carolina mountains. At a time when New Hampshire's Mt. Washington (6,288 ft.) was thought to be the tallest mountain in the east, he promoted the higher peaks in the Southern Appalachians.

Clingmans Dome Rd. was part of an aborted plan in the 1930s to build a Skyline Drive through the western part of the Smokies, similar to the road which traverses Virginia's Shenandoah National Park today.

The A.T. gently slopes downhill to the junction with the Fork Ridge Trail at 3.6 miles. Here the Mountains-to-Sea Trail leaves the A.T. and continues on the Fork Ridge Trail, crossing Clingmans Dome Rd. This is the turn-around point for hikers with just one vehicle.

The A.T. continues straight ahead. Root balls as big as cabins on enormous downed trees lie perpendicular to the ground. The trail is muddy but less rocky, banked by logs on both sides. This green spruce forest with moss-covered rocks, when wet, feels like Hobbit land—straight out of *The Lord of the Rings*. Cross sections of stumps have been

At 2.9 miles, (although you may not realize it) you'll reach the summit of Mt. Collins at 6,210 ft., an SB6K mountain in the trees, and then come down to a tunnel of fir and spruce on a rocky trail. At 3.3 miles, you'll pass the junction with the Sugarland Mountain Trail which leads to the Mt. Collins Shelter.

Thousands of people each year make the half-mile trek to see the view from Clingmans Dome.

Giant trees thrive in the cloud forest along the high ridges of the Smokies.

Beautiful spruces line the trail as it climbs gently back up from the gap. At 6.4 miles, you'll climb over a fence installed in 1984 to protect the beech forest from feral hogs.

At 6.7 miles, the trail starts a steady downhill to Newfound Gap at 5,048 ft. elev. The last 1.0 mile, on a well-maintained trail through spruce trees, is used by visitors who arrive at the Gap by car and want to stretch their legs.

As you approach the end, notice the first rhododendron on the trail. The stone wall on your right is Clingmans Dome Rd. Carefully cross US 441 to the parking lot to finish the hike.

placed in the wetter spots to keep hikers from having to wade through mud. The trail goes up a little here. It's up and down as you get closer to Newfound Gap in this green wonderland.

At 6.0 miles, the trail comes down to Indian Gap Rd. at Indian Gap and its intersection with Road Prong Trail. Indians, explorers, and Confederate soldiers came through here. In 1830, it was widened as a toll road. At that time, Indian Gap was thought to be the lowest point across the Smokies. In the 1850s, a shorter pass through the Smokies was found. It was named Newfound Gap.

Appendices

A: Hike Details

Hike	Chapter	Miles	Ascent
Camp Alice Loop	Mount Mitchell	4.5	1,170'
Mount Mitchell	Mount Mitchell	11.4	1,590'
Green Knob Tower	Mount Mitchell	5.7	2,310'
Pot Cove Loop	Black Mountain	6.1	1,200'
Lookout Rock	Black Mountain	4.7	1,040'
Graybeard Mtn	Black Mountain	8.0	2,180'
High Windy	Black Mountain	6.0	1,600'
Craggy Gardens	Mtns-to-Sea Tr	6.0	1,480'
Lane Pinnacle	Mtns-to-Sea Tr	10.0	2,900'
Folk Art Center	Mtns-to-Sea Tr	4.9	890'
Dupont Five Falls	Dupont/Flat Rock	11.2	1,240'
Bridal Veil Falls	Dupont/Flat Rock	6.3	900'
Stone Mtn Loop	Dupont/Flat Rock	9.0	1,620'
Carl Sandburg Home	Dupont/Flat Rock	5.4	1,000'
Green River GL	Dupont/Flat Rock	9.4	1,650'
Jones Gap Loop	Upstate SC	10.2	2,250'
Raven Cliff Falls Loop	Upstate SC	8.4	1,950'
Hospital Rock	Upstate SC	6.5	2,390'
Rim of the Gap	Upstate SC	9.9	2,540'
Paris Mountain SP	Upstate SC	6.6	1,380'
Table Rock	Upstate SC	11.2	3,900'
Sassafras Mtn	Upstate SC	9.0	2,380'
Ellicott Rock	Upstate SC	8.7	960'
US 276—Short Hikes	Pisgah—East	----	----
Mount Pisgah	Pisgah—East	5.0	1,190'
Hardtimes Loop	Pisgah—East	6.0	600'
Stradley Mountain	Pisgah—East	8.3	940'
Avery Creek Loop	Pisgah—East	9.5	1,680'
Coontree/Buckwheat	Pisgah—East	8.4	2,130'
Looking Glass Rock	Pisgah—West	6.2	1,530'

Highlights	Type	Page
Highest mountain, SB6K, history	Loop	28
Views, highest mountain, SB6K, history	Shuttle	32
Outstanding views, tower, solitude	O & B	37
Views, history, town and college	Loop	48
Ridge views, solitude, history	Loop	51
Views, history, shelter	Loop	54
Views, chimney	Loop	59
Ridge Views, heath balds, wildflowers	Shuttle	69
Mountain views, historical house remains	O & B	74
Folk Art Center, views	O & B	77
Waterfalls, covered bridge, cemetery	Loop	88
Waterfall, lakes, abandoned homes	Loop	93
Views, recent history	Loop	97
Mountain ridges, house, grounds, and goats	Loop	102
River, boulders	Loop	105
Waterfall, rocky cliffs, river walk	Lollipop	115
Waterfall, cable crossing, suspension bridge	Lollipop	118
Waterfall, rock formations	Shuttle	122
Rocky cliffs, waterfalls, ridge views	Loop	127
Lake, mountain ridges, stream	Fig. 8	131
Views, lakes, waterfall	Lollipop	135
Highest mountain in SC, boulders, winter views	O & B	139
History-Chattooga River	O & B	142
Waterfalls, history	O & B	153
Views, historical house remains	O & B	158
Views of ridges and the Biltmore Estate, river	Loop	163
Gentle trails, experimental forest	Loop	166
Views, creeks, Twin Falls	Loop	170
Ridgeline views, rock formations	Lollipop	174
Views, pluton	O & B	184

Hike	Chapter	Miles	Ascent
Cat Gap Loop	Pisgah—West	8.3	1,720'
Graveyard Fields	Pisgah—West	7.9	1,470'
Cold Mountain	Pisgah—West	9.8	3,500'
Shining Rock	Pisgah—West	10.7	2,200'
Sam Knob Loop	Pisgah—West	10.6	1,710'
Boogerman Trail	GSMNP	7.5	1,150'
Little Cataloochee	GSMNP	6.6	1,490'
Mount Sterling	GSMNP	13.3	3,260'
Hemphill Bald	GSMNP	9.6	1,910'
Smokemont Loop	GSMNP	6.2	1,400'
Deep Creek Loop	GSMNP	13.4	1,880'
Road to Nowhere	GSMNP	9.4	1,370'
Shuckstack-Lakeshore	GSMNP	11.7	3,010'
Horsepasture River	Nantahala NF	8.9	2,110'
Panthertown Loop	Nantahala NF	11.2	1,700'
Tsali Loop	Nantahala NF	12.3	1,140'
Joyce Kilmer	Nantahala NF	2.0	400'
Naked Ground	Nantahala NF	10.5	3,500'
Haoe Lead	Nantahala NF	10.2	2,640'
Wesser Bald	Nantahala NF	10.8	2,760'
Appletree Loop	Nantahala NF	12.2	2,170'
Grassy Ridge	Appalachian Trail	5.0	1,130'
Roan High Knob	Appalachian Trail	4.6	1,110'
Sams Gap	Appalachian Trail	8.2	1,700'
Lover's Leap	Appalachian Trail	5.4	1,050'
Max Patch	Appalachian Trail	10.5	2,640'
Clingmans Dome	Appalachian Trail	8.2	1,070'

Highlights	Type	Page
Views of Cedar Rock, waterfalls, shelter	Loop	188
Waterfalls, high-altitude meadow	Loop	192
Views, literary reference, SB6K	O & B	197
views, three SB6Ks	Loop	202
views, waterfall, creeks, SB6K	Loop	208
Streams, old-growth trees, artifacts	Lollipop	223
Artifacts, chapel, cabins, cemetery	Shuttle	227
Views, fire tower, cemetery, history	O & B	231
Views, flowers, bald	O & B	235
Stream, cemetery, church	Loop	238
Creeks, waterfalls, historic millstone	Loop	242
Tunnel, history, current events, Forney Creek	Fig. 8	247
Fontana Lake, history, current events, old cars	Loop	250
Waterfalls, waterfalls, waterfalls	O & B	260
Views of plutons, waterfalls	Loop	266
Views of ridges and Fontana Lake, gentle trails	Loop	271
Old-growth forest, spring wildflowers	Loop	275
Old-growth trees, stream, ridge views	Loop	277
Stream, ridge views, solitude	Lollipop	281
360-degree views, tower, cascades, flowers	Shuttle	285
Woodland walks, solitude, views	Loop	289
Heath bald, rare plants, SB6K	O & B	298
Shelter, hotel site, gardens, two SB6Ks	O & B	302
Shelter, waterfall, solitude	Shuttle	306
Ridge views, French Broad, town of Hot Springs	Lollipop	310
Views, spring flowers, creek, shelter	O & B	315
Views, ridge walk TN highest point, two SB6Ks	Shuttle	318

B: Resources

National Parks

- **Great Smoky Mountains National Park**
  107 Park Headquarters Rd.
  Gatlinburg, TN 37738
  (865) 436-1200
  (865) 436-1231 for backcountry information and permits
  www.nps.gov/grsm

- **Blue Ridge Parkway**
  199 Hemphill Knob Rd.
  Asheville, NC 28803
  (828) 298-0398
  www.nps.gov/blri

- **Carl Sandburg Home National Historic Site**
  81 Carl Sandburg Ln.
  Flat Rock, NC 28731
  (828) 693-4178
  www.nps.gov/carl

U.S. Forest Service Ranger Stations

- **Nantahala National Forest – Cheoah District**
  Route 1, Box 16A
  Robbinsville, NC 28771
  (828) 479-6431
  www.cs.unca.edu/ nfsnc/index.htm

- **Nantahala National Forest – Highlands District**
  2010 Flat Mountain Rd.
  Highlands, NC 28741
  (828) 526-3765
  www.cs.unca.edu/ nfsnc/index.htm

- **Nantahala National Forest – Wayah District**
  90 Sloan Rd.
  Franklin, NC 28734
  (828) 524-6441
  www.cs.unca.edu/ nfsnc/index.htm

- **Pisgah National Forest – Appalachian District/Hot Springs Station**
  P.O. Box 128
  Hot Springs, NC 28743
  (828) 622-3202
  www.cs.unca.edu/nfsnc

- **Pisgah National Forest – Appalachian District/Toecane Station**
  P.O. Box 128
  Burnsville, NC 28741
  (828) 682-6146
  www.cs.unca.edu/nfsnc

- **Pisgah National Forest – Pisgah District**
  1001 Pisgah Hwy.
  Pisgah Forest, NC 28768
  (828) 877-3265
  www.cs.unca.edu/nfsnc

- **Sumter National Forest – Andrew Pickens District**
  112 Andrew Pickens Cir.
  Mountain Rest, SC 29664
  (864) 638-9568
  www.fs.fed.us/r8/fms/ forest/about/ap.shtml

North Carolina State Forests and Parks

- **Dupont State Forest**
  P.O. Box 300
  Cedar Mountain, NC 28718
  (828) 877-6527
  www.dupontforest.com

- **Mount Mitchell State Park**
  2388 State Hwy. 128
  Burnsville, NC 28714
  (828) 675-4611
  www.ils.unc.edu/
  parkproject/visit/
  momi/home.html

- **North Carolina Arboretum**
  100 Frederick Law
  Olmstead Way
  Asheville, NC 28806
  (828) 665-2492
  www.ncarboreturm.org

- **N.C. Wildlife Resources Commission**
  NCSU Centennial Campus
  1751 Varsity Dr.
  Raleigh, NC 27606
  (919) 707-0050
  www.ncwildlife.org

South Carolina State Parks and Forests

- **Mountain Bridge Wilderness Area**
  8155 Greer Hwy.
  Cleveland, SC 29635
  (864) 836-6115
  www.southcarolinaparks.
  com

- **Paris Mountain State Park**
  2401 State Park Rd.
  Greenville, SC 29609
  (864) 244-5565
  www.southcarolinaparks.
  com

- **Table Rock State Park**
  158 E Ellison Ln.
  Pickens, SC 29671
  (864) 878-9813
  www.southcarolinaparks.
  com

- **South Carolina Department of Natural Resources**
  P.O Box 167
  Columbia, SC 29202
  (803) 734-9100
  www.dnr.sc.gov

C: Books & Movies

BOOKS

Adkins, Leonard M. *Walking the Blue Ridge: A Guide to the Trails of the Blue Ridge Parkway (Third edition).* The University of North Carolina Press, 2003. Adkins documents all the trails which go off from the Blue Ridge Parkway.

- Related hikes:
  Mountains-to-Sea Trail

Brown, Margaret Lynn. *The Wild East: A Biography of the Great Smoky Mountains.* University Press of Florida, 2000. A history of the Smokies, concentrating on the natural history.

- Related hikes:
  Great Smoky Mountains National Park

Brill, David. *As Far As the Eye Can See: Reflections of an Appalachian Trail Hiker (3rd ed.).* Appalachian Trail Conference, 2004. One of the more popular accounts of an A.T. thru-hike. Brill hiked the trail in 1979.

- Related hikes:
  Appalachian Trail

Bryson, Bill. *A Walk in the Woods.* Broadway; Reprint edition, 1999. Many books have been written by thru-hikers about their experiences on the Appalachian Trail. None are as famous or as funny as *this one*. It's worth noting that Bryson did not walk the whole trail and annoyed many who did; nevertheless, the book became a worldwide best-seller.

- Related hikes:
  Appalachian Trail

Crowe, Thomas Rain. *Zoro's Field: My Life in the Appalachian Woods.* University of Georgia Press, 2005. In the late 1970s, Crow lived on a patch of land he rented in the Green River area, where he grew vegetables, raised bees, and wrote about his experiences.

- Related hikes:
  Carl Sandburg Home, Green River Game Lands

de Hart, Allen. *Hiking North Carolina's Mountains-to-Sea Trail.* The University of North Carolina Press, 2000. The only complete trail guide to the MST, by one of the first hikers to complete the trail.

- Related hikes:
  Mountains-to-Sea Trail

Deeds, Jean. *There are Mountains to Climb.* Silverwood Press, 1996. A well-written account by a middle-aged woman who thru-hiked the A.T.

- Related hikes:
  Appalachian Trail

Dickey, James. *Deliverance.* Delta; Reprint edition, 1994. A classic story of four

Atlanta men who spend a weekend canoeing a fictional souteastern whitewater river. First published in 1970, the book depicts (and its title word has become shorthand for) an unflattering stereotype of Southern Appalachian mountaineers.

- Related hike:
  Ellicott Rock

Dykeman, Wilma. *The French Broad.* Wakestone Books, 1992. The author explores the people and towns along the river called the French Broad. Written in the 1950s and steeped in oral history, this classic book is part of the Rivers of America Series.

- Related hike:
  Lover's Leap

Frazier, Charles. *Cold Mountain.* Atlantic Monthly Press, 1997. *Cold Mountain* is the story of two parallel journeys: a Confederate soldier's physical trek across North Carolina and the internal odyssey of the woman he loves as she gains an understanding of herself.

- Related hike :
  Cold Mountain

Hays, Tommy. *The Pleasure was Mine.* St. Martin's Press, 2005. A sweet family story about a man whose wife of 50 years has Alzheimer's disease. It is set in Greenville, SC, with great scenes in Jones Gap State Park.

- Related hikes:
  Mountain Bridge
  Wilderness Area

Kephart, Horace. *Our Southern Highlanders.* University of Tennessee Press, 1984. This book, first published in 1913, is historical, sociological, and autobiographical. It concentrates on the Appalachian people and the author's interaction with them. In it, Kephart recounts stories of the land and people who lived in what is now the Great Smoky Mountains National Park.

- Related hike:
  Deep Creek Loop

Maxwell, Elizabeth. *A Flowing Stream: An Informal History of Montreat.* WorldComm, 1997. Growing up, Maxwell spent summers at Montreat, and as an adult, she taught at Montreat College for 35 years. The book is illustrated with many historical pictures.

- Related hikes:
  Montreat

Morgan, Robert. *Gap Creek.* Algonquin, 1999. The story follows Julie Harmon, who marries young and sets up housekeeping at Gap Creek at the end of the 19th century while her husband works in a cotton mill in Lyman, SC, between Greenville and Spartanburg. The novel was chosen as an Oprah Winfrey

C: Books & Movies (cont.)

book club selection, making it an instant national bestseller.

- Related hikes:
  Mountain Bridge Wilderness Area

Painter, Jacqueline Burgin. *The German Invasion of Western North Carolina* (2nd ed.). Overmountain Press, 1997. The book tells the history of Hot Springs circa WWI, with great pictures of the old hotels and the German prisoners of war.

- Related hike:
  Lover's Leap

Pierce, Daniel S. *The Great Smokies: From Natural Habitat to National Park.* University of Tennessee Press, 2000. This is the book to start with if you want to learn about the history of the Smokies. The book discusses the human and political history of the Great Smoky Mountains National Park.

- Related hikes:
  Great Smoky Mountains National Park

Rash, Ron. *One Foot in Eden.* Picador, 2002. This gripping novel about a murder, set in upstate South Carolina, is told from several points of view.

- Related hikes:
  Sassafras Mountain, Horsepasture River

Rash, Ron. *Saints at the River.* Picador, 2004. The story of what happens when a young girl drowns in the wild and scenic Chattooga River, and her parents want to dam up the river to retrieve her body.

- Related hike:
  Ellicott Rock Wilderness

Sandburg, Helga. *A Great and Glorious Romance: The Story of Carl Sandburg and Lilian Steichen.* Eastern National Park and Monument Association, 2002. Carl Sandburg's youngest daughter writes about her parents' marriage.

- Related hike:
  Carl Sandburg Home

Schenck, Carl Alwin. *Cradle of Forestry in America: The Biltmore Forest School, 1898-1913.* Forest History Society, 1983. An engaging memoir of Schenck's days working for George Vanderbilt. It was first published in 1955, years after Schenck left the Southern Appalachians.

- Related hikes:
  Pisgah National Forest, Pisgah Ranger District

Silver, Timothy. *Mount Mitchell & the Black Mountains: An Environmental History of the Highest Peaks in Eastern America.* University of North Carolina Press, 2003. Silver's book is a fascinating natural and human history of the area.

The author intersperses his own experiences throughout this exploration of the Blacks.

- Related hikes:
  Mt. Mitchell

Weber, Walt. *Trail Profiles: The Mountains-to-Sea Trail.* The Carolina Mountain Club, 1999. A trail profile of the MST, traditionally maintained by the Carolina Mountain Club, with a history of the area.

- Related hikes:
  Mountains-to-Sea Trail

Wright, Perrin. *Geographic Place Names In and Around Montreat, N.C.* Self-published, 2003. A history of the derivation of the place names in the Black Mountains.

- Related hikes:
  Montreat

MOVIES

28 Days (2000) with Sandra Bullock. The movie was shot on the grounds and in the buildings of the Blue Ridge Assembly. In the film, the conference center becomes a rehab center.

- Related hikes:
  High Windy – YMCA
  Blue Ridge Assembly

All the Real Girls (2003) with Paul Schneider. Filmed in Marshall, close to Hot Springs, this subtle movie gives you a good feel for the people in the area. The main character, Paul, known for having sexual relations with every girl in town, falls in love with his best friend's younger sister, who is a virgin. Paul must try to prove to everyone that this time he is really in love.

- Related hike:
  Lover's Leap

The Clearing (2004) with Robert Redford and Helen Mirren. The movie, filmed in Pisgah National Forest, tells of the kidnapping of a high-powered executive, as his wife works frantically with the FBI to have him released.

- Related hikes:
  Pisgah National Forest,
  Pisgah Ranger District

Cold Mountain (2003) with Nicole Kidman. Based on Charles Frazier's 1997 novel of the same name. However, the mountain scenes in the film were shot not in North Carolina, but in Romania.

- Related hike:
  Cold Mountain

Deliverance (1972) with Jon Voight and Burt Reynolds. This movie is based on James Dickey's novel about four men on the Chattooga River who are attacked by locals.

- Related hike:
  Ellicott Rock Wilderness

The Fugitive (1993) with Harrison Ford and Tommy Lee Jones. A surgeon is sent to prison, wrongly accused of murdering his wife. When he escapes from a prison bus after a train wreck, he is pursued by a U.S. Marshall, whom he eludes by jumping down Cheoah Dam in the Nantahala National Forest. The train scenes were filmed in Dillsboro, NC. If you take a ride on the Great Smoky Mountains Railroad, you can still see the wreck site from the making of the film, including the prison bus and the shell of the engine that crashed into the bus.

- Related hikes:
  Joyce Kilmer-Slickrock Wilderness Area

The Last of the Mohicans (1992) with Daniel Day-Lewis and Madeleine Stowe. The movie was partly filmed in Dupont State Forest with scenes at Triple Falls, High Falls, and Bridal Veil Falls. Based on the classic James Fenimore Cooper novel, the story revolves around the English and French who are battling for control of the North American colonies in the 18th century. War strategy dominates the film, but a love story develops between the daughter of an English officer and a white man raised as a Mohican. *The Last of the Mohicans* took place in upper New York state, but as viewers will see, authenticity did not seem to matter in the film. As a movie reviewer said, "How many people, even after seeing this movie, could correctly report that the French and Indian Wars were not between the French and the Indians?" Nonetheless, the Southern Appalachian scenery is breathtaking.

- Related hikes:
  Five Falls Loop and Bridal Veil Falls at Dupont

Nell (1994) with Jodie Foster. Nell grew up in a sheltered and isolated world and speaks her own private language. The movie was filmed at Fontana Lake and in Robbinsville.

- Related hikes:
  Shuckstack-Lakeshore, Joyce Kilmer-Slickrock Wilderness Area

Songcatcher (2001) with Janet McTeer and Aiden Quinn. A brilliant musicologist discovers a collection of ballads in the Southern Appalachian mountains, which she tries to record.

- Related hike:
  Hemphill Bald

D: Glossary of Hiking Terms

Bagging a peak – Reaching the summit of a mountain. The expression is used most often with a hiking challenge, such as the South Beyond 6000 (SB6K).

Bald – A bare mountain top, common in the Southern Appalachians. If left to nature, most balds will fill in with shrubs and eventually become covered with trees.

Basin – The entire tract of land drained by a river.

Bear bag – A bag used to store food by hanging on bear cables or poles.

Bear cables or bear poles A contraption set up in some backcountry campsites for campers to hang their food out of the reach of bears. Many campsites in the Great Smoky Mountains National Park have bear cables.

Bench – A flat, stable surface on a slope, either occurring naturally or cut for a trail.

Benchmark – A surveyor's mark affixed to a stationary object of previously determined position and elevation (often a flat rock) and used as a survey reference point.

Blaze – A paint mark on a tree, rock, or post, used to show the route of the trail

Blowdown – Trees that have been toppled by wind, creating an obstruction on the trail. If not cleared quickly, hikers tend to go off the trail and around the blowdown.

Bushwhack – To make your way through the woods without an official trail.

Cairn – A pile of rocks serving as a trail marker.

Contour – (v.) To follow an imaginary contour line traversing a mountainside. "You'll descend into a pine forest before emerging to contour around the hill."

Contour line – A line on a topo map which connects points of equal elevation.

Cove – A narrow gap or sheltered area between hills.

Crag – A steep, rugged mass of rock projecting upward or outward.

Divide – A ridge of land separating two valleys.

Duff – Humus, dirt, soil.

False summit – See *local top*.

Ford – A shallow place in a stream where it is usually easiest to cross.

Gaiters – A light-weight covering of the foot and leg from instep to the ankle or knee. Gaiters are meant to keep your feet dry and free of trail debris.

Gap – An opening through mountains; a pass.

Gorge – A small canyon with steep, rocky walls. In the Southern Appalachians, a stream usually runs through bottom of the gorge.

Gorp – Any mixture of nuts, dried fruit, and sweets,

also referred to as trail mix. Originally, it stood for Good Old Raisins and Peanuts.

GPS – Global Positioning System. A system that uses orbiting satellites to pinpoint your location on the globe. It allows you to record your route by dropping "electronic bread crumbs." You can then download your route on your computer and with the proper software, superimpose it on a topo map. A GPS is nice to have, but does not take the place of a map and compass.

Grade – The degree of slope of the trail. The percent grade is the relationship between horizontal distance and vertical gain.

Herd path – An unofficial trail made by the passage of people. Sometimes referred to as a manway.

High points – Shorthand for a challenge to reach all the high points in each state. Three high points are included in this book: Mt. Mitchell in North Carolina, Clingmans Dome in Tennessee, and Sassafras Mountain in South Carolina. Not all the high points require a lot of hiking. See www.highpointers.org.

Hiking challenge – An organized way of recognizing those who have hiked a specific group of trails or mountains. For example, the Appalachian Trail, the South Beyond 6000 (SB6K), or all the hikes in this book.

Lead – A long ridge or ridge spur that leads to higher ground.

Local top – You can't see anything higher, so you think you're on top of the mountain. Then, as you go down and turn the corner—surprise, surprise—there's the real top. Sometimes called false summit.

Minor summit – One of the peaks of a mountain but not the highest peak.

Monadnock – A mountain or rocky mass that has resisted erosion and stands isolated in an essentially level area, the most famous being Uluru (Ayers Rock) in Australia. Table Rock in upstate South Carolina is a monadnock.

Peak bagger – A hiker who is intent on getting to the top of the mountain, usually because s/he is doing a hiking challenge.

Pit stop – See *trail break*

Pluton – A body of igneous rock formed beneath the surface of the earth by consolidation of molten rock. Looking Glass Rock is a famous pluton in the Carolina mountains.

Quads – Topographic maps. Each map covers a four-sided area (quadrangle or quad) of 7.5 minutes of latitude and 7.5 minutes of longitude. See also *Topo map*.

Relo – Short for relocation of a trail.

Rhodo or rhodi - Short for rhododendron.

Ridge – A long narrow chain of hills or mountains. Also called a ridgeline.

Rock hop – To cross a stream by stepping from rock to rock to avoid getting your feet wet. Sometimes it is actually safer to just get wet instead of trying to balance on rocks.

SB6K – South Beyond 6000. A challenge program in which hikers climb by approved routes the 40 peaks over 6,000 ft. elev. in western North Carolina and eastern Tennessee. See *Appendix E* for more on SB6K.

Scout a hike – To do a hike on your own with an eye to bringing others along next time—a bit like a dress rehearsal. Most hiking clubs require that their leaders scout a hike before they lead it.

Scree – A steep mass of loose rock on the slope of the mountain.

Section hiker – A hiker who completes a trail, such as the Appalachian Trail, in a series of separate hikes.

Shoal – A shallow place in a body of water, a sandbar.

Slab – (v.) To go across the face of a hill in a mostly horizontal plane. "The trail slabs the mountainside shortly after it crosses the creek."

Summit – (v.) To reach the top of a peak. Most commonly used as a mountaineering term. "He summited Mt. Pisgah early in his life."

Sweep – On a group hike, a person designated to hike at the back of the group. All the hikers stay between the leader in front and the "sweep" in the back. Sometimes called "tail ender" or "tail-end Charlie."

Switchback – The zigzag course on a steep incline which allows a trail to maintain a reasonable grade of ascent. Switchbacks make the trail longer than if it went straight up the mountain, but they also make the hike less strenuous.

Thru-hiker – A hiker who completes the entire length of a trail, such as the Appalachian Trail, in one continuous hike.

Topo map – Short for topographic map. The best known USGS (U.S. Geological Survey) maps are the 1:24,000–scale topographic maps, also known as 7.5-minute quadrangles. This is the only uniform map series that covers the entire area of the United States in detail. Topo maps use contour lines to portray the shape and elevation of the land and render the three-dimensional ups and downs of the terrain on a two-dimensional surface. Topo maps are often referred to as quads.

Trail break – In some hiking clubs, a euphemism for going to the toilet in the woods. Also called a pit stop or separation.

Trailhead – The point where the hike begins.

Wand – A signed metal rod stuck in the ground, designating the trail and sometimes a turn in the trail.

Waterbar – Usually a rock or log barrier embedded at an angle in the trail to create proper drainage. Water flowing down the trail is diverted by the barrier and prevents erosion of the trail.

Watershed – Watersheds are the land areas that catch rain or snow and drain to specific rivers, lakes, or ground water sources.

Winter views – Views only available in winter, when the trees have shed their leaves.

E: South Beyond 6000

The South Beyond 6000 Hiking Challenge

Some people collect stamps or dolls, but hikers collect peaks and trails. In the Southern Appalachians, the best-known hiking challenge is the South Beyond 6000 (SB6K), the 40 mountains over 6,000 ft. in elevation located in western North Carolina and eastern Tennessee. Some mountains, like Clingmans Dome in the heart of the Smokies and Mt. Le Conte with its lodge, are famous. Others, such as Mt. Chapman and Marks Knob, are obscure bumps known only to peakbaggers. If you climb all 40 peaks via an approved route, you get bragging rights and a patch to sew on your pack.

Climbing these peaks encourages hikers to explore the area in a methodical manner. Without such a list, most of them would concentrate on the most popular destinations: Mt. Le Conte, Mt. Mitchell, and Cold Mountain.

SB6K FAQs

How do they check that you've hiked all 40 peaks?
They don't. Hiking the 40 peaks and other challenges depends on the honor system. To apply for a patch, you just list your date and route for each peak.

But can't you drive to some of the mountaintops?
The tower on Clingmans Dome is only a half-mile from the parking lot, and the top of Mt. Mitchell is even closer to where you can park a vehicle. A list of approved routes ensures that the hiker will walk at least 5 miles round trip and will ascend at least 500 ft. in elevation. In reality, though, most mountains require a lot more effort.

Why do it? Why set these goals?
As one peakbagger explained it, "I never would have explored some of the amazing mountains I've been to if it weren't for this program. I think it makes people more aware of...remote locations."

The Rules

Hike the 40 mountains over 6,000 ft., 15 of which have no maintained trail. Your total day hike must be at least 5 miles and ascend 500 ft. in elevationto qualify. See the Carolina Mountain Club website (www.carolinamtnclub.org) for the application form and other details. There are no time limits for this hiking challenge.

Mountain	Elev.	County	Page #
Mt. Mitchell	6,684	Yancey	p. 32
Mt. Craig	6,647	Yancey	
Clingmans Dome	6,643	Sevier (TN)/Swain	p. 318
Mt. Guyot	6,621	Sevier (TN)/Haywood	
Balsam Cone	6,611	Yancey	
Mt. LeConte	6,593	Sevier (TN)	
Mt. Gibbes	6,571	Yancey	
Potato Hill	6,475	Yancey	
Mt. Chapman	6,417	Sevier (TN)/Swain	
Richland Balsam	6,410	Haywood/Jackson	
Old Black	6,370	Sevier (TN), Cocke (TN)/Haywood	
Blackstock Knob	6,359	Yancey/Buncombe	
Celo Knob	6,327	Yancey	
Mt. Hallback	6,320	Yancey	
Waterrock Knob	6,292	Haywood/Jackson	
Roan High Knob	6,285	Carter (TN)/Mitchell	p. 302
Roan High Bluff	6,262	Mitchell	p. 302
Lyn Lowry	6,240	Haywood/Jackson	
Luftee Knob	6,234	Jackson/Swain	
Gibbs Mountain	6,224	Yancey	
Mt. Kephart	6,217	Sevier (TN)/Swain	
Black Balsam Knob	6,214	Haywood	p. 202
Winter Star Mtn.	6,212	Yancey	
Mt. Collins	6,188	Sevier (TN)/Swain	p. 318
Mark's Knob	6,169	Swain	
Grassy Ridge	6,160	Avery/Mitchell	p. 298
Big Cataloochee	6,155	Haywood	
Tricorner Knob	6.120	Haywood/Swain	
Mt. Hardy	6,110	Haywood/Jackson	
Plott Balsam	6,088	Haywood	
Craggy Dome	6,080	Buncombe	
Reinhart Knob	6,080	Haywood/Jackson	
Chestnut Bald	6,040	Haywood/Transylvania	
Grassy Cove Top	6,040	Haywood	
Sam Knob	6,040	Haywood	p. 208
Shining Rock	6,040	Haywood	p. 202
Tennent Mountain	6,040	Haywood	p. 202
Yellow Face	6,032	Jackson	
Cold Mountain	6,030	Haywood	p. 197
Mt. Sequoyah	6,003	Sevier (TN)/Swain	

F: Joining a Hiking Club

A great way to start

You want to start hiking but your partner isn't interested, your children would rather spend time hanging out with their friends, and your buddies don't get up until noon on weekends. It's time to join a hiking club.

When you hike with a club, you're not going on a guided tour. Hiking club leaders are volunteers, responsible only for picking out a hike, getting the right map for the area, knowing the distance and ascent of the hike, and scouting the trail before the hike. When you hike with a club, you are still responsible for yourself.

If you are new to a particular hiking club, even if you're an experienced hiker, here's how to get started:

• Look at the hike schedule on the web (or call the club's contact person for a schedule) and pick out an appropriate hike based on distance, altitude, and your own experience and fitness level.

• Contact the leader to make sure the hike is appropriate for guests in general and for you in particular.

• Bring the right gear for the hike.

• Confirm the time and location of the meeting point.

• Get to the meeting point at least 10 minutes before the stated starting time.

• If you get a ride to the trailhead from another hiker, be prepared to chip in for the cost of the ride. Have several small bills handy.

• Thank the leader at the end of the hike.

• If you have gone on two hikes with a club, it's time to join.

Finding a club to join

There are a number of local clubs in the area covered by this book. Should you live nearby, they are a great way to get started. To find a club in your area, check your local news media for scheduled club-related hikes and activities or follow the web links from the national associations listed below.

National Organizations

American Hiking Society
www.americanhiking.org

Appalachian Trail Conservancy
www.appalachiantrail.org

Hiking clubs in the region covered by this book

Carolina Mountain Club
www.carolinamtnclub.org

Georgia
Appalachian Trail Club
www.georgia-atclub.org

Greenville Natural History
Association
POB 26892
Greenville, SC 29616

High Country Hikers
www.main.nc.us/
highcountryhikers

Smoky Mountains
Hiking Club
www.smhclub.org

Tennessee Eastman
Hiking and Canoeing Club
www.tehcc.org

G: Recording Your Hikes

Challenge Yourself!

Record the date you complete each hike in this book. Finish them all and send a copy of this sheet to Milestone Press with your name, address, and email address, or visit www.hikertohiker.com to submit your list online. I'll send you a certificate of achievement.

Hike	Date Hiked	Notes
Camp Alice Loop		
Mount Mitchell		
Green Knob Tower		
Pot Cove Loop		
Lookout Rock		
Graybeard Mtn		
High Windy		
Craggy Gardens		
Lane Pinnacle		
Folk Art Center		
Dupont Five Falls		
Bridal Veil Falls Loop		
Stone Mtn Loop		
Carl Sandburg Home		
Green River GL		
Jones Gap Loop		
Raven Cliff Falls Loop		
Hospital Rock		
Rim of the Gap		
Paris Mountain SP		
Table Rock SP		
Sassafras Mountain		
Ellicott Rock		
US 276—Short Hikes		
Mt Pisgah		
Hardtimes Loop		
Stradley Mountain		

Hike	Date Hiked	Notes
Avery Creek Loop		
Coontree/Buckwheat		
Looking Glass Rock		
Cat Gap Loop		
Graveyard Fields		
Cold Mountain		
Shining Rock		
Sam Knob Loop		
Boogerman Trail		
Little Cataloochee		
Mount Sterling		
Hemphill Bald		
Smokemont Loop		
Deep Creek Loop		
Road to Nowhere		
Shuckstack-Lakeshore		
Horsepasture River		
Panthertown Loop		
Tsali Loop		
Joyce Kilmer		
Naked Ground Loop		
Haoe Lead		
Wesser Bald		
Appletree Loop		
Grassy Ridge		
Roan High Knob		
Sams Gap		
Lover's Leap		
Max Patch		
Clingmans Dome		

Index of Trails & Places

Field Notes

Field Notes

Field Notes

Milestone Press Adventure Guides

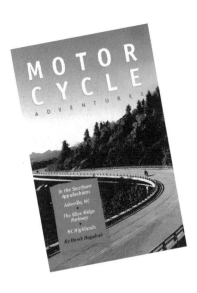

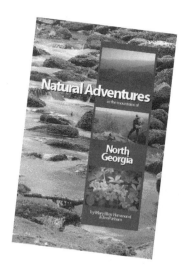

MOTORCYCLE ADVENTURE SERIES
by Hawk Hagebak

- Motorcycle Adventures in the Southern Appalachians– North GA, East TN, Western NC
- Motorcycle Adventures in the Southern Appalachians– Asheville, NC, Blue Ridge Parkway, NC High Country
- Motorcycle Adventures in the Central Appalachians– Virginia's Blue Ridge, Shenandoah Valley, West Virginia Highlands

FAMILY ADVENTURE
by Mary Ellen Hammond & Jim Parham

- Natural Adventures in the Mountains of North Georgia

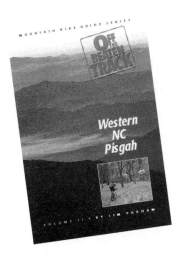

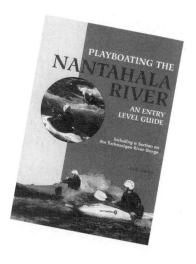

OFF THE BEATEN TRACK MOUNTAIN BIKE GUIDE SERIES
by Jim Parham

- Vol 1: Wetern NC–Smokies
- Vol 2: Western NC–Pisgah
- Vol 3: North Georgia
- Vol 4: East Tennessee
- Vol 5: Northern Virginia

- Tsali Mountain Bike Trails Map
- Bull Mountain Bike Trails Map

PLAYBOATING
by Kelly Fischer

- Playboating the Nantahala River– An Entry Level Guide

Can't find the Milestone Press book you want at a bookseller near you? Don't despair—you can order it directly from us.
Call us at 828-488-6601
or shop online at
www.milestonepress.com.

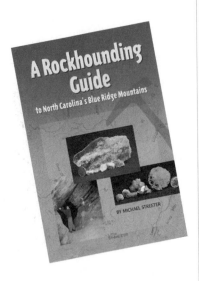

ROCKHOUNDING
by Michael Streeter

- A Rockhounding Guide to North Carolina's Blue Ridge Mountains

ROAD BIKE SERIES

- Road Bike Asheville, NC: Favorite Rides of the Blue Ridge Bicycle Club by The Blue Ridge Bicycle Club
- Road Bike the Smokies: 16 Great Rides in North Carolina's Great Smoky Mountains by Jim Parham
- Road Bike North Georgia: 25 Great Rides in the Mountains and Valleys of North Georgia by Jim Parham

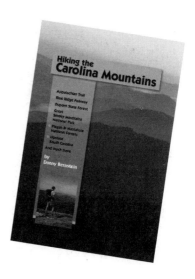

OUTDOOR EDUCATION

- Steve Longenecker's
  Wilderness Emergency
  Aid Book for Kids
  (& Their Adults)
  by Steve Longenecker

HIKING

- Hiking the Carolina
  Mountains
  by Danny Bernstein

Can't find the Milestone Press book you want at a bookseller
near you? Don't despair—you can order it directly from us.
Call us at 828-488-6601
or shop online at
www.milestonepress.com.